MAN HATING PSYCHO

IPHGENIA BAAL

Influx Press
2021

Published by Influx Press
The Greenhouse
49 Green Lanes, London, N16 9BU
www.influxpress.com / @InfluxPress

© Iphgenia Baal, 2021

First edition 2021. Printed and bound in the UK by TJBooks.

Paperback ISBN: 9781910312797

Ebook ISBN: 9781910312803

Editor: Kit Caless
Proofreader: Natasha Onwuemezi
Cover design: Keenan Designs
Interior design: Vince Haig

MAN HATING PSYCHO

Contents

CHANGE :)

+44 7723 018520 ~ Red Ed
Hi all. I know I've not been in touch with some of you for a long time so apologies for messaging out of the blue like this but I'd like your help to bring about CHANGE :) ! The election is coming and whether you love or hate Corbyn, we will either end up with a far-right hard Brexit under Boris Johnson or a 2nd referendum and Green Industrial Revolution for a carbon neutral economy by 2030, £10 minimum wage and free university education Norway-style social democracy under Labour. I would like to share links to help have an informed debate given the biased mainstream media. if you are able to share any of the media you agree with on your social media we can help have a more balanced and informed campaign than will be possible if people's main source of information is the BBC. If you don't want to receive these links please remove yourself from the group. Hope ur blossoming warm wishes, Eddie x

14.42

+44 7765 680205 left the group

+44 7904 924115 left the group

+44 7766 878263 left the group

+44 7950 241500 left the group

+44 7725 978362 left the group

+44 7793 045700 left the group

+44 7843 574429 left the group

+44 7743 504423 left the group

+44 7490 169709 left the group

+44 7980 908414 left the group

+44 7478 949166 left the group

+44 7762 320814 left the group

+44 7999 281079 left the group

+44 7545 265555 ~ Vegan Veritas
Hi Ed, thx for msg. I'll b voting labour even though I'm not sure about Corbyn. Anything to get this lot out and maybe get a second ref.

14.42

+44 7779 286544 left the group

+44 7716 016664 left the group

+44 7453 779030 left the group

+44 7775 308146 left the group

+44 7800 569507 left the group

+44 7595 707622 left the group

+44 7539 764992 left the group

+44 7505 900824 left the group

+44 7525 430943 left the group

+44 7545 265555 left the group

+44 7956 859558 ~ Lowercase_Guy
Who is Ed? Who added me? Britain does not need a general election. What it needs is a military general!

14.48

[jpg: shrugging man]

14.48

+44 7979 008162 ~ Marshmellow Man
Who dis? Can we get a Norway style Brexit?

14.49

+44 7843 585476 left the group

+44 7801 149075 left the group

+44 7958 742368 left the group

+44 7816 604484 left the group

+44 7958 045388 left the group

+44 7903 590639 left the group

+44 7950 931268 left the group

+44 7769 357858 ~ GlitterSparklePuss
Hey @Red_Ed. Haven't heard from you since I told you I didn't want to sleep with u and u got upset. Hope ur doing better and aren't so predatory. Will def be voting labour though, look forward to the links :)

15.00

+32 475 92 86 35 left the group

+44 7956 859558 ~ Lowercase_Guy
Who is Eddie? Show ur face! People are leaving this group like Brexit !!

15.12

+44 7905 935694 left the group

+44 7956 859558 ~ Lowercase_Guy

> **+44 7769 357858 ~ GlitterSparklePuss**
> Hey @Red_Ed. Haven't heard from you since I told you I didn't want to sleep with u and u got upset. Hope ur doing better and aren't so predatory. Will def be voting labour though, look forward to the links :)

Lol who is @Red_Ed??

15.30

+44 7979 008162 ~ Marshmellow Man
Hahahahaha @GlitterSparklePuss, whoever you are that was fucking legendary

15.31

+44 7849 393034 left the group

+44 7816 624481 left the group

+44 7702 778680 left the group

+44 7776 006006 left the group

+44 7956 859558 ~ Lowercase_Guy
If Ed does not identify who they are I am out of here

15.36

+49 1525 9798906 ~ Random Idiot
Would like to see the manifestos first in order to make an informed deicsion. Definitely do not trust cons. Lib dem are more likely to have a referendum than labour (corbyn does not look favourably at the eu). Cheers!

15.36

+44 7979 998219 left the group

+44 7815 654484 left the group

+44 7979 008162 ~ Marshmellow Man
Anyone here from Canterbury?

5.38

+44 7460 682464 ~ Lollipop Princess
What the hell

15.38

+44 7411 844985 left the group

+44 7460 682464 ~ Lollipop Princess
Do not add me without my consent first

15.38

+32 492 39 47 68 left the group

+44 7717 285670 ~ Eve *Stop HS2*
It's so funny someone already mentioned no more contact since refusing to sleep with Eddie... This was also me. Wouldn't call you predatory though... Quite passionate and somewhat sleazy yes. But that passion shows in your politics too ;)

15.38

+44 7460 682464 left the group

+44 7834 862716 ~ Yors Tru Lee

I'm voting labour. C ya on the other side Eddie. Thnks for the effort

15.39

+44 7904 049491~ Piotr El Gryko

Hi Ed, thanks for adding me to this group. I plan to vote against the tories/hard right government. This means ideally libdem or labour depending on which works out for tactical voting.

15.39

+44 7506 433203 ~ Name is a Country

I don't vote. Thnx.

15.39

+44 7979 008162 ~ Marshmellow Man

Why am I in Red Ed's failed hareem group text?

15.39

+44 7723 018520 ~ Red Ed

:)

15.39

+44 7921 925111 left the group

+44 7506 433203 left the group

+44 7470 041911 ~ Muchos Muchos Marley

Sending you love and supporting Corbyn... But I'm on too many social messaging groups. Ciao .)

15.40

+44 7956 859558 ~ Lowercase_Guy

Okay am out this group is strange thats two people refusing to sleep with Red Ed

15.40

+44 7470 041911 left the group

+44 7971 032074 left the group

+44 7723 018520 ~ Red Ed
Thanks okay

15.40

Thanks for the messages

15.40

+44 7857 165138 left the group

+44 7555 718015 left the group

+44 7734 533827 left the group

+44 7508 024130 ~ Yuliana Not Juliana
Dunno what this is but will vote for labour

15.41

+44 7932 142975 ~ Kareema Gopta
Good luck with the campaign. I will also be voting against far right politics. Don't want to receive updates here. Hope you are well.

15.41

+44 7932 142975 left the group

+44 7508 024130 left the group

+44 7728 919449 left the group

+44 7757 365306 left the group

+44 7956 859558 ~ Lowercase_Guy
Please who is Eddie?

15.42

+44 7850 466910 ~ iHole
Who cares?

15.42

> *+44 7850 466910 left the group*

> *+44 7804 426556 left the group*

+44 7854 488586 ~ Kristy 'Power-Ballad' Turlington
Hi Edward, I also haven't seen you since I was 17 (back in 2013, I believe?) when at least you weren't actually sure whether or not you wanted to sleep with me. I would leave the group but am finding this all too entertaining…

15.42

+44 7817 732542 ~ Jess

> **+44 7956 859558 ~ Lowercase_Guy**
> Please who is Eddie?

Seriously I'd love to know too :)

15.42

> *+44 7814 032502 left the group*

+44 7979 008162 ~ Marshmellow Man
Burning man, group texting, corbyn voting Casanova

15.42

I'm guessing i'm here because some girl gave him a random number?

15.43

> *+44 7592 949791 left the group*

+44 7956 859558 ~ Lowercase_Guy
Who is he where did he get my number from? What kind of fuckery is this

15.43

+44 7446 039423 ~ Lil Kikko

Hey Ed, why have you never tried to sleep with me? I'm offended

15.44

+44769 357858 ~ GlitterSparklePuss

:D :D

15.45

+44 7446 039423 ~ Lil Kikko

[gif: girl sticking out tongue]

15.45

+44 7817 732542 ~ Jess

> **+44 7446 039423 ~ Lil Kikko**
> Hey @Red_Ed, why have you never tried to sleep with me? I'm offended

:D:D:D:D:D:D

15.45

+44 7979 008162 changed the group description. Tap to view.

+44 7920 056935 left the group

+44 7723 018520 ~ Red Ed

> **+44 7956 859558 ~ Lowercase_Guy**
> Please who is Eddie?

@Lowercase_Guy it's Ed from self-empowerment spoken word event years ago

15.45

+44 7813 708108 left the group

+44 7577 985854 left the group

+44 7817 732542 left the group

+44 7834 767654 left the group

+ 44 7956 859 558 ~ Lowercase_Guy
Haha yeeeaaaars ago and you are only just getting in touch?
All politicians are the same. We need to cancel democracy

15.47

+44 7835 323882 left the group

+44 7598 144209 left the group

+44 7847 035174 left the group

+44 7723 018520 ~ Red Ed
https://mirror.co.uk/news/politics/furious-theresa-
snaps-2075633

Furious Theresa May snaps at Tory MPs for mocking
Jeremy Corbyn's Grenfell tie
As families of those who died looked on from the
public galleries, some Tory MPs decided to mock the
bright green tie

15.47

+44 7761 963737 ~ Tech Bro
I've slept with Ed loads of times. He's pretty good. You lot
are missing out.

15.47

+44 7723 018520 ~ Red Ed
Oh guys this is really really embarrassing

15.48

+44 7979 008162 ~ Marshmellow Man
I would sleep with him if I had any idea who the fuck he was

15.48

+44 7769 357858 ~ GlitterSparklePuss

> **+44 7761 963737 ~ Tech Bro**
> I've slept with Ed loads of times. He's pretty good. You lot are missing out.

Not really that funny

15.48

+44 7723 018520 ~ Red Ed
I thought I'd make a big Whatsapp group and do my bit to help with the election.

15.48

+44 7979 008162 ~ Marshmellow Man
Mate this is definitely going on reddit

15.49

+44 7904 839543 left the group

+44 7723 018520 ~ Red Ed
@GlitterSparklePuss I don't know how to respond to your message apart from it's years since I've seen u and I wish you'd have said at the time

15.49

+44 7474 454151 left the group

+44 7956 859558 left the group

+44 7981 273084 left the group

+44 7889 364743 ~ Butt Smasher
I want an environmentally sustainable economy, human rights for everyone, end to the arms trade, no more borders, a free and fair society. I'm voting labour.

15.52

+44 7723 018520 removed +44 7583 117701

+44 7723 018520 removed +44 7903 584041

+44 7723 018520 removed +44 7979 008162

+44 7723 018520 removed +44 7769 357858

+49 1525 9798906 ~ Random Idiot
Please do not close this group... this has honestly made my day

16.00

+44 7932 972424 left the group

+44 7761 963737 ~ Tech Bro
Ed may have ended up swinging the election for the tories the way this is going.

16.01

+44 7723 018520 left the group

+44 7811 943148 left the group

+44 7905 795311 left the group

+44 7948 245803 left the group

+44 7954 158322 ~ Liam
Hey Ed! how are you? Been ages! I like your dream for 2030 may it happen! Will be voting tactically for remain. Either libdem or labour i'm delighted lab offering peoples vote if they win that's a good move i will watch for updates with interest xliam

16.01

+44 7790 781498 left the group

+44 7977 511075 left the group

+44 7988 420263 left the group

+44 7472 476389 left the group

+44 7593 104049 left the group

+44 7551 225315 left the group

+44 7792 057381 left the group

+44 7920 004590 ~ lotusoftheskies

> **+44 7761 963737 ~ Tech Bro**
> Ed may have end up swinging the election for the tories the way this is going.

Definitely 'swinging'

16.20

+44 7760 504393 left the group

+44 7904 049491 left the group

+61 439 306 357 left the group

+44 7929 302796 left the group

+44 7717 285670 left the group

+44 7701 072434 ~ Jody
Good luck with this! I am not yet eligible to vote yet but sad to see the way the conversation is going,. Right wing trolls r real.

16.26

+44 7701 072434 left the group

+49 1525 9798906 ~ Paul
Have not met 'ed' yet...but we have spoken a few times on the phone to discuss my parties. He comes across as a very thoughtful guy. I like to think some of those comments

above are about the younger version of him... He seems very likeable. just thought I would be a little more positive...

16.26

+44 7735 234045 left the group

+44 7880 760451 left the group

+44 7861 293426 ~ Anna Lisa
Sending all good wishes to you ed.

16.27

+44 7801 547859 left the group

+44 7861 293426 left the group

+44 7763 668549 ~ Guen Benedetto
Hi ed! I can't vote as not british but i usually canvass and do outreach with other groups - I've gathered this is about labour ... fingers crossed folks!

16.28

+44 7763 668549 left the group

+44 7765 356372 ~ Anita Sixsmith
Who is this ?

16.31

+44 7544 045014 left the group

+44 7738 091530 left the group

+44 7514 732885 left the group

+44 7760 193337 left the group

+44 7459 822331 left the group

+44 7479 859275 left the group

+44 7772 174155 left the group

+44 7734 204705 left the group

+44 7776 351705 left the group

+44 7532 032823 left the group

+44 7814 737028 left the group

+44 7927 132522 left the group

+44 7765 356372 ~ Anita Sixsmith
This isnt eds number

17.16

Your sending messages to the wrong number

17.16

+44 7952 645236 left the group

+44 7551 939242 left the group

+44 7910 675357 left the group

+44 7766 395558 ~ Chazzy ChaChing
Going to vote! Let's make a change

18.02

+44 7765 356372 ~ Anita Sixsmith
We are not eddie

18.02

+44 7834 862716 ~ Yors Tru Lee
@GlitterSparklePuss.. u r missing out... Ed's got a huge cucumber!..

18.10

+44 7765 356372 ~ Anita Sixsmith
Your sending messages to the wrong number we are not eddie

18.12

+44 7512 843141 ~ Star O'Reilly
This is a group chat Anita

18.12

+44 7765 356372 ~ Anita Sixsmith
Group chat with who?

18.13

+44 7512 843141 ~ Star O'Reilly
Group chat with everyone in the group. What year r u living in?

18.13

+44 7980 500548 left the group

+44 7712 421368 ~ Imogen
Failed harem indeed! @GlitterSparklePuss & eve and I had a similar experience, think of all the other women whom have found themselves in a predatory situation with Ed. I thought we could be friends until I realised being female meant I didn't have a choice in his advances. My friend also experienced his unwelcome advances. We agreed to stay away.

18.30

It looks as though your address book is full of bad decisions Eddie. Hope you change your ways.

18.34

+44 7570 852899 left the group

+44 7853 677808 left the group

+44 7789 740193 ~ El Duccio
Anyone up for a halloween party?
https://www.facebook.com/events/686369241858633

18.37

+44 7453 859858 left the group

+44 7766 395558 changed the group description. Click to view.

+44 7766 395558 ~ Chazzy ChaChing
IVE JUST SPOKEN TO ED ON THE PHONE. ED IS NO
LONGER A MEMBER OF THIS GROUP! HE TRIED TO
DELETE THE GROUP BUT ACCIDENTALLY DELETED
HIMSELF. LOL. HE IS UN-ABLE TO DELETE OR POST
TO THE GROUP. HE SENDS DEEPEST APOLOGIES TO
ANYONE HE MIGHT OF ANNOYED OR UPSET. IN
SHORT. VOTE LABOUR! END POVERTY (END OF MEMO)
18.56

+44 7972 715090 left the group

+49 1525 9798906 ~ Paul
I am actually looking for a halloween party... Anyone going?
19.04

+44 7765 356372 ~ Anita Sixsmith
We are opting out

19.04

+49 1525 9798906 ~ Paul
(I was talking about the facebook party above).

19.06

+44 7765 356372 ~ Anita Sixsmith
We dont even know you people

19.07

+44 7882 255838 ~ EnglishTwerkingClass
That's what the parties are for, to meet people :)

19.08

+49 1525 9798906 ~ Paul
For those who are open-minded, adventurous, not judgmental

19.10

> *+44 7508 845467 left the group*
>
> *+44 7766 003730 left the group*
>
> *+44 7545 153472 left the group*
>
> *+44 7584 132143 changed this group's settings to allow only admins to edit this group's info.*
>
> *+44 7584 132143 changed this group's settings to allow only admins to send messages to this group.*

+44 7584 132143 ~ TrustMeLondon
Eddie has asked me to forward the following. Last messages ever on the group, promise. Contact each other directly from here perhaps

20.15

Forwarded>
Hi everyone. I added you to this group intending to send information around for the general election. I selected my whole address book and two women @GlitterSparklePuss and Imogeon sent messages to the group says I was predatory, while another woman Eva said I had not stayed in touch with her after she said she was not interested and a string of messages were sent about who had or had not slept with me. I deleted the group from my phone but the group has continued somehow even though i cannot access it and it's not on my phone and the name of the group was changed. I want to share my perspective on what occurred and @TrustMeLondon has agreed to

26

forward this on my behalf. Some of this is personal and some of you I do not know well but I think it's best I share openly and honestly.

20.16

Forwarded>

I have not been in touch with GlitterSparklePuss who I know as Daniella since 2013, and after seeing her message I contacted her. I attach screen-shots below of the conversation as this is the most open way I can share what occurred.

20.16

Forwarded> _____

<21 Daniella Kilsby

last seen today at 15.26

and i am really sorry 15.02 √√

Daniella Kilsby

Do you not remember taking your pants off to play the touching game? 15.03

I've seen your genitals 15.03

Ok, thank you for acknowledging that
15.03

You

Now you remind me yes but i don't remember it being nonconsensual and when you made it clear you didn't want that i remember getting dressed again
15.04 √√

do you remember that? 15.04 √√

Daniella Kilsby

> yes though i don't appreciate having to
> say it more than once before you listen
> 15.04

You

> yes i'm sure youre right but it's complicated
> and i was young and inexperienced 15.05 ✓✓

> i had a lot to learn 15.05 ✓✓

Daniella Kilsby

> So was I Edward... and far more
> trusting of the intentions of people that
> i thought were

20.17

Forwarded>

Imogeon I do not know, I've looked at my contact book and I have her contact but I do now know where we met. She gives no details of why she believes me to be predatory and I've messaged to ask her if she can help me understand and I hope she will reply. Eva again I do not remember other than it says I met her in night club in my phone book and that she says it was in 2013. She says I did not stay in touch with her after she says she was not interested in me and I'm not sure why imogeon believes that means I was predatory. I was young and immature in 2013 and it's clear I must have made GlitterSparklePuss, Imogeon and Eva very uncomfortable for them to remember and be moved to post all these years later. I feel deeply ashamed. I believe I have learned since then and done a lot of work on myself and I now have long term stable and positive relationships.... Read More

20.16

Forwarded >

I promise I will think deeply about this and would really welcome any feedback that can enable me to reflect and learn and grow to avoid such situations happening again, please do feel free to message me

20.16

+44 7584 132143 added +44 7723 018520

+44 7584 132143 made +44 7723 018520 an admin

+44 7723 018520 ~ Red Ed
I'm sorry everyone. Eddie.

20.22

+44 7723 018520 removed +44 7939 183520

+44 7723 018520 removed +44 7751 787927

+44 7723 018520 removed +351 914 250 485

+44 7723 018520 removed +44 7852 590177

+44 7723 018520 removed +44 7919 336065

+44 7723 018520 removed +44 7921 437923

+44 7723 018520 removed +44 7453 923365

+44 7723 018520 removed +44 7415 605445

+44 7723 018520 removed +1 (917) 678-9446

+44 7723 018520 removed +44 7956 196973

+44 7723 018520 removed +44 7800 938842

+44 7723 018520 removed +44 7745 521975

+44 7723 018520 removed +44 7435 356752

+44 7723 018520 removed +44 7913 321273

+44 7723 018520 removed +44 7887 553374

+44 7723 018520 removed +44 7424 102910

+44 7723 018520 removed +44 7950 143356

+44 7723 018520 removed +44 7969 466494

+44 7723 018520 removed +44 7789 740193

+44 7723 018520 removed +44 7834 862716

+44 7723 018520 removed +44 7786 860954

+44 7723 018520 removed +44 7745 291380

+44 7723 018520 removed +44 7988 810092

+44 7723 018520 removed +44 7772 709860

+44 7723 018520 removed +44 7957 169127

+44 7723 018520 removed +44 7766 395558

+44 7723 018520 removed +44 7790 109028

+44 7723 018520 removed +49 1525 9798906

+44 7723 018520 removed +44 7923 841497

+44 7723 018520 removed +44 7766 011605

+44 7723 018520 removed +45 93 98 04 12

+44 7723 018520 removed +44 7712 421368

+44 7723 018520 removed +44 7765 356372

+44 7723 018520 removed you

LINE

Can be literal or implied and may refer to: a concept which includes but is not limited to an infinitely extended one-dimensional figure with no curvature and negligible width or depth (line); a notional limit or boundary (out-line, top-line, sky-line, red line, dead-line, Equator); a mark delineating ownership (border-line, to sign on the dotted line); transmission/text (by-line, punch-line), also the fundamental unit of poetic composition; emphasis (under-line); of measure (base-line, waist-line, hair-line, hem-line); umbilical cord (mascu-line?); circuit: for travel (bus-line, railway-line, air-line, shipping-line), for communication (phone-line, land-line, hot-line, date-line, pipe-line, on-line); indicator (life-line, bee-line); prepared dose of a powdered narcotic drug (main-line); a dance formation (side-line); fishing equipment; the former unit measuring flux; a direction, course or channel (inc-line, rec-line, bass-line, stream-line); a standard military formation; an offensive or defensive position in sport. In cricket, the direction of delivery; a length of cord or cable (washing line, tow-line, drag-line); dialogue to be spoken (pl. lines); islands in the Pacific; the police (disicip-line, to cross the line, to walk the line, the thin blue line); element of a stave; sign of age (pl. lines); old school punishment (pl. lines); a number of things or people in a straight row (front-line, bread-line); ancestry, descent (blood-line, aqui-line, line-age); conversation (chat up line, to spin a line, lie); to act in accordance with others (to tow the line, the party line); a throng edging a parade; the trajectory of a bullet. Also the point beyond which one will not fire; words to be spoken (off-line); of thought (hard-line); of sight (dec-line); of vision (flat-line); marking the starting or finishing point (gaso-line, end of the line).

Pain in the Neck

When Matey's number came up, I'm not gonna lie, I thought twice about picking up. Not because we were on bad terms or anything silly like that, just that everything involving Matey had a way of turning out good for Matey, at the expense of everyone else. It was never anything major. Ordering a round then not having his wallet, sharing a cab and jumping out halfway, that kinda thing. I don't think he did it on purpose but his obliviousness didn't make hanging out with Matey any less expensive. I couldn't think why he'd be calling either because although Matey and I were mates, we'd never been the sorta mates who spoke on the phone. Curiosity as to what he might be after got the better of me.

— Matey? I said, picking up.

— Long time no speak, Matey said, sounding jovial. — How you doing?

— I'm alright, I said, finding his enthusiasm a little disconcerting. — What's up?

— Well... Matey drew out the vowel, building up to something. — This is gonna sound weird but hey, do you know I've got a new girlfriend?

As it happened I *did* recall hearing someone in the pub a few weeks back saying something about Matey having bagged himself 'another rich bird with a flat'. The daughter of a far-right Spanish politician, if I was remembering that right.

— Yeah, I said. — I did hear something. She's Spanish?

— She's really cool, Matey said, statement of fact. — I think you two would get on…

— Oh really? I said, and laughed. — And why is that?

— Well, she found one of your books, Matey said. — When we were unpacking. Did I tell you we got a flat?

— No, I said. — You didn't.

But I don't think Matey heard because he carried on talking without pausing for breath.

— It's a fucking wicked little place, he said. — It's really near you. She really liked your book.

— Which one? I said.

— I don't know, Matey said. — The little one. But anyway, she looked you up online and watched the film you made with Anna. It's so sick. It's like Adam Curtis.

— Except not funded by the BBC, I said.

Matey talked over me again. — And she was like, you know she wants to do set design? But she doesn't know many people in London, so I thought maybe if you were doing something, I don't know…

— I don't think I'm gonna be hiring any set designers soon, I said, amused at what Matey thought making zero-budget satirical shorts destined for 700 views on Vimeo entailed.

— No, no, Matey said. — Sure, sure. But maybe you two could chat. She really likes your stuff.

Sceptical as ever about the idea of working with someone I didn't know, I wasn't gonna pretend I wasn't flattered.

— So what you saying? Matey said.

— Sure, I said, not entirely sure what I was agreeing to. — Why not.

— Wicked, Matey said. — Well, if it isn't too short notice, you could come over now.

— Now? I said.

— Yeah, now, Matey said. — We're having a few people over tonight, a housewarming. You can stick around if you like.

I'd promised myself I was gonna work that afternoon. The book I was working on was horribly close to deadline and nowhere close to finished, but the thing had been giving me a headache because I'd rewritten it and rewritten it and couldn't work out what it was about and truth be told, I'd've taken any excuse to get away from it, let alone the rare opportunity of meeting a fan.

— I'm not busy, I said. — Send me the address.

I hung up the call, wondering what exactly Matey'd meant by 'you can stick around if you like'. If it was an invite it was pretty blasé plus if he'd organised a housewarming party he would've invited people before the day of the party so why, I wondered, hadn't I been included in those invitations?

Matey texted a postcode. I stuck it into Google Maps, which showed a walking route through the estates and across the park, estimated to take fifteen minutes. The address was on a side of the park I'd not been to so I dropped into Street View to take a look. A curious cul-de-sac, mostly garages and lock-ups, but at the far end was a standalone two-storey Georgian house. It had a yellow front door and a pointy roof and it was clear from the outside that the flats inside were expensive.

While I was clawing at the screen, trying to zoom in to see the upstairs windows, Matey texted again.

— Forgot to say

— Do u still have my records????

Matey's records, left behind after a long Hackney Wick weekend (coincidentally the weekend Matey and I had had sex, if you can call three sleepy seconds sex. What a mistake that'd been), had been in the flat for so long it took me a minute to get what was he talking about. Then the records and the sad sex came back to me. I went into the hallway and opened the cupboard by the front door where the hoover and winter coats were kept. I rummaged through until I came to the record box underneath a pile of bin bags that should've been taken to a charity shops years ago. I snapped a picture of the silver box and texted it to Matey.

— Still here, I wrote.

I lifted the box out of the cupboard and flicked through the 12"s to if there was anything worth stealing. Heads High - Mr Vegas, Big Pimpin' - Jay Z, white labels I guessed were drum 'n' bass. DJ Matey staples. Fine for a party but quite frankly I could live without them in my personal collection.

— Nice 1, Matey texted back.

— Bring them with.

Annoyed by his bossiness, I was about to text back with the word, 'pls' but, noticing my low battery, didn't bother. There was little point policing Matey's manners. Nothing ever went in. Instead, I plugged my phone in to charge then went through to the bedroom to dress. With sunshine streaming through the windows, thoughts of a party later and assuming Matey's rich Spanish girlfriend was hot, I ditched my usual jeans and t-shirt combo and opted for a short, tight mini-dress that made my bum look excellent. I knew it was lame to dress up and I didn't fancy Matey or anything, I just wanted to look my best. Or at least that's what I told myself.

As soon as I left the house, I regretted my choice of outfit. It was much colder outside than it'd looked. My arms and legs came up in goosebumps. By the time I reached the park my teeth were chattering. Why had I worn a stupid dress? And why had I agreed to bring Matey's records? The box was heavy and impossible to carry.

Fingers red-raw from clasping the plastic handle, I struggled through the park until, alternating the box from my right hand to my left, I bashed the funny bone in my knee with one of the metal corners. I dropped the box with a screech then picked it up again and limped over a park bench to inspect the damage. The impact had, disappointingly, left no trace.

Thinking I should text Matey, I felt where my pockets usually were and realised I'd left my phone behind. I could see it in my mind's eye, next to the toaster, lighting up, getting calls. Or not. Half of me wanted to go back and get it but the half that didn't want to lug the stupid box all the way back to mine won out. I could see the corner of Matey's street from where I was so decided I'd either survive the evening without it or, if I was really that desperate, could pop back and pick my phone up later on. I picked up the box, this time forgoing the handle and carrying it in both arms held against my chest the rest of the way.

I arrived at the yellow front door and rang the bell. I heard noises from inside but no one came down. I rang the bell again. More noises, footsteps this time, then the front door was opened by a girl, much younger than me (and so much younger than Matey), who looked exactly how you'd expect the daughter of a disgraced far-right Spanish politician to look: 90s raver undercut, pierced lip, expression on her face like it was expecting an apology.

— Hey, I said, and smiled.

Matey's rich Spanish girlfriend looked blank.

— Are you a friend of Matey's? she said, speaking slowly.

I was confused. Hadn't Matey said his rich Spanish girlfriend looked me up on the Internet? I'd looked myself up on the Internet and there were plenty of pictures of me that looked just like me. Maybe this wasn't Matey's rich Spanish girlfriend, maybe it was her sister, or one of her friends.

— Yeah, I said. — He told me to come round to meet his girl…

— 'Ees gone out, the girl said.

— Friend… I said, then trailed off expecting her to elaborate further but she didn't. — Well, these are his records. He asked me to bring them over. Are you his girlfriend?

Matey's rich Spanish girlfriend bristled.

— Yes, she said, looking me up and down. She was in tracksuit bottoms and a vest but even if she hadn't been I'd've felt overdressed.

— It's just Matey said you'd read my book, I said then stopped, feeling like a total idiot. — Actually, d'you know what? Don't worry. I'll come back later, this evening.

— Ohhhh, Matey's rich Spanish girlfriend suddenly changed tack, grabbing my arm. — 'Ees you! Matey's friend who makes the books. I'm sorry. Please.

She stood aside and gestured for me to come in, then stopped me on the threshold and pointed at the box of records, which I'd left on the pavement.

— If you don't mind, she said. — I've carried so many of Matey's boxes from when we moved in.

We sat in the living room, where Matey's rich Spanish girlfriend was halfway through assembling an Ikea shelving unit and a bottle of port. With nowhere to sit and my skirt too-short for me to sit cross-legged on the floor, I perched on the windowsill, watching Matey's rich Spanish girlfriend breeze over the instructions.

— So, she said. —How do you know Matey?

How did I know Matey?

— I don't know, I said. — Just from around, people. Matey told me you're a set designer. Where's he gone anyway?

Matey's rich Spanish girlfriend shrugged.

— What time are people supposed to be coming?

This time she didn't even look up. I made a couple more lame attempts at conversation but was starting to get the feeling that Matey's rich Spanish girlfriend didn't like me and hadn't read any of my books. I started to fidget, thinking I should just head back to mine and come back later, when the party started, rather than loitering like a spare part.

— You okay? Matey's rich Spanish girlfriend said, noticing my restlessness.

— Yeah, I said. — I…

— You want a drink? she said, picking up the bottle of port.

Before I could answer yes or no, Matey's rich Spanish girlfriend plucked a watermarked tumbler out of a cardboard box that said 'kitchen' and filled it. Then, asking me to pass an allen key, a screw, a piece of MDF, roped me into helping her assemble the shelves. It wasn't what I'd had in mind for my afternoon but as it turned out, it was fun. The shared activity and the booze made conversation flow a little more easily. I quickly ascertained that Matey's rich Spanish girlfriend had neither read my books nor looked me up online (what a weird lie for Matey to tell), but other than that Matey was right. We got on pretty well. She laughed at all the right bits of my jokes and I listened with interest to her reasons for wanting to live anywhere other than Spain. She bemoaned her father and Spain's rigid class structures, saying that England was so much better because no one cared if you were posh. I begged to differ but Matey's rich Spanish girlfriend was so insistent I let it drop.

The drunker we got, the more careless we became, discarding the instructions for assembling the shelves in favour of working intuitively. All well and good until we came to slotting the shelves into the frame. They didn't fit. I searched the mess we'd made for the instruction booklet but Matey's rich Spanish girlfriend, who was drunker than me, slurred for me not to bother.

— Look, she said, — Watch.

She jammed shelf after shelf into the frame, each at a different at a wonky angle, snapping pegs.

— See, she said, shaking the shelving unit to test its resilience.

If the shelving unit had belonged to me, I might've objected but what did I care if Matey and his rich Spanish girlfriend had wonky shelves?

— If you say so, I said, then, noticing dusk setting in outside, — where the fuck is Matey?

Matey's rich Spanish girlfriend, still slurring, said Matey was an 'arseholio' for inviting me over then going out all afternoon and for leaving her here alone to unpack. I pointed out that we hadn't done any unpacking. There were boxes everywhere and nowhere to sit. The flat was in no way ready for a party. Matey's rich Spanish girlfriend draped a heavy arm around my shoulder and prodded me in the ribs, saying that I was a really good person no matter what Matey said.

— What do you mean? I said.

But she dismissed my question with a wave, saying I shouldn't care what people said about me because she thought I was ok.

— Ok, I said.

Seeing I was bothered by the remark, Matey's rich Spanish girlfriend started stroking my face, saying that she liked me more than she liked Matey and when he got back, if he ever got back, she was gonna kick him out and tell him I was moving in instead. From the way she said it I got the feeling that she (or at least her fascist father) was the one paying the rent. Then Matey's rich Spanish girlfriend grabbed my forearm and squeezed it hard, eyes popping excitedly open.

— Wait! she said. — I forget! We can get up on the roof.

Before I knew what was happening, Matey's rich Spanish girlfriend was dragging the Ikea shelving unit we'd just assembled into the hall. She pointed up at a skylight in the ceiling.

— See? Matey's rich Spanish girlfriend said.

She climbed the shelves, which trembled under her weight, creaking ominously.

— Hold them, she said, sounding every bit as bossy as Matey scrambling over a rig.

Standing on its top shelf she reached up her arms and pulled a catch, which opened the skylight to reveal a square of dark neon sky.

— Ooooh, Matey's rich Spanish girlfriend said.

She went up on tiptoe but was well shy of the roof.

— Get more things, she said. — A chair.

I fetched a chair from the kitchen and passed it up then held the shelves. Matey's rich Spanish girlfriend put one foot on the back of the chair and jacked herself up, catching the roof. The chair wobbled. The Ikea shelving unit wobbled. Her scissoring legs disappeared out of the skylight. I heard her cockcrow laugh then her face appeared above me grinning and telling me to come up.

I climbed the Ikea shelving unit and stood on the seat of the chair but I had a problem. There was no one to hold the chair for me, so I wasn't gonna be able to jump without it tumbling over. Seeing the issue, Matey's rich Spanish lowered her arms through the skylight towards me.

— I pull you up, she said.

I didn't think Matey's rich Spanish girlfriend looked strong enough to lift my entire bodyweight from above but raised my arms all the same.

— I don't think… I said.

— Ready? Matey's rich Spanish girlfriend interrupted.

— No, I… I said.

But Matey's rich Spanish girlfriend yanked my arms and my feet lifted off of the chair. My head emerged into the fast-approaching evening but Matey's rich Spanish girlfriend's hands were sweaty and one of my wrists slipped from her grasp. For a dizzy moment I dangled from one arm like a rag doll, legs cycling in the hallway below, before Matey's rich Spanish girlfriend reached down to scoop me up by my waist and haul me to safety.

I flopped down on the asphalt, reeling from my melodramatic ascent, feeling the coldness of the tiles seep into my clothes like damp. Matey's rich Spanish girlfriend brought her face level with mine.

— You ok? she said, laughing through port-stained lips.

My shoulder was throbbing.

— I think I've done something to my shoulder, I said, wanting to say, 'I think you've done something to my shoulder', but not having the guts.

But Matey's rich Spanish girlfriend was off, scrambling up the incline to the chimney pots, where she started pointing out obvious landmarks and going on about how beautiful London is. While I was in agreement with her that London sometimes looked beautiful, I wasn't able to give the city my full attention because whatever was going on my shoulder was getting worse. It twitched. It spasmed.

— I think I'm gonna go back in, I said.

— Noooo. Come up, come up, come up! Matey's rich Spanish girlfriend shouted. — Just two minutes, please, then we go in. Come on, you're a writer.

Against my better judgement and not understanding what being a writer had to do with anything, I joined Matey's rich Spanish girlfriend by the chimney pots, taking more care with the old house than she had. We sat arm in arm and watched the sun go down. The temperature went down with it. The port was wearing off. Soon we were both shivering.

— Now we go back in, Matey's rich Spanish girlfriend said, blatantly pleased at having got her way. — Come back again later, with more people.

I didn't need asking twice. We slid down the tiles and returned to the skylight where Matey's rich Spanish girlfriend decided she would go first. Holding herself on braced arms, hands to either side of the skylight, she lowered herself through the opening, giggling. It seemed like she was in control until her arms buckled and she slipped. She grabbed my ankles to stop herself falling but her flailing left leg clipped the chair. A crash sounded from below. I helped Matey's rich Spanish girlfriend to her feet then we both peered through the skylight. The chair had fallen upside down, legs in the air, and the Ikea shelving unit had smashed into something close to the flat-pack form it'd arrived in.

— We are stuck, Matey's rich Spanish girlfriend said.

She seemed to think it was hilarious but I failed to see the funny side.

— How are we gonna get back in? I said. — It's freezing.

Matey's rich Spanish girlfriend, high on adrenaline, suggested we scale the building's exterior.

— If we want to die, I said.

She scurried to the roof's edge and for a second I worried I was going to have to forcibly stop her climbing down but she just leaned into the street and yelled at a pair of market traders filling their lock-up for the night.

— Hey, she shouted. — Help. We're stuck. This woman is hurt.

This woman?

— Why don't you just call Matey? I said, trying not to sound snappy and failing. I really wanted to get off the roof. I didn't want to get ill.

Matey's rich Spanish girlfriend smacked her forehead with an open palm.

— Of course! she said, ran her hands over her pockets. — But I think I left my phone. You call him...

There was nothing else for it but to wait.

— Matey will be back soon, Matey's rich Spanish girlfriend said.

— Yeah, I said. — For the party.

But Matey wasn't back soon. We sat huddled together for warmth underneath the brown sky listening to the sounds of the city for one hour, two hours, maybe more. Without a phone it was hard to tell. Conversation stalled, our lips turned blue, I think we both began to fall asleep but not restful sleep like from being tired, sleep like hypothermia setting in, organs shutting down.

We woke to loud, drunk voices echoing in the dead end street.

— Ees Matey, Matey's rich Spanish girlfriend said, untangling her limbs from mine and gettting up and shouting. — Matey! Matey.

Cheers came from below. Matey clearly had the party with him but I couldn't stand up to see because my limbs were so cold they'd gone dead. Matey's rich Spanish girlfriend hung over the edge of the roof shouting down to the crowd while I did my best to bring my body back to life. Huffing warm breath on my fingers until I could feel them again. Rubbing my legs until the feeling came back. But my shoulder had completely seized up, so solid and immovable it was as if the muscle had started to calcify and turn into bone.

Once Matey grasped that we weren't up on the roof out of choice, he was, even drunk, astonishingly efficient. He got the partygoers indoors and shut them in the living room out of the way before removing the chair and broken Ikea shelving unit. Then, under his rich Spanish girlfriend's instruction, he fashioned a landing pad out of a mattress and cushions and pillows and blankets.

— Ok, Matey said, plumping the array. — I think we're good.

Matey's rich Spanish girlfriend wasted no time. She plunged through the skylight feet first without a word to me. I was impressed by her bravery until I watched her crash land. The mattress skidded across the floor, she landed hard on her bum. Dangling my legs through the skylight, I watcher her writhe around. The floor looked miles away and I was starting to wish I'd gone first.

— Is she ok? I said. —Are you okay?

But Matey and his rich Spanish girlfriend, wrapped up in one another, either ignored me or didn't hear.

— You tell me you go half an hour, Matey's rich Spanish girlfriend said. — You leave me all day to look after your friend.

— Hey, I said. — Guys. Guys.

Matey looked up at me then back at his rich Spanish girlfriend.

— Come, let's get out of the way, he said.

— I don't think I can do it, I said.

— Don't be a pussy, Matey said. — Here, I'll catch you.

He opened his arms wide and grinned.

— My shoulder, I said. — I can't move it.

Just then, a guest who must've escaped from the front room, appeared in the hall. He whispered in Matey's ear and though I couldn't hear what he said it was obvious he was offering Matey a line of cocaine, because he put two fingers to his nostril, rolled his head and sniffed, then nodded at Matey's rich Spanish girlfriend. Matey looked up at me.

— One minute, he said, then all three of them vanished.

— Matey! I shouted. — The mattress. Don't leave me here. Matey.

I waited, hoping Matey would return to catch me or at least move the mattress back underneath the skylight but when I heard the damp fuzz of an amp being switched on, followed by the crackle of vinyl and Heads High - Mr Vegas, I knew I was on my own.

I shifted my bum to the edge of the skylight. Then, holding my bad shoulder, counted down in my head from ten. Nine, eight, seven, six, five, four. I tricked myself and went on three. I heard my scream but wasn't aware of making it as I plummeted to the floor, tucking and rolling off of my bad shoulder on impact. I heard applause and looked up to see a pair of vintage sportswear wankers who raised their drinks at me. Hadn't they heard me calling for help? Why hadn't they helped me?

— That was wicked, one of them said.

Relieved as I was to be back inside, I was not in the mood for a party. I couldn't believe Matey had left me like that, never mind inviting me over then going out all day, never mind that he'd spun me some yarn about his girlfriend reading my books. What was that about? If he'd wanted someone to babysit he should've just asked straight out, not won me over with flattery. I stalked from room to room intent on holding Matey to account but when I found him, in the bathroom on the phone ordering drugs, he shushed me before I could say anything. I stood there like a lemon for five, ten minutes, but the more I thawed out the clearer it became that there was something seriously wrong with my shoulder. It didn't hurt but things kept happening. Little spasms, little throbs, then a feeling like there was liquid glugging through it.

I gave up on Matey finishing the call and went to find Matey's rich Spanish girlfriend instead to see if I could borrow a jumper or jacket for the walk back to mine. She was in the kitchen doing tequila shots with a group of people more her own age, talking loudly in Spanish. It looked to me like she had plenty of friends.

— I think I'm gonna go, I said.

A couple of the people Matey's rich Spanish girlfriend was doing shots with looked round but she didn't.

— Hey, I said, unable for the life of me to remember her name. Had she even said it? Had Matey?

— Could you maybe lend me a jumper for the walk home? I said. — I'll bring it back.

Matey's rich Spanish girlfriend turned and grabbed the hand on the side of my bad shoulder and held it aloft, like we were champions.

— Yes! she said. — Roof legeeeeend.

I yowled in pain but Matey's rich Spanish girlfriend didn't seem to get that I was yowling because it hurt and started yowling with me.

— Yowl! she yelled then did a shot.

— Yowl! the Spaniards yelled and did theirs.

I withdrew my bad arm away, cradling it with my good one. I had to get away from these people.

Nicking a jumper a partygoer had discarded, I slunk off without saying goodbye and walked back across the park thinking what a pair of obnoxious cunts Matey and his rich

Spanish girlfriend were and annoyed at myself for wasting a whole day and night on such horrendously selfish people.

When I woke the next morning my first thought was of Matey and Matey's rich Spanish girlfriend's living room. It appeared to me like a vision, full of cigarette smoke and empty wraps. What a beautiful morning not to have been up all night, I thought, but my smugness was short-lived because kicking off the covers and sitting up, a jolt of electric, synapse-y pain that'd been lurking in my fingertips awaiting its opportunity, shot up my arm, into my neck and I yelped like a dog that'd been stood on. Not daring to move for fear of whatever had just happened happening again, I lay pinned to the sheets. My thoughts, like the thoughts of many an incapacitated person before me, returned to yesterday's misadventure. If only I hadn't gone along with Matey's rich Spanish girlfriend's stupid idea to go up on the roof. If only she hadn't kicked the stupid chair and stranded us up there for hours. If only Matey hadn't done a stupid disappearing act and been there when he said he would be. Why hadn't he just invited me to the stupid party instead of telling me to come over in the stupid afternoon when he wouldn't even be there? My poor, poor neck! Those stupid arseholes! This was all their fault.

Several further failed attempts at elevation followed. Putting my hands behind my head and interlacing my fingers to carry its weight; rolling onto my side and trying to scoop my head up; rolling onto my front and leaving my head hanging. All resulted in the same outcome: me thrashing around in distress and cursing Matey and Matey's rich Spanish girlfriend. It was only after I took a pause and gave the matter more serious thought, that I deduced the problem I was having was getting up, but what with the floor, which I was aiming for, being below the bed, I could potentially forgo getting up and instead, get down. As I shifted my body to the mattress edge, I recalled shifting my bum to the edge of the skylight and the anticipation before dropping. My legs dropped to the floor. Kneeling, like I'd keeled over saying my prayers, face-down on the sheets, I recalled lying face-down on the asphalt up on the roof to catch my breath. I put each hand on the corner of the mattress, elbows up, remembering Matey's rich Spanish girlfriend's braced arms before her fumbled ascent. Then, with a sharp inhale of breath, I pushed away from the bed. A high-pitched mewling noise came out of my mouth but I made it to standing.

Head held high, like I was balancing a stack of books on it, one hand protectively supporting neck, I made my way to the bathroom, wincing with the impact of my feet meeting the floor. The vibrations jarred my shoulder with every step. I remembered sitting on the roof hearing the amp get turned on… I mean, I knew Matey could be selfish but who abandons a woman in distress like that? In the bathroom I pinged on the light but catching sight of my reflection in the bathroom mirror, lips pursed in self-pity, I pinged it off again. I tugged my knickers down one-handed, one side then the other, feeling the strain rippling across my shoulders. I sat heavily on the toilet, moaning with relief at taking the weight off of my feet, but instead of the delayed tinkle of wee hitting water, I felt a prickly warmth that instantly turned cold spread under my bum cheeks. The toilet lid was down and wee was going everywhere but I didn't have the strength to stop it. I'd never felt so weak, so incapable. I dropped my head to my hands in despair. Why was this happening to me? I wasn't a bad person. I hadn't stayed up all night and done coke. All I'd done was go round to see my friend's new place. All I'd done was bring him his records so he had music for his housewarming party.

A Jiminey Cricket voice whispered, *maybe that was the only reason Matey called you, maybe that was why he invited you over in the afternoon and ditched. All he wanted was his records, he didn't want to see you, he didn't care whether or not you were at the party, he hadn't cared enough to wait for you to get down from the roof, or even say goodbye.*

In the state I was in there was little to be done about the bathroom floor so after dabbing my bum dry I left it in a state of its own and drifted into the kitchen where, overwhelmed from the effort it took to do anything, I slumped down the kitchen counter. I couldn't believe how fucked I was... My eyes came to rest on my phone. Surely Matey must've noticed I'd gone by now. I extended one arm, groaning at the expenditure of energy it took to unplug my phone and slide it toward me. I unlocked the screen but there were no missed calls, no new messages. Matey either hadn't noticed or didn't care about my disappearance. For a brief, delusional second I thought about calling him, I even opened Recent Calls and hovered over his name in the list but in my heart of hearts I knew it was pointless. Matey'd either be asleep or still awake and high and even if he wasn't either of things his behaviour yesterday had made it pretty clear he didn't give a shit about me. All he'd wanted was his records and a babysitter and he'd got what he wanted. I thought about texting but what would I say? Your rich Spanish girlfriend has hurt my neck? You lied to me about her reading my books? Have you noticed I've not been there all night? Did you notice I was there at all or did your records just miraculously appear in time for your party?

I found myself wishing there was something more wrong with me than just a cricked neck, like if Matey's rich Spanish girlfriend had broken my arm or something. If she'd broken my arm they'd've had to give a shit. I'd've had to go hospital. It'd've been a massive drama. There wouldn't have been a party. They wouldn't've just been able to ignore me all night if I'd been screaming in agony, showing bone. But even as I fantasied about worse case scenarios, full-body paralysis and severed tendons, that I could lay at Matey's and Matey's rich Spanish girlfriend's feet, I knew I was wasting my time. I didn't need Matey or Matey's rich Spanish girlfriend and I didn't want their sympathy either. What I needed was information.

My thumb came down on Safari. Google came up. Watching my trembling hands with a mixture of alarm and curiosity, like they were someone else's hands, I one-finger typed, 'can't move' into the search bar. A drop-down list of suggestions appeared, the first one was 'can't move neck'.

Taking some comfort from the algorithm's correct prediction, which made me feel less alone because for 'neck' to be the top result it meant there were millions of people just like me, suffering. I scrolled through the search results until I came to the official guidance from the NHS. They'd kept me alive this long, I thought, and clicked.

The NHS website loaded a short article written in text set at a large enough point-size to ward off complaints from the shortest-sighted. One bullet-pointed list detailed extraordinarily precise ways a cricked neck might be achieved:

'Hunching over a phone or computer'

'A cold breeze while sleeping'

'Vigorous hair brushing'

No entry for being assaulted by a minor league Spanish aristocrat.

A second list described symptoms:

'Loss of movement'

'Sharp sensation'

'Stabbing pain'

'Bulge'

None did it justice.

Do's & Don't's followed.

'Do: over-the-counter medication, hot compress/cold compress, rest.'

'Don't: wear a neck collar, do anything dangerous'.

I thumbed the screen hoping for clarification of what 'anything dangerous' might be but the page contained no further information.

Abandoning the safety of the kitchen counter, I stumbled round the kitchen, opening drawers and rifling through cupboards like a malfunctioning automaton. My awkward movements unleashed chaos. Cutlery flew through the air, the pat of butter dropped into the bin, the stack of important letters got wet but somehow, I managed to neck a couple of codeine and fill a hot water bottle before, cursing Matey and his rich Spanish girlfriend for the third, fourth, maybe even fifth time that day, I retreated defeated to the bedroom.

But the bed, with its sweaty sheets and duvet peeling out of its cover, didn't look too inviting, and I recalled reading somewhere that a hard surface was better for bad backs than a soft one. I dropped the hot water bottle to the floor.

It landed with a thud, its contents sloshing from side to side inside it. I went down after it, onto my hands and knees then onto my stomach before rolling ungracefully over onto my back. I wedged the hot water bottle under my neck and felt around for my phone.

I scrolled through Contacts to see if I could think of anyone other than Matey to call. Someone who might be willing to come over and help, maybe bring food... I tried my mum. She didn't answer. I tried my sister. She picked up to whisper that she was busy but would call me back and hung up. Georgia was at work, Maz was babysitting, JRTC had a foreign ringtone, Su's phone was off. Angrily recalling all the times I'd dropped everything to help my friends out, gone round their house to wait for a delivery for them while they were out, listened to hours of them crying over cheating boyfriends, brought them soup to make them feel better, brought them flowers to cheer them up, I gave up. Fuck people. My thumb meandered from icon to icon, came unthinkingly down on Instagram. First post was a picture of people crowded into Matey's living room, followed by a picture of people up on Matey's roof at dawn. The scene of the crime. Matey and his rich Spanish girlfriend were there and the sportswear wankers and some dude with his cock out who was pissing into the street and loads of my friends. People who hadn't been there when I left so must've turned up later. Iris, Eka, Hannah, Kieron, Ben, Naomi, Jesse, Dan, Victor, Jones, Matty, Eva. Practically everyone I knew. All minutes from where they knew I lived and not one had thought to call me. I clicked through the tags below the post to check people's profiles. Selfies, sunsets, satirical leftwing memes.

What a bunch of cunts. Didn't they know anything? Didn't they understand? I struck them off one by one, unfollow, block, making a promise to myself that I knew I would have no trouble keeping: that once I was better, *if* I got better, I'd remember this. The next time someone called *me* up ill or homeless or asking to borrow money they could sit and spin. They weren't my friends, or at least not in any way that meant anything, not in any way that could be counted upon. They were just people I knew. People I wish I didn't. People I wish I'd never let have the privilege of coming near me, of knowing me. Self-regarding, self-involved, self-serving. First world pricks with first world problems. To hell with them and their jobs and their babies and their boyfriends and their mortgages and their discounted gym memberships and their political leanings and their opinions on art and their taste in music and their taking up of fusion cooking and their interest in vintage motorcycles and their vinyl collections and their customised denim. None of it would last! The day would come when their back or their eyesight or their heart or their brain or their bladder or their bowels or their bones would give out, give way, and when that day came it wouldn't be *me* that came to their rescue. It wouldn't be anyone! Because that's what happens in a world where giving a shit is conditional, where people are only important to other people according to what those people can do for them. Social standing, career opportunity. A world where nobody cares about people as people is a world where nobody cares about you. This is why people had children. This is what they were for. An insurance policy taken out by spineless, shallow cowardy custards so that when the day did come around there'd be someone there to take care of them. But children were no insurance. Children can grow up to hate their parents. Or move abroad. And rightly so! Who wants someone they know holding the bed pan anyway? No, better to go and die in peace. Better to die alone. Find a cave somewhere, crawl in and hope for the best.

Reaching the end of New Posts, I double-clicked and swiped up closing Instagram. My horrible mood vanished with it. My fucked neck wasn't any of these people's fault. I knew that. It was Matey's and Matey's rich Spanish girlfriend's. And it'd already been established that Matey and Matey's rich Spanish girlfriend didn't give a toss, so why was I even looking at their shit? Why was I even thinking about them? Hadn't I wasted enough time and energy on people who couldn't spare so much as thought for me? Let them do their coke and have their parties and climb on their roofs and post their nonsense, what I needed to do was get better.

Banishing thoughts of Matey and his rich Spanish girlfriend, I closed my eyes and tried to focus on the sensation of heat permeating my body, fixing me. I imagined the painkillers hitting my empty stomach, dissolving in acid, digesting, pain receptor blockers being absorbed into my bloodstream, circulating towards my brain. Dark dots meandered against the orange, veiny backlit backdrop of my eyelids, as slowly and senselessly as bluebottle flies. A blush of static formed. Resonant fractals spiralling like a magic eye. They moved in and out and in and out and were pulling me in and out with them. The static grew noisier. It got so intense I could hear its effervescent hiss. The pulsing in and out got stronger and was starting to make me dizzy and the only way I can describe it is that it was like a head-rush, only reality was the head and I was the rush. It was like being plucked out of this world, a nauseating feeling, like sitting in the passenger seat of a car that has really good suspension. And as I rushed along feeling sick, I was looking back and could see myself in the middle of it all, lying on my back on the floor in my duvet in my bedroom in my flat on my street in my borough in my city in my country in the seas on the continent in the world in the universe in outer space then outside of space and outside of time where I teetered for a non-moment before, helpless to resist the pull back down, I tumbled back into time, into place, only further in than where I'd started. Deep, deep down inside, like that song. What it felt like was that I was someone or some*thing* that lived inside my body but wasn't me. A seldom-seen vole- or mole-like creature peering at the world from within.

I opened my eyes and peered around the room, taking in the curious new perspective. Disgusting bales of hair matted into the carpet, dust running along the skirting, chipped paint where wall met wall. The hot water bottle'd gone cold, which meant I must've been out for a couple of hours. Assuming the codeine had kicked in, I threw caution to the wind and sat up without supporting my neck. My head lolled backwards, making a crunch that seemed to come from the depths of my skull. In a panic, I scrabbled around for my phone. Two o'clock and still no word from Matey. I re-opened Safari. A pop-up window had sprung up, vibrating like an alarm clock. 'Did you find this website useful?' I took little satisfaction in clicking the box marked, 'No' before returning to Google to tweak my search.

'Cricked neck blurred vision' warned of spinal meningitis and stroke but both were 'rare'. Other symptoms included pins and needles. I definitely had those. I tweaked my search again, tried 'cricked neck danger', then 'cricked neck death', then 'cricked neck massage', then 'cricked neck treatment'. Clicking from osteopath's blog to chronic neck pain forum, I skimmed concertinaing threads peppered with hyperlinks and medical jargon that warned of bony spurs and herniated discs and spinal stenosis and sudden death following incorrect spinal manipulations and the partial-paralysis of a 34-year-old man that prompted a malpractice suit and misaligned chakras and biblical scares.

'The experience of an illness reveals a mistake that we have made in life so an important aspect of treatment is to understand the message it carries.'

The mistake I'd made was thinking Matey was my friend.

'The neck signifies that which conjoins the higher things in man, concerning the head, and the communication of the lower things that occur in the rest of the body, so the energy of the neck area is concerned with the energy of communication and expression. A pain in the neck often signifies one is being neglected, or ignored.'

I thought of all the times I'd been blanked in the past twenty-four hours, from talking to Matey on the phone to trying to talk to his rich Spanish girlfriend, to being left on the roof, to Matey not being there in the first place.

'To put the neck under the yoke of the king of Babylon and serve him, is to be devastated as to truth.'

The truth is that we live in a society compromised of self-serving wankers who given the opportunity wouldn't think twice about treading on, enslaving, maiming, crippling anybody else if they thought there was something in it for them.

Much as I found reading accounts of the horrible things happening to other people soothing, it didn't take long for me to reach the conclusion that I didn't have spinal bifida or early on-set arthritis. All I had was a cricked neck and while trigger point massage and soft tissue decompression sounded swell, maybe the only thing I needed to do was allow it. Allow the hot water bottle, allow the codeine, allow doing anything at all. Just lie on my bedroom floor like a fasting monk. Submit to whatever was happening to me. Discarding the phone, I stared at the cracks in the ceiling, wondering how long I could stay here for. Days, weeks, maybe forever, until I was a crumbly heap of bones. The idea of never moving again, of never having to deal with assholes like Matey or fascists like Matey's rich Spanish girlfriend or vintage sportswear wankers or social media or shopping for food or checking up on old friends, of just giving up, was delightful.

MIDDLE ENGLISH BESTIARY

A wilde der is, that is ful of fele wiles, / Fox is hire to name, for hire qwethsipe. / Husebondes hire haten for hire harmdedes. / The coc and te capun / Ge feccheth ofte in the tun, / And te gandre and te gos / Hi the necke and bi the nos / Haleth is to hire hole. For-thi man hire hatieth, / Hatien and huten bothe men and fules. / Listneth nu a wunder that tis der doth for hunger. / Goth o felde to a furg and falleth thar-inne, / In eried lond er in erthchine forto bilirten fugeles. / Ne stereth ge nogt of the stede a god stund deies, / Oc dareth so ge ded were, ne drageth ge non onde. / The raven is swithe redi, weneth that ge rotieth / And othre fules hire fallen bi for to winnen fode, / Derflike withuten dred he wenen that ge ded beth. / He wullen on this foxes fel, and ge it wel feleth. / Ligtlike ge lepeth up and letteth hem sone, / Gelt hem here billing / Rathe with illing, / Tetoggeth and tetireth hem mid hire teth sarpe, / Fret hire fille / And goth than ther ge wille. / Twifold forbisne in this der / To frame we mugen finden her, / Warsipe and wisedom / With devel and with ivel man. / The devel dereth dernelike, / He lat he ne wile us nogt biswike; / He lat he ne wile us don non loth / And bringeth us in sinne and ter he us sloth. / He bit us don ure bukes wille, / Eten and drinken with unskil, / And in ure skemting / He doth rathe a foxing: / He billeth one the foxes fel, / Wo-so telleth idel spel, / And he tireth on his ket, / Wo-so him with sinne fet. / And devel geld swilk billing / With same and with sending, / And for his sinfule werk / Ledeth man to helle merk. / The devel is tus the fox ilik / Mith ivele breides and with swik; / And mani al-so the foxes name / Arn wurthi haven to same. / For wo-so seieth other god / And thenketh ivel on his mod, / Fox he is and fend iwis - / The boc ne legeth nogt of this. / So was Herodes fox and flerd / Tho Crist kam into this middel-erd: / He seide he wulde him leven on / And thogte he wulde him fordon.

I never got what X__ saw in J__ but then I rarely got what anyone saw in the person they were shagging. Sometimes I didn't even get what *I* saw in the person *I* was shagging, so it was no skin off my nose that J__ and X__ were going out.

J__ was short and squishy, with a face straight off the boat from the Isle of Shite. One of the we've-been-here-since-1066 lot. The inbreds. He cut hair for a living in a swanky salon in town, charging £200+ a haircut, which supplied him with a steady supply of badly fitted jeans, diamanté t-shirts and single stud earrings. Exactly the sort of numpty you'd expect to step out of a secondhand Porsche. I suppose in a way X__ and J__ suited each other because X__ wasn't much to look at either. What you might call an English Rose. Face like butter. When they turned up places together I always thought of a pair of trolls who'd been relieved from bridge duty and let loose in H&M.

They'd been together for a year or two, when gossip started circulating that J__ was cheating. I listened to the 'proof' (leaky theories founded on X__'s reports of J__'s erratic behaviour) with interest but found it unlikely mainly because I couldn't imagine anyone other than X__ wanting to have sex with J__. But then I ran into J__ on Hoxton Street with this insanely beautiful but obviously insane Iranian girl on his arm. The kind of crazy you can tell on sight. Heavy contouring, hella voluptuous, real fur coat. Made sense. When J__ saw me he panicked and blurted out a lame explanation about them being second cousins. He needn't have bothered because if my time on the London 'dating' scene (lots of sex, very few dates) had taught me anything, it was that when it came to other people's relationships, you mind your business. You know the person sticking his dick in your friend is a slimeball? All well and good. He made a pass at you? So be it. Whatever inside info you think you've got, you keep it to yourself. If your friend calls you crying, asking if you think they should dump him, *even then* you keep your mouth shut. Because, nine times out ten, your friend and the slimeball will work it out. They'll stay together and instead of the slimeball being ditched it'll be you, because all the things you said about the slimeball being a slimeball will make you a threat. A threat to their happiness and an exterior factor to blame for the ultimate failure of their relationship. No, the thing to do is to let things play out of their own accord… Which is exactly what I did.

A couple of months after that, coming up to Christmas when I was due to leave London for three+ months, I heard that X__ was pregnant. Now, I find it disturbing whenever I hear that the news that anyone is pregnant but found the news of X__'s pregnancy no more or less disturbing than I would've found it had it been anyone else. I jetted off to Rajasthan and forgot all about it. Arriving back in Blighty in the Spring, full of stories of stoned bubbas on mountaintops with hacked Sky subscriptions who chanted lines from *The Simpsons* like mantras, I found my travel anecdotes trounced by the latest cataclysm. J__ and X__ had split up and bigger than that, X__ wasn't pregnant anymore. The break-up had been bad. Other people had got involved and the Porsche'd got trashed. Groupthink eventually sided with X__ , meaning J__ was history. I enquired after the foetus but was met with muted response. I didn't press the point but doing the maths in my head, X__'d been three months gone when I left, which meant an abortion was out of the question. But, whatever the weather, it wasn't my business. I accepted the group consolidating behind X__ and ditching J__ in theory but in practise I didn't make any effort to see either of them.

I ran into X__ a few weeks later. She showed up at lunch, tagging along with L__ and C__ , who I'd heard she'd moved in with after splitting up with J__ , but if I'm honest, I almost didn't recognise her. She looked so different. I could tell L__ had done her make-up, because their faces looked identical and her clothes were definitely a bit of C__. Black, black, black, black, black. She'd pierced her nose, straightened her hair, might've been wearing a corset but what did I care? Dump boyfriend, get makeover was such standard procedure it barely warranted mentioning. I accepted the new X__ like I'd accepted the old X__. With minimal interest.

After lunch I ran a couple of debt collecting errands, popping in to the 'offices' of 'magazines' that owed me money, when, as is so often the way with these of things, I ran into slap bang J__. I was about to blurt out how weird it was to bump into him because I'd literally just seen X__ but then I took in *his* change in appearance. Not as dramatic as X's, or at least he was still wearing the same clothes. Exactly the same clothes, by the looks of things. The elastic of his skinny jeans sagged at the knee, a couple of diamanté pieces were missing from the dragon design on his t-shirt, his trainers were dirty and most shocking of all, the Nike tick on the side of his head that had grown out.

J__ seemed overly pleased to see me. He gave me a long hug and when he spoke, made earnest eye contact. Much friendlier than usual, taking more interest in me than he'd ever done before. Asked about India, asked about the writing, said he was gonna buy one of my books (yeah right), the whole preamble… But I knew where it was headed.

— Have you, he said, — spoken to X__?

When he said her name, a shadow passed over his face, highlighting the crow's feet at the corner of his eyes and indents between his eyebrows.

I shrugged and said, — You guys not speaking then?

J__ nodded, shook his head, nodded and said, — I don't know, I really don't know.

He started trying to thank me for not saying anything about the Iranian but he was stumbling over his words and was hard to understand. I caught 'the only one', 'second cousin' again and 'undermined trust' before I stopped him.

— It wasn't my business, I said.

J__ carried on talking, saying how he loved X__ , he'd let her down, he was an idiot, he couldn't lie to her anymore, he thought they were friends but that maybe she had something mentally wrong with her, he didn't trust C__ , he didn't trust L__. It was clear he wasn't going to let the opportunity of speaking to someone who knew X__ pass, so I suggested the Lamb & Lion, a charming ex-BNP boozer that was always empty and which I very much enjoyed spending time in. J__ got the drinks in, two pints each, and we took a corner table.

— We were friends more than anything else, J__ said, instantly calmed by two big gulps of flat lager. — That's why we stayed in it for so long. Even when it was obvious it wasn't working. We actually liked each other, that's why.

— I'm sure you guys will work something out, I said.

— I dunno, J__ said, — I loved her you know? But I don't know, if I'd any idea of the way she'd act over us splitting up I never would've got into anything with her in the first place. Everything from Farzeen to the baby flung in my face, like it'd never been talked about, as if nothing we'd said before counted for anything.

— So you guys got an abortion? I said.

J__ looked at me like he didn't understand the question.

— It was, she was, mental, he said. — She just tore the thing to shreds. I said I'd take her to Italy but I never took her to Italy. She gave me blowjobs all the time but I wouldn't give her cuddles. She told me I'd ruined her life, that I had blood on my hands. She got in touch with my boss. She got me fired! I mean can you believe that shit? Five in the morning messages accusing me of rape, *rape for fuck's sake*? We were going out!

— That doesn't preclude rape, I said, unable to stop myself chiming in on my favourite topic.

— I never raped her, J__ said.

— People have different definitions of rape, I said. — You know, sometimes if a person tells a big enough lie while having sex with you, it might not be rape in the eyes of the law but it is still kinda rape, because it's like you're not who you say you are.

— I. Did. Not. Rape. My. Girlfriend, J__ said.

— Ok, I said. — Sorry.

— I went to her dad's funeral and now she'd never come to my dad's funeral, I mean, what the fuck? Who wants to go to someone who raped her's dad's funeral? It's like…

J__ slapped his forehead with his fingertips.

— Crazy. Crazy! I tried to engage, I really did. I replied to *all* the mental emails with rational questions, like, 'why does this matter now when it didn't before?', 'yes of course I loved her', 'no I wasn't seeing anyone else', 'yes, we'd always be friends', but it didn't matter what I said because I knew her fuckwit flatmates were pouring poison about me into her ear.

— L__ and C__? I asked.

— Fucked in the head, J__ said.

— C__'s alright, I said. — She's funny.

J__ raised an eyebrow.

— So one minute it's all hell breaking loose and then I get this text, like, 'it's done'.

— What's done? I said.

— Exactly, J__ said, — exactly. I called, no answer. I texted. I even went round to the house because it's like, I needed to know what'd happened and I could hear someone in there but whoever it was wouldn't open the door. No one would talk to me. No one.

— Sometimes things just get fucked up, I said, the sentiment sounding wise as a thought but coming out sounding kinda stupid.

J__ finished the dregs of his first pint and slid it to the edge of the table.

— I don't know man, he said, starting his second pint. — It's like one minute I'm gonna be a dad, which I didn't have any say in, and next minute I'm not and I don't know why. I'm telling you my head was a mess. No one would chat to me or tell me anything. No one. And I thought about you, because, you know, it was really safe the way you didn't say anything about... J__ waggled his eyebrows. — But you were away and everyone else just shut down on me.

I'd seen this group of friends do this to people before. One minute someone was in, the next they were out. School playground rules preserved far beyond school playground boundaries.

— The only person who'd chat to me was P___. P___ was a proper mate. Didn't say a word about any of the shit that'd happened only that the D must've been good.

J__ laughed the laugh of a man for whom erections are a thing of the past.

— He listened to all my shit, helped me sort out the flat, got me a gig with this agency who sent me round to people's flats, like old people and shit, to give them trims. It wasn't salon prices, more like thirty, forty quid, but it kept me going. Anyway eventually P___ gets sick of listening to me bang on about X__. He gives it to me straight. Says X__ is damaged goods, that he'd seen her round and she'd gone whacko anyway so whatever things had been between us before, I was better off out of it. So I'm like, okay, I hear you, you know? It's like months obsessing over what? But I'm, like, so out of the game I don't even know and P__ tells me the thing to do is get on Tinder, like 'this is what you wanna be doing mate'.

J__ picks up his phone from the table and holds up the blank screen.

— He shows me his account and there were some proper sorts. Girls coming straight out and asking for it, no strings. And peng. So, we were pretty pissed and just went for it, made this jokes profile like with pictures of me skiing and that one of me with Kylie Minogue. I wasn't taking any of it too seriously but then next morning I wake up, completely forgetting about making any profile and when I switch my phone on it's like ding, ding, ding! Keisha, Cara, Danielle. You ever done this?

I shake my head. — No.

J__ finishes his second pint as I'm starting mine.

— Another? he said.

I demurred. He strode towards the bar, returning minutes later with a pint and whiskey chaser. He knocked back his whiskey and settled in his seat, his manner shifting, and for the first time in the conversation, sounding relaxed.

— Pretty soon I'm pinging messages back and forth with this one girl and we make a plan to meet. China Town on a Saturday afternoon. I wasn't expecting sex, I wasn't expecting anything. I wasn't taking it seriously, you know, but a couple of hours in and we're at it in the Burger King toilets.

A big grin spread across J__'s face.

— Sorry. He said. — Anyway, my point is, is that it was nice to have the company of a woman whose chief desire was something other than cutting off me bollocks.

He raised his pint. I met his glass with mine.

— Anyway this girl ends up coming back to mine and we're at it all night. In the kitchen, on the sofa, in the hall. Wake up in bed next morning and bam! A text from the Ex. *Like she knew.* All it said was, 'How are you?' but I'm telling you man, it threw me. Not a word for months and then… I'm not exaggerating when I say I had a full on panic attack. I used to get them when I was a kid. Super Skunk. But I haven't smoked in years. Had to lock myself in the bathroom and this girl's, like, knocking and asking me what's wrong and I just didn't come out, you know? Stayed in there 'til she left.

— J__ , I said.

— I know, I know, he said. — Terrible. But anyway, once she's gone, I calm down a bit. I jump in the shower and then, sorry to be crass but I get this banging hard on. It was like someone had given me Viagra or something, like something had taken over my body, like something had taken over my mind. Because I was suddenly remembering all this shit that I'd kind of forgotten before. Like the night me and X__ got together and I fingerbanged her in Spoons. D'you know that story?

I nodded, I did, curious to see where J__ was going with all this.

— And not just sex stuff, other stuff. Fighting. When she threw my Blackberry in the sea in Southend and her smashing up the bathroom and then all this stuff that never happened, like us on a cruise liner in the Arctic and in a wood that was kinda the woods behind my parents house, but wasn't. It was like a flashback or a trip or something. The two of us fucking in this ancient woodland with all, like, elves and shit and yeah, J__ laughs, — I just sploodge everywhere but then I'm telling you, it was bare freaky. I've never felt anything like that before. It was like my mind was riding on this, like, monorail. I get out the shower and go to the bedroom. No towel, dripping wet, and I pick up the phone and I call her. I'm telling you, it was really weird, whatever was going on. It was something strong.

J__ and I finish our drinks at the same time. J__ gets to his feet.

— What do you say we switch to white? he said.

I shrugged in agreement. He went to the bar, I went for a wee, taking my phone with me and sending a couple of texts. One to C__ telling her I'd bumped into J__ and it seemed like he'd lost it. I returned to the table where J__ had poured two giant glasses out of a bottle.

— So I'm like, 'hello, are you there?', J__ continues without missing a beat. — And suddenly we're talking, chatting on the phone like normal, like nothing has happened. I'm making jokes, she's laughing at them and I'm like 'woah'. We talk for like an hour and then, just as we're getting off the phone, she drops it in. Some foxes had made a nest in her garden.

— Foxes? I said.

— Yeah, he said. — Foxes. Random I know but that's what she said. Two hours later I'm stood in X__'s kitchen looking at these foxes, only there's not much to see. I can make out the white tips of their tails and bits of fur but they're basically hidden behind stinging nettles.

— That garden, I said, — is a disaster.

— From what the Ex'd said on the phone I expected a fox extravaganza, J__ said, waving his arms like he was conducting an imaginary orchestra. Pissed. — You know, all singing, all dancing but whatever, it was nice to be there and if a couple of foxes at the end of the garden was the excuse we needed to make friends then I was glad of the foxes. The flatmates were being proper dizzy though. C__ kept going on about how they were in love then L__ said she thought they were pregnant and when she said it they all three turned to look at me and it was super awk. But then it was kinda okay again. Like it was forgotten. So we sit around shooting the shit and d'you know what? It was alright. It was like none of any of the fucked up shit that happened had happened, like old times again. The girls persuaded me to stay for dinner, got some beers in and I end up passing out in front of the telly, then, get this, I wake and all three of them are there, standing over me, like they were watching me sleep, so I'm like shit, you know? But then X__ is all like, 'shhh' and 'follow me', so we all four of us go through the kitchen and she points out at the garden and there they were. It was kinda amazing. The foxes were out on the lawn, up on their hind legs and they were dancing. I've never seen anything like it, well maybe in those picture books, you know, where the animals wear clothes and go around doing shit. It was like that. They were doing, like, eskimo kisses. It was amazing actually, seeing them close up like that, and then before I knew it, we are holding hands and the flatmates are just standing there watching and X__ leans in and I think she's gonna kiss me and I'm thinking of all the reasons I shouldn't — the baby, Tinder girl — but then she just does what the foxes are doing. She gives me an eskimo kiss.

J__ closed his eyes and nuzzled the air, wasted but then I wasn't feeling too sober myself.

— Anyway, he said, setting his elbows on the table and topping up our glasses, — I didn't hear from X__ for the rest of week and I don't hear from Tinder girl either. But I was feeling alright about things. I was pleased things were cool between me and X__ and figured that as far as Tinder girl was concerned, a hook up was a hook up. But then, that Friday, the Ex texts and, you guessed it…

J__ leaves the sentence hanging.

— What? I said.

— So does Tinder girl, J__ said. — And it's such a friendly, straight up message that I'd have to be a total dickhead not to reply, I mean, I fucked this girl, you know? So I write back apologising for a being a weirdo, said that I had some stuff going on, 'it's not you it's me' kinda thing, and I press send but then, the same second, X__ calls. I freaked, thought I'd sent the message to her by mistake and meant to decline the call but pressed the wrong button and then she's just on the line yammering away about C__ being right about the foxes being pregnant because they'd woken up to babies and she was like, 'they're so cute' and 'you gotta come see', and I was like, 'errrr, I dunno', but I knew she wasn't gonna take no for an answer so I tell her, 'I'll swing by later on', with zero intention of actually doing it. The phone hockey had weirded me out. Anyway, when I got off the phone there's a text from Tinder girl suggesting a drink at the Nelson that evening. First, I was like, maybe I shouldn't, I mean me and X__ had almost kissed and I wasn't exactly sure what was, you know, going on… But then, I don't know, I just thought about what P__ said and thought, 'what are you doing man?' It's over, you know. We were friends, or trying to be and that was good but there wasn't gonna be any funny business. Not after everything. So I texted Tinder girl, 'see you there', and figured I'd text X__ later to cancel. Simple. Only it wasn't simple because half an hour later I get another call. Hysterical. Apopo-, apoplectic. Is that how you say it? I swear, for a second I thought I'd looped back in time because X__ was just hyperventilating into the receiver and I could hear the others in the background telling her to hang up and then, when she could talk again, she just kept saying, 'dead, dead, he's dead', and the only person I could imagine she was talking about was her fucking dad. She was just crying and crying and I don't know, I guess that's the thing, isn't it? Once you've been through something with someone, when you think they need you, you go.

J__'s face creased with concern.

— I ran all the way, he said — And you know what I was thinking? I was thinking, 'here we go again'. Arrived expecting the worst and knocked on the door. Half of me was wondering what carnage I was about to walk into and the other half of me was thinking I should text Tinder girl and cancel but then the door opened and man, the sight of three women who'd spent an hour or more crying, all like hugging each other and swaying back and forth, that's a sight no one needs to see. But what can I do? I'm there and X__ throws herself into my arms, like, 'I'm so glad you're here', and 'thank you, thank you', and I'm telling her it's gonna be alright and I'm like, looking out into the back garden, which is when I see it and mate, it was brutal.

— What was? I said.

— The fox, J__ said. — One of the baby foxes. Swear down I've never seen so much blood. The women were wailing about how I had to do something because I was a man and how I should know what to do because I grew up in the countryside so what choice did I have? I went out to have a look at this thing. Blood coming out of its mouth, its nose, its eyes, its ears. The women wouldn't come out, huddled in the doorway like, 'the father killed it because it was the runt of the litter'. I nudged it with my trainer and then this hiss came from the stinging nettles. The mum. I saw her, teeth bared, tail wrapped round the rest of the babies.

— Jesus, I said.

— You're telling me, J__ said. — Another?

The bottle of wine was finished and I was pretty pissed.

— I dunno, I said. — I kinda need to eat.

— One more then we'll go somewhere, J__ said.

Too drunk to disagree, I accepted. J__ went to the bar and came back with another bottle and two packets of crisps, which he opened and tore down the side then set in the middle of the table.

— Where was I? J__ said.

— You'd just kicked the dead fox, I said.

— Oh yeah, J__ said, — So the women are like, 'what do we do?' And I'm like, 'bag it and bin it', but the women are like, 'no fucking way', and come up with some fucking insanity like we, meaning I, had to bury it. So they give me a spade and send me into the garden and tell me to dig.

— Fucking hell, I said.

— Innit, J__ said. — So I'm about to say, 'this is crazy', when I catch sight of X__ and it's just like, I don't know, there was something really off about it. She was so pale and just staring at me in trance and so I'm like, 'ok, I wasn't there for you before and if this is what you need from me, I'll do it'. So I'm out in the garden and I'm digging and I dig this fuck off big hole. None of them help, mind. They go back inside and I can see them through the kitchen window sat around the table, drinking tea and I could tell they were talking about something important because they were sitting really close together and every now and then one of them turns to look at me. So, eventually I go back inside, like, 'I'm done', so they all come out and look at the hole and then they look at each other and they're shaking their heads and they're all like, 'bigger, it's got to be bigger'. They go back inside and I don't know what else to do. I carry on digging. I'm digging and digging and I'm telling you, I dig this hole so big you could fit a person in it.

— Creepy, I said.

— You're telling me, J__ said. — So it's starting to get dark and I look in through the window and the women have vanished and I'm about to go inside and look for them when they just appear, like materialise next to me. They've got all this shit with them. X__ has a wooden drawer and C__'s got a tea towel and all these candles and they tell me we're going to have a funeral.

— Are you serious? I said.

— That's what they said, J__ said. — So I'm there thinking, 'how'm I gonna get out of this?', you know. I nip off to the bathroom to text Tinder girl. It's too late to cancel but I let her know I'm gonna be late when there's a knock at the door and it's X__ and she's like, 'come with me', and takes me to her bedroom and makes me sit on the bed and I'm all like, 'I don't think this a good idea', but she ignores me, starts rummaging around under the bed. I'm watching the others out the window, lighting candles 'n' shit so when X__ hands me this box I'm not even thinking, I'm still like, you know, 'if you wanna talk', 'I think we should talk', but she hands me this box, a shoebox, and is just like, 'open it'.

J__ stopped talking. Leaning back in my chair I looked at him through my glass of wine, his face distorted like a grotesque, his blonde hair tinged green by the drink.

— Well? I said. — What was in the box?

J__ shook his head.

— Fuck, he said.

— What? I said.

— It was the baby, J__ said.

— What? I said, sitting up in my seat.

— No, J__ said. — I mean, it was the box they gave her, you know, afterwards. To remember. The scan and a piece of paper with handprints and footprints.

— Shit, I said. — I didn't realise... I trailed off, not wanting to put into words that I hadn't realised the abortion or miscarriage or whatever it was had been so late, late enough to make it an actual baby and not just a blood clot. — Heavy.

— Nor did I, J__ said. — It was so fucking heavy. I had no idea, you know, she hadn't told me anything and there I was worrying about what to say to Tinder girl and she's showing me this and I feel like a proper cunt. Like, who even am I? But then I look at X__ and it's like I don't even know. Like she's a different person, somebody else, and she's holding up this piece of paper with these tiny footprints and she's staring at me, pale as fuck, and when I touch her, she's cold. I don't know what I'm doing but I'm like, 'fuck the box', try and take the piece of paper and give her a hug, you know, tell her, I don't know, that she shouldn't have gone through all that alone, that I was sorry, and I'm choking up because it's like, what the fuck? But then the others start calling for us to come down and X__ is like, snap, box away, straight back to normal, and goes downstairs so I follow her, of course, try to take her hand but she shrugs me off and then we're in the garden and the others have arranged it all. They've put the tea towel over the fox and there's a patch of blood seeping through and they've put coins on its eyes and flowers all round it and man, I just felt like I was in over my head, you know? I wanted to duck out, but then X__ just shoots me this look, like, 'you owe me', so I don't say anything, you know?

— OMG, I laughed in bemusement. — This is insane.

— You're telling me, J__ said but doesn't laugh. — So somehow I'm roped into being the undertaker and I lower this coffin thing into the hole and obviously the hole is way bigger than it needs to be and I was gonna say something when C__ starts reading. Wait. Reading this.

J__ takes out his phone and types.

— What is it?

J__ puts his phone on the table and slides it over, rotating it so the screen faces me. It is open on a website called English Bestiary.

— Scroll down, he said. — To fox.

I ran my fingers along the screen until I came to an entry written in italics.

— I like 'feely wiles', I said, reading the first line. — What are they?

J__ shrugged. — No idea, he said. — It's a load of fucking nonsense, but this is what they decide they're gonna read. They do this whole ceremony.

— I think it's Middle English, I said. — Like, the fox is a wily animal that people hate because of its harmful deeds…

— You understand that? J__ said.

I shook my head. — No, just guessing.

J__ shivers.

— Don't tell me you're one of them?

I laughed.

— Anyway they're reading this shit and X__ is like crying and they were really freaking me out. It was like none of them would look at me but I could tell they were watching and I'm really not getting it. I'm just waiting for it to be over so I can go but it goes on and on and then, when the funeral, or whatever, was done they're like, 'now you've got to fill it in'.

— Man, I said. — You know, I saw X__ just before I bumped into you. I wasn't gonna say but it was kinda weird.

— She's different, right? said J__.

— She's different, I said.

— Yeah, well, so then it's like I fill up the hole and when I'm done I don't even go in to say goodbye, just slip out the alley at the side of the house and vanish. Make it to the pub to meet Tinder girl and I'm only five minutes late but yeah, the date was a total disaster.

J__ sits back in his seat, his manner shifting.

— So was this it? I said. — Have you spoken to X__ since?

J__ pours more wine, finishing the bottle.

— Not even. I don't hear from X__ for the rest of the week and I don't hear from Tinder girl either and to be honest I was glad of the headspace but then Saturday night I get another call. Another fox has snuffed it. A dog got into the garden. They'd been in the kitchen at the time and watched the whole thing. X__ begged me to come, said crows kept coming down and pecking at the carcass, that there wasn't anyone else. So, of course I go round, and I'm ready to do whatever I've got to do but fuck, if you thought last time was bad, this was beyond, just beyond. There's fox all over the lawn, guts, entrails, but they weren't red, they were black. I don't know, is that bile? Whatever it was, it was rancid. And the girls, well, they had lost it. X__ was like lying under a blanket shivering, C__ had been sick, L__'d legged it to her boyfriend's. And you know, the weather had turned, it was one of the first warm days so the smell was rank, gutsy. I almost hurled. This thick, black shit smeared all over the grass, all over the patio. Like Marmite, only there was no way so much Marmite could exist in one place. It was like the equivalent of how much Marmite the whole country eats in a year. It looked like the time the rats got into the bins and left the lawn covered in strings of black bin liner and the week's rubbish, only this wasn't teabags and plastic, it was animal. Ribbons of intestine. Gross. Gross. Gross. And worst of all its head, which was the only part of it still intact, had one eye open staring up at the sky.

The bartender rings the bell for last orders and this time I offer to get the drinks in, half in protest at being told I can't drink anymore and half because I want to hear the end of the story. I get us a large glass of red each and return to the table.

— So? I said. — What did you do?

— I did my best to sort it out, J__ said. Put the fox in a bin liner.

— Where was the mum?

— No sign, J__ said. — No sign of either of the parents, just one of the kids asleep on its own. Anyway, I open up the hole and put the fox in with its brother…

— Or sister, I said.

— Or sister, J__ said.

— And was there a funeral? I said.

— No funeral, J__ said. — The girls didn't even come out. X__ stays up in her bedroom and I can feel her watching me out the window but each time I look up she's not there. When I'm done and I go back inside, there's no sign of anyone so I just let myself out but I knew it was just a matter of time…

— A matter of time until what? I said.

— A matter of time until the last one, J__ said. — And sure enough, I got the call a few days later. The parents never came back, just left the last surviving of the litter on its own. The women'd gone maternal and tried to feed it warm milk on a platter but the fox wasn't having any of it. It starved to death. They'd found it on the patio, skin and bones, right outside the back door, like it'd been knocking or scratching, trying to get in…

— Fuck, I said, thinking that in all my years in London, a city full of foxes, I'd never heard a story like this.

— This time I arrived to find X__ home alone but surprisingly chill. We sat and talked while I put the fox in a bin liner. Not about anything heavy, just what I'd been up to, what she'd been up to, that it was cool we were talking, how this was all a bit weird. So, I went out and opened the grave, put the bag in, covered it up. I could see X__ through the kitchen window, standing by the sink, so I went in to tell her it was done, which is when I saw it nestled in the long grass like a lost shoe.

— Saw what? I said.

— A paw, J__ said. — I guess the cub must've chewed it off in the throes of starvation or something. It was so tiny and so perfect, claws still soft, like a baby and I dunno, I saw it, like, set in a clasp or something, surrounded by semi-precious stones, like one of those things that Victorians used to wear, you know?

I nodded, thinking I knew what he meant.

— And then I thought about the box, the shoebox under her bed, and I just thought the whole episode seemed so symbolic I thought maybe she'd want to keep it, the handprints, the footprints, like a talisman, a good luck charm.

J__'s words are slurred. The bartender rings the second bell. J__ wobbles to his feet.

— Let's get outta here, he says. — You got any ciggies?

I finish my wine. — No, I say. — But I'm sure we can ponce one.

We go outside and succeed in liberating a couple of fags.

— Which way are you walking? J__ said, lighting up.

I nodded in the direction of home. J__ looped his arm through mine and we started to walk, not talking.

— So? I said.

— So what? J__ said.

— So what happened with the paw?

— Oh, J__ said. — Yeah... so I went inside and I'm like, 'look what I found', and X__ takes her time, putting down the sponge and pulling off rubber gloves, finger by finger, before turning to look at me. I'm like, clueless, 'this is for you'. I'm holding the paw, holding it out for her in the palm of my hand but when she sees it, I dunno. First, she kinda froze and I couldn't tell if she was looking at it, had taken it in or what. Then I thought she was gonna cry but she doesn't. She just stares at it and stares at it and stares it. Then bam! She slaps the thing out of my hand and comes for me, screaming, hammering her fists into my chest, scratching my face, totally mental, shouting, screaming in my face like 'get the fuck out. Get. The. Fuck. Out. Getthefuckoutofmyfuckingkitchen'.

VODAFONE.CO.UK/HEEELP

Most nights I remember to switch the ringer to silent when I go to bed, but that evening I'd come home drunk, passed out in all my clothes, and forgotten to do it. It wasn't the shrill, persistent and usually un-ignorable ringtone that woke me up though, it was the electronic shivers of the thing vibrating in my pocket and dissipating into my guts.

The call was from a number that wasn't in my Contacts. That in itself didn't mean much. I'd got a new phone a couple of weeks ago and not been able to figure out how to auto-transfer the address book. Too lazy to enter the hundred and twenty-one numbers manually, I'd saved the important numbers — work, family, boyfriend — and figured that my actual friends would call me, when I would save their number, while anyone who didn't call wasn't my actual friend.

The call rang off and the screen locked. In the darkness an impression of an iPhone floated, scarred onto my retina, like when you accidentally look straight at the sun.

I dimmed the brightness, unlocked the screen and opened Missed Calls. The number seemed familiar, like a number I'd dialled before. If that was the case it meant the caller was someone I'd known for time, since my pager days, when I'd known all my friends' numbers off by heart because I was always having to punch them into phone box keys.

The number called again.

I picked up but didn't say anything, just in case.

— Hello? Hello? Hello? a voice said.

I put the call on mute.

— Are you there? the voice said.

I listened, not to the words, which were standard phone call fare, but to the sound of the voice. Male, breathless, in an enclosed space...

— I know you're there baby. And I'm here too. Hello? Hello?

I felt like I recognised the voice, especially when it said 'baby'.

I unmuted the call.

— Who is this? I said.

The line went dead.

Laying the phone aside, I struggled out of my jacket and jeans, paused to guiltily remember I hadn't brushed my teeth then got under the duvet and tried to sleep, but tomorrow's hangover was already kicking in. I tossed and turned for a couple of minutes then unthinkingly reached, once more, for my phone.

I selected the number from my Call List to save it, entering it as 'Who' before going into WhatsApp to see if 'Who' had an account with a profile picture. I found that they did but the picture wasn't of 'Who', it was an Internet meme of a cat that said, 'I'm not bipolar I jus remember shit out of nowhere and my mood changes'. Sounded pretty bipolar to me. A text notification.

— Ding!

> *Can't say i don't miss u bitch*

The message threw me. Not because it was rude but because I couldn't think of anyone who talked like that, like 'bitch', unless they were joking. I got a disorientating feeling of there being something, or someone, I was forgetting. A situation I'd ignored, a person I'd insulted or neglected.

— Ding!

> *Hey*

— Ding!

> *Don't ignore me*

— Ding!

> *I know ur there*

When the number called again I let it ring out, not wanting to encourage Who by letting them know I was there while I tried to figure out who they were. Sitting up in bed. Giving the screen my full attention.

— Ding!

> *Call me back*

With the message thread open the notifications from this point turned from a ding to a whoop!

— Whoop!

> *I just miss you babe*

— Whoop!

> *I know ur getting my calls*

— Whoop!

I tink we are meant to be

Flicking the switch on the side of the phone, I turned the ringer to silent.

U n me

I know I'm fucked up

But I need u

I love u

Another call.

U will always be mine

Another text.

I'm gonna find who trew him out the window

That message settled it. I must've been mistaken when I thought I recognised the number or thought I recognised the voice because this message was clearly not intended for me. I didn't know anything about any window or anyone who'd been thrown out of one.

Starting to feel sorry for whoever it was, who was clearly having a time of it, I decided to intervene.

Yo. I think u've got the wrong number...

The reply was immediate.

No.

I'm not sure what to say to that. I reply with a single character.

?

Who doesn't reply for long enough that I'm about to put the phone away again but then another message arrived.

> *All I wanted to say is that I saw u ok*

> *I saw you with him*

> *U didn't see me tho*

The first two messages are whatever. Who thinks he saw whoever he thinks he is talking to talking to someone else. So what? But the last message is creepy. What was Who doing? Hiding behind trees following his ex-girlfriend (it had to be an ex) around on a date?

The number called again. It rang twice then disconnected before another call came through from a withheld number. Who was clearly stupid and his antics were starting to grate.

I sent a message.

> *I don't know you.*

I sent another.

> *Stop harassing me.*

Bad move on my part. The messages start arriving in droves.

> *I don't mind*

> *But it would've been nice if u let me know*

> *Disrespectful to not*

> *U looked butters btw*

> *I just wanted u to know that*

'Butters' stirred something. The use of archaic slang made me wonder again if I maybe did know this person. They were definitely around my age and clearly from London and…

> *With ur fucking shit flower*

> *On ur fucking shit head*

> *On ur fucking shit infested body*

I was lost again. I hadn't, as far as I could recollect, worn any shit flower or any other kind of flower on my shit head.

I texted back again.

> *LOL. Bit strong!*

But Who was on one.

> *I was shocked at how baff u are*

> *So baff*

I tried one last intervention.

> *Yo. I don't know you. Stop messaging me.*

I don't know if Who saw my messages or not but the rate he was sending them at made me think that even if he did see them, he wasn't taking them in.

> *I'm going to find u n trow U off a balcony*

> *Fate of every posh cunt hahaha*

> *I'd feel bad doing this to anyone else but u deserve it*

I love fighting with what iv got

My mind and my body

U fight with nothing

Becos u r nothing

I opened message settings and turned off 'read' notifications then returned to the thread, which was growing by the second.

I should call ur mother n tell her

Tell her what a stank ass ho her dgahuter is

Mind u she's probably just as bad

On a crack ting

Dirty girl

I bet ur pum be st8nking

Why you blocking my messages?

A call, then back to messaging.

Why do i still even see u on my feed?

Why do i still even here of u

Dead bit

Dead out

Shit head

Now i know why OJ did it

Diiiiiiickhead

We're so fucking dun

U fucking deadout person

Dead

Out

Baff

I screen grabbed a few sections of the thread. I don't know why I did it. Being a person who has herself expressed many a panic attack via text message I can't say I was worried. I wasn't afraid these messages would materialise into a physical threat to my person. What I felt more was something closer to a sense of power or control over Who (a couple of screen grabs of this sort of shit was enough to get someone arrested) combined with a dash of sadistic amusement at the thought of someone in their flat going totally crazy.

I never thought I hated anyone til I saw ur dirty crack looking shit stained face

All the best ones hate u know that

And the rest

They arent real

Probably cos u fucked them all is why

Everyone i know came in that stank hole

Now they disgusted with theyself

U owt to be shot and killed

I should hunt you down

Cos me I got nothing but time

Hate fuck you

Pillowbiterzzzz anonymous pahahahaha

Ur gonna have ur lips wrapped round this cock before the days out either way

Mark my words

Watch them eyes bug out ur skull

And ur gonna like it

A call.

Whatever

Ignore me den

Mek no difference

I just can't stand liars and emotional bullies

And that's what you are

And don't worry

Already called a lawyer

Criminal lawyer

Brief pause.

Last chance

Call.

Ok den

See you in court

A speech bubble appeared going dot, dot, dot then disappeared, reappeared again, and disappeared again. The screen locked.

Next morning, there's a voicemail.

I called my answering machine to listen.

— Welcome to Vodafone voicemail, the answerphone said. — You have one new message and three saved messages. To listen to your messages...

I cut the answering machine off by pressing 'one'.

The voicemail was long and peculiar. Some rustling, a door or cupboard being shut, distant voices. It was a pocket call but something about it made me think it was made on purpose. Running water. Something scraping the receiver. The phone being carried from an inside space to an outside space. Distant traffic.

— That was your last new message, the answerphone said. — Saved messages.

I hung up.

My WhatsApp icon alerted me to twelve new messages. Why had Who switched from text to WhatsApp?

On the case for cunt and cunty

Jojake

Kofuck

Transpasay

Blasting clearways

I'm fucked

Sorry

Im so sorry

I really am

I'm sorry

Love u

I'm messed up

As soon as I opened the WhatsApp messages, Who called. The clairvoyance of insanity, or had he been online watching and waiting for the blue ticks?

I should've ignored the call, or at the very least waited until I was more awake, but I was too hungover to get up and too hungover to sleep and was up for the entertainment.

— Hello, I said, when the call was answered.

— Hello, said the voice I kinda recognised.

Neither of us said anything. In the background I could hear a slow, steady beep, like a measured heartbeat.

— Thanks for calling me back, the voice said. — Sorry about last night.

— Are you gonna tell me who I'm speaking to? I said. — Or are you gonna make me guess?

— It's me, the voice said, sounding offended.

— Me who? I said.

The voice doesn't say anything.

— Why are you calling me? I said.

— You called me, the voice said, still offended.

— Yes but you called me, I said. — You've been calling me and sending me crazy texts all night!

The voice doesn't say anything.

—Hello-o? I said. — Are you hearing me?

— I tried to kill myself last night, the voice said.

My turn to go silent.

—I *said*, the voice said, sounding hard-done-by, — *I tried to kill myself last night.*

— Oh, I said. — Sorry. But, you know, I still don't know who I'm speaking to.

— No, the voice said.

—No? I said.

— No. I tried to kill myself and the only person I wanted was you… I'm okay, in case you were wondering.

— Ok, I said. — Well, I'm glad you're okay and I'm sorry for, you know, whatever, but this is not who you think it is. I'm not whoever you need to be speaking to.

— Please don't get angry, the voice said, going up an octave.

— I'm not angry, I said. — But I'm gonna go.

— You don't understand, the voice said. — I heard voices... Actual voices. You. My mum. And I don't know, I just had to get out, get out. Please don't hang up. Don't hang up. Don't hang up. Please. Just listen. Understand. I went to the Joiners, where we had our first date. Do you remember? I know you do.

The sound of something hitting the phone or the phone being hit against something.

— Stupid. Stupid, stupid, stupid, the voice said. — The footie was on. Liverpool lost and the Fulham boys were gloating and I told them, just leave it, you know babe? You know me. I just wanna sit here and drink my pint... I don't want trouble.

The voice was babbling.

— Sorry, I said. — I'm hanging up now. Ok. Goodbye, goodbye.

— Please don't interrupt, the voice said. — It's really important you understand.

— Sorry, I said. — But I just don't get why are you telling me this? I think you need to talk to someone, you know, professional.

— Just lissen, the voice said. — Please. Fletcher persuaded me to go halves on a ticket.

I rolled over in bed and the reception dipped making the voice drop in and out.

— Taxi back to Fulham… Everyone at the same time… On my own… Everyone at the same time… Decided to do it… So calm… Bathroom… On my own… Decided to do it… Bathroom… So calm.

I held the phone up for better signal.

— I was so calm, the voice said. — That's how I knew it was right. The right thing to do. I went into the bathroom and turned on the tap and I was gonna do it right there. That's when I called you, you know. To say sorry, to let you know it wasn't your fault. I had my razor and I was gonna do it but then Sean, I could hear Sean getting ready for work. Sean, Sean… it wasn't fair doing it where Sean would find me, where he'd come home from work, and find me, dead, and covered in blood.

Static on the line detracts from the melodrama. I didn't know any Sean.

— So I went out to the alley behind the house, you know the one where we… There, I thought, at least someone else would find me. The cut was deep, brer, deep. The blood bubbled out, like spurting. There was *loads* of blood. I did it right, I did it properly. The way you're s'posed to. I don't fuck about, you know? Up, not across, the way you're s'posed to. Then I just lay there watching the blood come out for ages. I must've lain there, I don't know, for, like, forty-five minutes…

The voice stopped. It felt like he's was waiting for me to say something.

— I severed three tendons, the voice ventured, as if it might help.

— I'm not sure, I say, — What you want me to say. I don't really get why you're telling me this.

— I didn't do it, the voice shouted. — You have to understand. I decided to live. I decided I wanted to live. And this woman, this woman, this old girl, this old woman, man, if it wasn't for her. She called the ambulance. She got blood on her nice coat. I told her I'd buy her a new one but I don't even know who she is like. Like her name. They took me to hospital. I'm here now. I severed three tendons...

The voice stops. I don't fill the silence.

— Please, the voice said. — You've got to understand. They asked me, they asked me who I should call, and, I don't know, Fletcher, Fletcher seemed like the best person.

— Look, I said. — I'm really sorry but can you just put yourself in my shoes for one second?

Sulky silence.

— What d'you mean? the voice said.

— I don't know you! I said. — How many times? You're telling me all this stuff and I don't think you even know who I am.

— Please don't get angry. Please don't go, the voice said.

— Ok, I said. — If you know me, what's my name?

— He found the letter, the voice said.

— What fucking letter? I said.

— The letter to you, the voice said. — He came round to mine before he came to the hospital, to get clothes. I needed clothes because they'd had to cut up my t-shirt and my jeans were covered in blood and I didn't have shoes or a jacket or anything... Don't get angry. Please. Please don't get angry. Please. Please. Please. Please. I wrote it ages ago. He went through my things. It wasn't like it was out. It's really important that you understand. He went through my things. I was never gonna send it or anything. I swear.

A different voice. The mysterious Fletcher?

— Who are you talking to? it said. — Are you talking to her? I told you stay the…

The receiver is covered and the shouting which ensues is intermittently beeped out by the sound of buttons being pressed.

— How many *beeeeep* do I *beep* *beep* *beeeeeeep* when you only wanna *beep* for the *beep* *beep* *beeeeep*.

NOTHING OLD, NOTHING NEW, NOTHING BORROWED, NOTHING BLUE

— Look at your kitchen, look at your kitchen, ohmygod look at your kitchen. It's delightful... only wait 'til you hear what my husband said, how it's all very well if all you've got to do is look after kids, I mean, he doesn't have to get up in the night, he doesn't have to get up in the morning, so I get it in early. Going from being a full-time event manager with a social life, a very fulfilling life, to being a full-time mum is a big shift. I spend a lot of time mourning my old life. I mean, I'm very happy, I wouldn't change a thing, but it's hard, it's difficult, it's lonely. Even though I'm doing the most important job in the world, I feel like a sack of shit. but it's fine. I've been doing some volunteering. Not doing a huge amount. Cold calling. Funny, 'cos that's why I had a baby in the first place, to get away from that shit.

Oh, and then the festival was this weekend. Did I tell you about that? For me, it was work, I mean, I was going to enjoy myself, not get too fucked, and I could always go back to feed the baby. So Friday night is fine, but then Saturday night Lloyd dis-a-ppears. He calls two hours later, like, 'I'm in Luton bleurgh'. So I was like, 'What you doing in Luton?'

and he was like, 'Dunno'. He said he was at the airport but I could hear people laughing in the background so I just said, 'Remember that in two and a half hours you've *got* to *take* the *baby*.' An hour later he called again. This time he was in Gatwick. 'What you doing in Gatwick?' I said, and he was like, 'Dunno'. So, six-thirty comes and the door opens. He's soaked in booze. Stinking. Ten minutes later, he's asleep. So I do breakfast and sort out the baby and at seven-thirty I go up to wake him, and I'm like, 'Honey, I, I think you should get up', and it's just so bad, I'm already that type of person. I thought the transition was going to be slower, but I'm settled I guess. Anyway, guess who i met at the festival?? Probably one of the most famous people in the world.

But I mean it's the fucking principle. I have to go to the festival with my baby because he's been on a booze binge round London's airports. I just felt like such a gooner. Really bad. Really really really bad. I told him, your responsibility, your child, you've known about this for three fucking months. I was so angry... But then he has been really good since then. It's just a shame that it manifests itself like this. But, yeah, since then he's been really good, really interactive. With the baby, I mean. I really like him. He's a good dad. And you know, I'm fine, I'm fine. I just don't get to see my friends so much. Yeah. I'm okay. It's just good to see you.

But you know what I really want is friends who are mums. I've got a few people I see at the moment, but there isn't anyone that's like ohmygodwecanbebestfriends, I haven't met that person yet.

Course we do loads of baby shit together. But we do need to do some real shit. Like last night, after we made up... It was really nice. God, it's so embarrassing... In front of

Ritchie. That's our terrier. Sometimes, I swear, we're really naughty.

I mean, I'm very lucky. I've got a lovely kitchen. Things are lovely. I'm proud. I'm going to join the Rotary Club. Hope to find like-minded people. They do mountain biking and climbing and a bit of rambling as well, and we're going to go to the grey water sports club up the road, take up canoeing, so hopefully that will open things up. And my mum, she comes everyday. Do you have a car?

My mum's really helpful but very opinionated, so I told her, 'You care for you'.

Let me check, I've got some photos. Look at thaaaat. My favourite pic, and it's crazy, she literally has golden hair.

And this one's from the lawyers' weekend. Trident. My mum was so angry but I was like, 'Hello-o, your daughter's joining the Rotary Club, what do you expect?'

Then, after the festival my bosses came to dinner and they're like, 'This is fucking great innit?' and we were like, 'Yeah, welcome to our happy world in Maidenhead. How's it working out for you? Your 'holiday' in London?' Wait until you're married, wait until you have kids. It changes your relationship so much. Lloyd won't even put a plate in the dishwasher. Says he doesn't have the time, but he has time to lie in bed for an hour every morning. So I told him, 'I'm not asking you to *do* the dishes, I'm simply asking you to take your plate over to the machine, open it and bend over —'

PRO LIFE

There were four of us to start with. M___ , V_____ , A_____
and me. A friendship cemented in the back row of Miss
Wilder's maths class via notes passed back and forth.

M___: *Miss Wilder sux big balls!!*
Quiz?
A_____: *Yes*
Me: *Ego*
V_____: *Go on then!!!*

M___: *Ok. Don't think about the answers too much. Just write*
1st thing that comes to mind ok??? 1. If you could fuck any famous
person alive or dead who would it be?
A_____: *River <3 dead or alive*
Me: *LIAM DUR!*
V_____: *Courtney Love*

M___: *2. If you could be a famous person who would it be?*
A_____: *Bob Marley*
Me: *Patsy Kensit hahaha no not really. Maybe Marlene*
Dietrich ?

V_____: *Poly Styrene. Wot is this anyway???*

M__: *You'll see… Ok last question. If you could KILL another person who would it be?*

A____: *Killing in the Name of dah dah dah! Can't wait for next weeeeeek*

Guy from Ocean Colour Scene

Me: *Myself*

V_____: *Miss Wilder*

M__: *Got to be famous!!!*

V_____: *Ok then… maybe Gary Lineker*

M__: *So… The first person is how you see yourself, the second person is how people see you and the last person is who you really are :)*

A____: *Haha V_____ is Miss Wilder*

V_____: *Fuck You*

Me: *I'm myself :)*

When not incarcerated in lessons we spent our time shoplifting from Topshop, Boots, C&A; trying to identify persons who were likely to respond positively to our asking for 20p 'to use the payphone' (a ruse that lost its effectiveness with age and was finally permanently discontinued by the rise of mobile phones); snogging people (sometimes each other); trying to sort fake IDs; bunnin' zoots; playing *Crash Bandicoot* on PlayStation.

It wasn't long before our behaviour came to the attention of the authorities. One afternoon, at the back of maths again (I recall probability trees drawn on the whiteboard) we decided to give ourselves DIY tattoos using a compass and a biro (fountain pen would've been better but no one had one with ink). I was gonna do Oasis but didn't go past the 'O' before deciding I was satisfied with a circle. V_____ did the Nirvana smiley face, two crosses and a wiggly line but we were busted before she could finish. A_____ did KoЯn on her wrist in a font admirably similar to their actual logo. M___ did Metallica, really big, all the way up her forearm. Pretty impressive but even I, in my most crazed, rebellious mindset, had misgivings. (Amusingly, out of all of us M___ was the straightest and least into music, but she must've been the most enthusiastic of us when it came to self-harm, because everyone else's tattoo faded in a matter of weeks while, to the best of my knowledge, hers remains to this day.)

We were expelled one by one.

When my turn came around and I was called in to the headmistress's office and told to explain myself, I responded to the open-ended question with a question. What aspect of myself was I supposed to be explaining? I didn't get a response. The headmistress, an enormous woman with a girth to rival a St. Paul's Cathedral bell, and I sat in silence for several minutes. She broke the silence, asked me if I had anything at all I wanted to say. I told her I didn't. She told me I was expelled. Her actual words, 'your career within this establishment has come to an end'. Pompous twat. I got up and walked to the office door in silence, opened it then stopped. Maybe I *did* have something to say after all.

— Actually, I said, — Yeah. You're a big fat fucking BITCH!

As soon as the last syllable dropped I was gone, slamming the door behind me. I ran down the teachers' stairs, legged it along the corridor shaking with adrenaline. I burst into the classroom, where Miss Wilder was still mid-flow, and went to my locker. I opened it and pulled out textbooks and exercise books letting them tumble to the floor. I put my Walkman, my English and History exercise books and a copy of *Jude the Obscure* into my school bag and left the rest where it lay. I gave Miss Wilder the finger, slung my bag over my shoulder and was gone.

It took me years to discover what I was expelled for. My parents never divulged what the headmistress told them, just kept me grounded until they could find another school to send me to. It was *two decades later*, when I was 35-years-old, that the subject came up in conversation. My mum told me she'd been informed that I'd brought a replica gun into school and waved it around. News to me! And imagine the position it put me in. Nearly 40 and still needing to rant and rave about the petty injustices of yore! My life = an actual joke.

I told my mother in no uncertain terms, — That did not happen.

Did she believe me? Did she fuck.

Following that pointless conversation I racked my brain for any incident that could even vaguely be interpreted as me bringing a replica gun into school and waving it around. I couldn't think of anything.

I called V_____ , the only member of my old girl gang I was still in touch with, to ask if she could think of anything. At first she was equally stumped and equally offended by the ludicrousness of it all, but then she had a brainwave.

— Maybe it was the water pistols we all had? V_____ said.

— What water pistols? I said.

— You remember, V_____ said. — From McDonalds.

That was the summer McDonalds was giving away dinosaur-shaped water pistols with Happy Meals. Dinosaur-shaped water pistols that had a surprisingly powerful squirt. We were friends with a guy who worked there (A_____ had kissed him in his previous carnation, which was coming into the school twice a week to change the sanitary bins) and he would sneak us free water pistols without us having to purchase burgers and chips. My favourite was the pterodactyl. Hard blue plastic body with an orange beak. Mystery solved. Kind of. I considered calling my mother to tell her but what would be the point? It was so clearly a set-up and a cack-handed one at that that I decided to let the whole embarrassing incident lie. On their heads be it.

Our tight-knit faction diffused into a looser, more decentralised affiliation. We each ended up at a different London crammer, the only places that would take us if we didn't want to start the year over. And the thing with London crammers is that they were where ALL the fucks up were sent. Four weirdoes became eight, eight became ten, and in fact eleven, because one of the new people had boyfriend.

From my end there was H_____ , a mad alcoholic who would down bottles of Bacardi Breezer during break. She threw up in Geography on my first day, winning my admiration. And P__ , a big, quiet softie who liked his Moschino and went on to take too many psychedelics in Thailand and never be the same again.

From M___'s end there was T__ , an oversized lumbering boy who, when he was first introduced to the group, everyone thought was a woman cos he had long red hair and was fat enough to have tits.

From A_____'s end there was D_____ , a crazed Bulgarian skateboarder who dressed half-punk, half-traditional gypsy.

Baggy skate pants twinned with embroidered waistcoats and a handkerchief tying back luminous green hair. D_____ was going out with B__ , a nondescript west London boy who had taken up skateboarding to impress D_____ and turned out to be pretty good at it.

V_____ brought in X_ , a Malaysian lesbian who looked, spoke and dressed like Sonic the Hedgehog. An utterly charming person, who would go on to sort some of us out with our first jobs in a Covent Garden skate shop (not the good one).

Last of all there was S____. No one was sure where S____ came from or at least no one wanted to take responsibility for her because she was horrible. But for some reason, whenever we met up, there she'd be.

With her giant forehead, pointy nose and total absence of chin or cheekbones, S____ might've done alright in Tudor times but by 1998 standards she was considered butters. Her natural ugliness was enhanced by a spiteful personality, the dress sense of a psychotic clown (think multi-coloured patchwork pants held up by thick red braces) and a chronic addiction to Super Skunk that left her with permanent red eye but thankfully rendered her speechless a lot of the time. Still, you could see the nasty thoughts she was thinking written all over her ugly face.

S____'s only popularity card was her mother's absentee parenting. S____'s mother, L_____ , was cuckoo, la-la, totally out to lunch, meaning S____'s flat became the place to go to smoke/drink/screw with zero 'stress'. We would spend days on end at S____'s flat, three or four of us sleeping in S____'s bed, others on the sofa in the front room, hotboxing the kitchen, without ever catching sight of L_____. On the rare occasions where L_____ did surface (her open bedroom door being the warning sign), she appeared to be oblivious to the boys and booze and blazin'. Well, maybe that's not entirely true… The drugs and the liquor meant nothing to L_____ but she *did* have a nose for there being a boy in the house. She'd loiter in the dark recess of the corridor in a sheer dressing gown and suspenders, waiting to pounce. It was the only thing that made me feel sorry for S____ because it was awful.

When quizzed about her mother's paedophilic tendencies, S____ told us L_____ had grown up in Rhodesia where L_____'s mother, sick with malaria, spent the entire time in bed. Her father, bereft by lack of wife, took to dressing L_____ in her mother's clothes, slathering her in her mother's make-up and taking her to what S____ said her grandfather called 'nigger bars', where he would parade his daughter in front of the locals before taking her home to fuck her.

This story is undeniably horrific. Pedophilia, racism, incest, neglect, colonialism. *More* than enough to forgive L_____ any psychosexual problems she might have. But at the time, with all of us suffering from a terrible case of teenage brain, none of us were able to properly understand it or its implications. We saw L_____ as authority, so the thought of any abuse or humiliation she might have suffered struck us as hilarious. What can I say? Teenage girls are brutal.

S____'s status as Venue Provider might have secured her presence at our pathetic gatherings, but when it came to group politics (of which there were plenty, always stemming from people fancying the same people), S____ was less than an afterthought. Ugly as she was, it looked unlikely S____ would ever get laid, so in the mad scramble to cash in our virginities, no one considered her a threat.

This changed one half-term in suitably melodramatic fashion...

The plan was to meet at Queensway Bowling Alley, I forget the occasion. Being underage, we went there a lot. It was one of the few places that would serve us alcohol without asking for ID.

I arrived and spotted A_____'s blue afro pigtails right away. Hoping she (considerably wealthier and more adult-looking than I) would buy me a drink, I hurried to the bar where she was chatting to a woman who I kinda recognised, brandishing an unlit cigarette. Was she famous?

I kissed A_____ on the cheek then the maybe-famous woman brandishing an unlit cigarette came in for one as well. I hesitated.

— It's me, she said and smiled revealing pointed incisors, which I recognised right away.

S____.

Gone were the baggy pants and braces. In their place were a black, fitted, knicker-skimming dress, an astonishing pair of red leather fuck-me boots and a yard of thigh. Her normally frizzy, mousy hair was dark with product, ringlets gelled down onto her forehead, Sugababes-style. Her moon-face was thick with foundation, which stopped in a sharp line at her chin (early contouring). Her cheeks were rouged, eyelashes heavy with goopy mascara... It didn't take me long to deduce that S____ had raided her mother's make-up cabinet as well as her wardrobe. The overall effect was terrifying. S____ looked more clownish and psychotic than ever, but in one of my first successful deployments of social etiquette, I said, — You look nice, S____.

S____ leaned back on the bar, unlit cigarette dangling between pouted lips. She lifted a leg to rest a high-heeled boot on the barstool, hitching up her skirt to reveal a glimpse of white thong. Yikes!

Her eyes darted from me and A_____ to the door and back again. A smug expression tightened her features. I turned to look at the door to see D_____ and B__ , holding hands like always and, like always, dangling skateboards at their sides.

D_____ and B__ were the only solid, non-lesbian couple in our group. They'd been going out since they were fourteen and had only recently consummated their affair, incidentally at S____'s. We'd all been in on it and helped with the 'arrangements', like the little pervs we were. We'd conferred on what D_____'s sacrificial outfit should be, mood-lit the room then sat next door while they did it, tittering and speculating about what positions they were doing. When it was over, we dragged D_____ to the bathroom to press her for details. Intense.

The result of this shared rite of passage was that we, as a group, were deeply invested in D_____ and B__'s relationship. None of us could imagine a world in which they weren't together.

Amazingly, D_____ recognised S____ straightaway and greeted her with big, effusive Eastern European gesticulations. She plucked at the hemline of S____'s dress, got her to twirl to reveal the full ensemble and aimed compliment after compliment at the hair, the eyeshadow, the boots, all delivered in her sweet, clumsy accent.

B__ hung back from the interaction. He nodded hello to us then dashed into the gents. A_____ and I exchanged a look. Something was up, for sure.

Other people started showing up, each as stunned by S____'s makeover as the next.

V_____ was like, —Why d'you do it?

T__ told her she looked like Courtney, which was true.

P__ , who clocked it but was unphased, shrugged.

M___ pretended like it was all good to S____'s face but mouthed, 'what the fuck?' in our direction, making little circles around her ear with her index finger insinuating that she thought S____ was insane.

We went to sit in a booth. Booths were preferable to the tables in the middle of the room because they were private and sometimes Security would pop its head round the door and if he couldn't see us then he couldn't think to check our IDs.

S____ bought two jugs of frozen margaritas. Unusual as S____ was usually tight. She never bought drinks and frequently demanded 'tax' off people for the use of her house, usually two tokes on a spliff every time it was passed. Plus, when she did drink it was always Red Stripe. Every surface of her room was covered in empty tins, which I think she kept just to wind up her mother.

S____ put the jugs on the table but didn't sit down. She poured herself a tumbler then started parading round the bar area. It was some performance! Going up to blokes sitting at tables and leaning over them to show her (admittedly tiny) cleavage, grabbing a chair and spinning it round then sitting on it the wrong way round, legs apart.

— What the fuck is she doing? someone said.

The rest of us shrugged in bafflement.

S____ continued, doing sexy drinking and sexy walking and sexy leaning over.

— She's lost the plot, someone said.

The rest of us winced in horror.

— She's turned into her mother, someone said.

The rest of us nodded in agreement.

B__ , who we'd forgotten about because of S____'s erratic behaviour, returned from the toilets. At the sight of S____ cavorting he went visibly pale.

— Something's happening, someone said.

Everyone turned to look at B__ , who S____ hadn't seen yet. He made his way towards us, trying to avoid S____ but when reached where the tables and chairs began, S____ turned and saw him. She made a beeline for him. B__ changed direction in an attempt to avoid her. S____ altered her route, prompting a panicked pantomime where B__ circled round tables clearly trying to get away from S____ and S____ dodged to the left, to the right, trying to second guess him. D_____ stood but she was three people deep so couldn't get out of the booth without everyone else moving.

— What is she doing? D_____ said. — Let me out!

S____ finally cornered B__ beside a family slurping down Slush Puppies. They looked on in horror (as did we) as S____ looped a leg round B__'s waist, ensnaring him. She grabbed his face with both hands, forcing his mouth into a pout, and shoved her thick, stubby tongue into the hole.

D_____ crushed my hand as she scrambled over us to get out.

S____ was still tonguing B__ , slobbering all over him. She took his hand and placed it on her bum.

— Oh god, someone said.

A song came on the jukebox. The Sign by Ace of Base. Tinny beat, wavy audio.

The father of the family decided his kids had seen enough and ushered them out of their seats. He went to the bar to ask for the manager but needn't have bothered because the barman would've noticed in two seconds anyway because D____ started freaking. She wasn't even saying words, just made strange yelps like she was being strangled.

I, I got a new life, you would hardly recognise me, I'm so glad…

B__ pushed S____ , sending her tumbling to the floor where she landed with legs splayed and where she stayed.

How could a person like me care for you?

D____ ran over and grabbed B__'s arm. We could all see she how hard she was squeezing it.

Why, why do I bother when you're not the one for me?

— Say it is not! D_____ said.

B__'s face was a sight to see. He opened his mouth to speak but no sound came out.

Is enough enough?

S____ began to get up from the floor, her monstrous expression visible even through the make-up. M___ ran over to prevent S____ doing whatever she was about to do.

There was a brief stand off with M___ holding S____, S____ getting off on her bondage, B__ holding D_____. S____ went limp. M___ relaxed her grip. S____ slipped free. S____ lunged at B__ , pushing D_____ out of his arms and throwing her own arms round him. I watched it all, taking gulps of my frozen margarita as fast I could manage, sure it was only a matter of minutes before we all got kicked out.

— We are in love, S____ spat.

I saw the sign and it opened up my eyes…

B__ visibly shook.

— Well? Tell them, S____ said to B__.

B__ stared at D_____.

Life is demanding without understanding….

— We've been fucking for months, S____ said. — So your first time wasn't his. Was it baby? Tell her.

No one's gonna drag you up to get into the light where you belo-ong…

— Don't call him fucking baby! D_____ said, shoving S____ hard in the chest.

S____ looked triumphant.

— Is it true? Tell me! Is it true?

D_____ turned to B__.

B__ shook his head 'no', caught sight of S____ in doing so, whereupon the shake became a reluctant nod 'yes', then a bow in shame.

But where do you belo-ong?

D_____ looked from B__ to S____ to M___ to B__ to S____.

U-under the pale moon…

S____ picked up her drink and took a sexy sip through the straw, finishing it and loudly slurping the ends.

— I'm sorry, B__ said.

For so many years I've wondered who you are…

— Oh my god, whispered A_____ , sat beside me.

Security opened the swing doors and assessed the scene. Went over and spoke to B__. — Can I see some ID son?

B__ shrugged, defeated.

— Ok, well, you know I know you lot are underage so let's make this easy shall we?

How could a person like you bring me joy?

— I don't love her. I love you, B__ said to D_____.

— I can see you've got, Security looked at S____ , — a situation here, lad, but best work it out elsewhere. Okay?

Under the pale moon where I see a lot of stars...

B__ turned his back on S____ and Security, and dropped to his knees at D_____'s feet. Teenage melodrama in a bowling alley. Sweet. Everyone, even Security, waited to see what D_____ was gonna do.

— Come on, D_____ said, — we're going.

She pulled B__ to his feet and dragged him over to the booth.

— You okay? someone asked.

D_____ didn't reply.

They grabbed their skateboards and headed for the exit. We downed our drinks, gathered our things and followed suit. I stepped out of the booth, looked at S____, straw still in mouth. She was watching D_____ and B__'s every move. I nudged A_____ to alert her.

I saw the sign, I saw the si-ee-i-ee-ign...

— Uh oh, said A_____.

I saw the sign, I saw the si-ee-i-ee-ign...

D_____ and B__ had the swing doors open when S____ climbed onto a chair.

I saw the sign, I saw the si-ee-i-ee-i...

— Listen, kid, you've got to get down, said Security — Showtime's over.

I saw the sign and it opened up my eyes, I saw the sign!

— I'm pregnant, S____ said.

I don't remember how the rest of the evening went other than that at the end of it, I walked home with T__ who lived kinda near me.

— Poor D____ , I said.

— B__'s a fucking weirdo, T__ said.

— Do you think S____ is really pregnant? I said.

— Do you think she would lie about something like that?
T__ said.

We exchanged a look of silent agreement.

— Do you think B__ and D_____ will split up or stay
together? T__ said.

I ate dinner with my parents without breathing a word
of what had happened, half because I wasn't sure exactly
what *had* happened and anything I said would only prompt
questions I didn't have the answers to, and half because I
knew that the grown-up-ness of it (Adultery! Babies!) would
most likely upset them.

After dinner, the obligatory phone calls began.

A_____ called to say she was with D_____ who had
decided to forgive B__ and make a go of it. She said B__
said S____ was lying about being pregnant because they'd
actually only slept together once and that was months ago
so it was almost impossible.

M___ called to say she had spoken to A_____ and didn't
believe S____ about the baby either. She thought we should
all stop speaking to S____ because she was a 'psycho'. M___
rang off saying she was going to call S____ to tell her to stay
away from all of us.

I called V_____. Out of all of us V_____ was the
least interested in sex, so although we talked about what
happened, the only feeling she expressed was how insane she
thought everyone was. She tried to move the conversation
on to other things but I forced it back, thinking I should
let V_____ know the consensus: S____ was out. Upon

receiving the news V_____ stayed quiet for a minute then said, 'alright' but that, by-the-by, she didn't think S____ was lying. There was something in the way V_____ spoke that arrested me, and for the first time I considered the possibility that S might telling the truth. An actual baby. Fucking hell.

I called A_____ back to say, 'what if S____ isn't lying?' and, 'don't you think we should find out?'

It was decided a few of us girls would meet the next day and go round to S____'s with a pregnancy test and make her do it, but that we wouldn't mention it to D_____ or B__ until we'd found out either way.

The pregnancy test intervention never happened. In fact no one saw or heard from S____ for weeks. She didn't show up at school and when we tried to call her house, the call either rang out or L_____ would answer to say S____ wasn't available.

With S____ not around things went back to normal. D_____ and B__ seemed more together than ever, although everyone was careful not to mention S____ in their company. Course we talked about it amongst ourselves all the time, but eventually ran out of aspects to speculate on. S____ was a bitch, probably wasn't preggo, was hiding because she'd humiliated herself and we probs wouldn't see her again. Despite a fair number of us *being* teenage girls, we were decidedly ill-versed in teenage girl behaviour.

It was around this time that I started drifting away from the group. I got a boyfriend, Ricardo, who no one liked but was probably one of the best boyfriends I've had. (To this day I am glad I lost my virginity to him over any of the twats that followed.) My friends called him Ricardo

Retardo, which he didn't mind but I didn't like. And then there was the magic mushrooms.

We got the shrooms off M___'s dad, who sent them from America. Freeze-dried, vacuum-packed to be made into tea. We waited for a free house to do them, which came round one Easter weekend. The tea was made, the spliffs were rolled and we went out to the garden.

We sat sipping mushroom tea, asking each other every ten minutes or so whether we felt anything. Eventually I did. It was like reality was twinging, which I interpreted as a muscular spasm of my eye muscle rather than anything spiritual or other-worldly. Then things went like when you sit right in front of the telly and can see the thousands of kaleidoscopes that make up the screen.

— I can definitely feel something, I said.

The others started to laugh. They laughed and laughed and laughed and laughed until I started to feel uncomfortable.

— What? I said. — What's so funny?

— We've given you an extra strong dose, someone said.

They were creasing, finding it hilarious (probably tripping a bit themselves) but I didn't find it funny. I still don't. Not that anything bad happened. It was an amazing first trip with blue owls and tin foil cherry blossom and my skin turning the colour of molasses. What I didn't like was them *telling* me they'd given me an extra strong dose just as I was coming up. A much nastier thing to do than just doing it, but happily I didn't freak out.

A couple of days after the mushrooms, I met up with Ricardo and told him what had happened. He listened and when I was done he said, — I don't think these people like you very much.

It was a weird thing to hear. I'd assumed 'these people' would be my friends for life but suddenly the thought occurred to me that they might not be. Also, that I'd never really chosen them. Our parents sent us to the same schools. We were forced together. But school was done and there was a whole world of people out there…

I won't say it was a clean break (when is it ever?) but as summer rolled on I saw less and less of 'these people' and by the time Autumn came round I wasn't hanging out with them at all. I broke up with Ricardo and got a new boyfriend. He was older than me so his life was much more interesting than mine and I adopted it wholeheartedly. Pretty soon I'd as good as forgotten my old friends altogether, so, imagine my surprise when, walking through Camden the following Spring, who should I see but S____? Spliff in mouth, charging along the high street like a crackhead, pushing a buggy. S____ didn't notice me and I considered letting her pass unheeded, but curiosity to see the contents of the buggy got the better of me.

— S____! I called out to her.

— Fucking hell, how are you? S____ said, skidding to a halt.

— I'm alright, I said. — You had a baby!

— Yeah, that's what happens after you're pregnant, S____ said.

— We thought you were making it up, I said.

A flicker of something crossed S____'s face but I couldn't tell what.

S____ pulled back the hood of the buggy and presented the child.

— She's called D_____ , S____ said.

I didn't say anything but failed to disguise my surprise.

— I live round the corner. You should come over. B__'s home, S____ said, a fat little smile flickering across her thin lips.

— You're alright, I said. — I've gotta go.

— Well, why don't you give me your number? S____ said. — It's been too long.

My teenage concern that S____ was 'uncool' resurfaced momentarily. Bumping into her was one thing but did I actually want to hang out with her? Be friends? But then I remembered that S____ being 'uncool' was a verdict that had been reached by a group of people who were pretty uncool themselves. Feeling grown up and gregarious, I dictated my number to S____ , who punched the digits into her phone then read the number back to me.

Over the following months we texted a few times. S____ sent pictures of the baby. I replied to say they were cute. She invited me round. I made sounds that sounded like I was up for it but never went so far as to confirm a date.

It was about a year later that I caught my boyfriend in bed with someone else. Not yet having developed the self-worth which makes it possible to espouse and practise more liberal positions on monogamy, I went from being in love, well-travelled and popular to being single, broke and homeless.

I sat on the doorstep of my ex-boyfriend's house trying to sort somewhere to go. Having ditched my old friends I couldn't very well call them up out of the blue and ask to move in and all the rest of my address book were my boyfriend's friends, so no go. I got to S____'s number, remembered her saying that her dad had bought her a three-bedroom house in Camden. It was getting cold. It was getting late. I called her, explained my predicament and was relieved when she said I was welcome to come over. There was a spare room, which I could have for as long as I wanted. I got off the phone and two seconds later she'd texted through the address.

I replied, thanking her and giving an ETA of two hours max. I steeled myself for facing my ex then went inside to gather my possessions. Gathering my possessions unsurprisingly turned into a massive row that ate into the whole two hours before I finally fled. I caught the train to Camden, composing a long text to the ex, detailing just how few orgasms I'd had during sex on the journey and sent it as I emerged onto Camden High Street. I followed S____'s directions to thirty-four Rousden Road.

As I turned into the street I could heard a baby screaming. S____'s baby? I reached number thirty-four and yes, the screaming was coming from inside. The front door to the house was ajar. I went in. The baby's screams got louder still. I closed the door, flicking up the latch to lock it behind me.

— Hello? I said.

— Hello, a voice said.

It made me jump. I looked up and saw B__ sat at the top stairs with his head in his hands.

— Hey B__! I said. — I didn't realise you'd be here.

B__ looked up.

— I'm not, he said.

Baby still screaming.

— You're not what? I said.

— I'm not here, he said. — Or at least I won't be in a minute.

Baby still screaming.

— Is the kid alright? I said.

— Am I? he said.

— Hmmm, I said, — Well, S____ said I could take the spare room for a bit. Is that cool?

— Nothing to do with me, B__ said.

— Alright, I said. — Where's S____?

B__ shrugged then put his head back in his hands.

Baby still screaming.

— Is D____ ok? I said, remembering its name.

There was a knock on the door.

— That'll be Dad, he said.

Picking up the rucksack at his feet B__ took the stairs two at a time.

I opened the door to a man who middle-age had rendered entirely nondescript. He walked past me into the house without even basic acknowledgement.

— Come on then, let's get you off, B__'s dad said.

— I'm sorry Dad, he said.

Baby still screaming.

B__'s dad picked up a book from the hall and tutted loudly.

— Someone needs to take proper care of that child! B__'s dad said at a level just short of shouting, aimed along the corridor.

— Don't Dad, just don't, B__ said. He looked scared.

With no idea what was going on and bristling at the insult of this old sap blanking me, I stood in the way while B__ and his dad carried his bags out to an Audi Passat double-parked outside. They made several journeys back and forth. Then B__ got in the car and B__'s dad returned to the front door alone.

— Are you a friend of S____'s? he said.

I shrugged.

— I guess, I said.

— Well, B__'s dad said, raising his voice again clearly hoping S____ could hear, — You tell that drugged-up trollop she should be expecting a call from social services any day now. The Morleys don't go down without a fight.

He shook his fist in an unconvincing display of assertiveness then slammed the door shut.

Going through into the kitchen I find a purple-faced baby strapped into a high chair. Multi-coloured slops splatter its face, the tray in front of it and the floor and walls around it. When it sees me it stops crying, gives a little sigh, whimpers, then starts crying again.

— Hey mate, I said. — Hey.

I unstrapped the baby and lifted it out of its chair. It leant its hot head against my neck.

We go from room to room and finally discover S____ upstairs. I almost don't see her because she's lying in a pile of clothes with a tea towel over her face in a dark room that reeks of skunk. Actual skunk and smoked skunk. Also the way a person who smokes skunk smells, which is like skunk.

Baby D_____ sees S____ and starts bawling louder. I try and hand the baby to its mother.

— I think she wants you, I said.

— Just put her on the bed, S____ said, pulling the tea towel off her face.

I put the baby down. It carries on crying and wriggling, legs bicycling the air.

— Are you okay? I said — What the fuck's going on?

S____ sits up and reaches over to retrieve a giant spliff

from the ashtray and lights it. She takes two short, sharp inhales then one long toke.

— Fucking bastard's left me, she said, doing her best Pat Butcher impression.

Baby D_____ is still screaming and thrashing around. She starts to slide off the bed. I catch her just as she goes over the side. I hold the child in my arms and bounce her gently up and down.

— Shush, I said, — Shush.

— I think she likes you, S____ said.

S____ dropped the still-burning spliff into an ashtray, lay back down, tea towel over face... And somehow I end up being the one left holding the baby.

TAYLOR WIMPEY '99' HORROR

99. Elegant articulation of contemporary horror
98. Diverse urban horror
97. Local artisan horror
96. Refined city haven horror
95. Curated selection of horror
94. Property investment portfolio horror
93. Friendly addition to bustling horror
92. Independent boutique horror
91. Creative hub horror
90. Abundant green space horror
89. Tranquil outdoor horror
88. Award-winning horror
87. Iconic landmark horror
86. Exclusive postcode horror
85. Desirable lifestyle horror
84. Comfortable practical horror
83. Thoughtfully designed horror
82. Stunning feature wall horror
81. Timeless horror
80. Perfectly-positioned horror
79. Double-dug basement horror
78. Dedicated to lateral living horror

77. Michelin star horror

76. Third party service horror

27. 24-hour concierge horror

74. Secure mail and delivery service horror

73. Electronic controlled access horror

72. Video door entry system horror

71. Secure cycle storage horror

70. CCTV horror

69. Private courtyard horror

68. Comfort cooling horror

67. On-site facility horror

66. Residents' lounge horror

65. Sommunal games room horror

64. Open-plan studios for fast-paced horror

63. Generous duplex apartments for family horror

62. Penthouse horror

62. Floor-to-ceiling horror

60. Private terrace with decking horror

59. Sunken garden horror

58. Double-glazed horror

57. Sliding door horror

56. View of the city's financial horror

55. Programmable mood horror

54. Multi-functional horror

53. Antique bronze finish horror

52. Free-standing brass-wrapped island horror

51. Investment interior piece horror

50. Premium fixture horror

49. Glass balustrade horror

48. Designer door furniture horror

47. Engineered hardwood horror

46. Fitted broadloom horror

45. Sleek brand-conscious horror

44. Composite natural stone kitchen horror

43. Tiled splash-back horror

42. Gloss lacquered storage horror

41. Induction hob with extractor hood horror

40. Fully-integrated stainless steel horror

39. Fully-integrated eco horror

38. Fully-integrated fridge-freezer horror

37. Washing machine and spin dryer horror

36. Free-standing glass-fronted horror

35. Segregated waste disposal horror

34. Master en-suite horror

33. High-end porcelain in wet area horror

32. Underfloor heating horror

31. Statement black fitting horror

30. Twin basin horror

29. Heated towel rail horror

28. Dual flush WC with concealed cistern horror

27. Walk-in shower horror

26. Frosted glass bathscreen horror

25. Wall-mounted mirrored vanity unit horror

24. Glass-interior shelving stainless steel cabinet horror

23. Bespoke fitted wood-effect veneer wardrobe horror

22. Bespoke matching drawer set horror

21. Automated blind horror

20. BT socket and 5-volt powerpoint horror

19. Hyperoptic broadband horror

18. Access to shared satellite (subscription required) horror

17. Commerce-meets-culture horror

16. Entrepreneurial artistic horror

15. Weekend brunch and cocktail horror

14. Showcase horror

13. Ambitious horror

12. Undisputed centre of luxury horror

11. Effortlessly accessible horror

10. Fast and efficient horror

9. Heart of the capital horror

8. Crossrail, a casual stride away horror

7. Better connected horror

6. Carefully managed horror

5. Tailored package purchase horror

4. Being part of something special horror

3. Professional personalised horror

2. Property sale aftercare horror

1. Taylor Wimpey Central London customer journey horror

I JUST WANT TO PULL DOWN YOUR PANTIES AND FUCK YOU

In the ten years they'd known each other there'd been countless opportunities for them to do it. Times when neither were attached to anyone else, when there was nowhere to go and nothing doing. Like the night they broke into the derelict church on Walworth Road or the time they drove up to Nottingham for the Stop HS2 protest and slept in the trees. But for one reason or another it never happened and after a certain amount of time had passed any friction that might've existed between them on the basis of him being a boy and her being a girl vanished. In its place friendship blossomed. A friendship where bad behaviour, lewd comments, racist jokes and other non-PC parlance were permissible and where the micro-politics of every social situation going was scrutinised to the extreme. Sometimes they argued, like when he had a go at her for doing an event at the Serpentine because, he said, the Serpentine was funded by the Sacklers. She told him she didn't see what difference her doing or not doing an event there made to the millions of people addicted to Valium. Or when she had a go at him for tagging the walls of Old St. Pancras churchyard, which, she said was just a dickish thing to do. But on the whole, whether in agreement on a subject or not, they always arrived at the same conclusion: that while her politics were in theory libertarian and his anarchic, in practise there was so much overlap in their ways of thinking, so not being friends would be mental.

Any sexual tension that might've reared its head was kept at bay by the stories he told her about his frequent (and sometimes bizarre) sexual encounters. He always had a couple of women on the go. Around the time in question he was sleeping with one of the head honchos in XR who was, he said, the first 'black black' person he'd ever had sex with. ('Black black' meaning her skin was dark, a clarification that needed to be made in view of the increasing popularity of the American 'one drop' definition of black, more expansive and including quadroons, octoroons, high yellow, etc.) XR Woman flew him to eco-conferences in Austria, Belgium, Italy, France and fucked him in hotel rooms, claiming him on expenses as her assistant. He said he thought it was 'hot' because it made him feel 'objectified, like a girl' but also used it as evidence for the total fraudulence of XR's claimed agenda.

— The sex was amazing, he said. — But afterwards she feel asleep on the bed like this. He flailed his arms and began to grunt. — Snoring like a big, black pig.

His slapstick impression was funny and she laughed briefly and involuntarily. She hated XR as much as he did and had no difficulty believing the people with access to their coffers were not halal, but she also thought it wise to warn him (in case he didn't know) that comparing black people and women you've slept with to pigs was no go.

— You should be careful, she said.

— Why's that? he said.

— Well, she said, — People are getting cancelled left, right and centre for far softer statements.

— Are you saying I'm racist? he said.

— Maybe, she said. — I don't know. But it's a bit *Vice magazine* circa 2006…

— Fuck *Vice*! he said, his face reddening. — They don't pay their journalists you know.

— Again, she said, — old news. Why d'you even write for them anyway? They're clowns.

He shrugged. — A lot of people read it. I'm trying to get my message out.

She raised an eyebrow. — A lot of morons, she said. — But whatever, all I'm saying is you should be careful. I wouldn't want to see all the good work you do undermined over something stupid.

— Oh yeah, he said, jibing her, — I forgot you think you're black.

— It isn't that, she said. Then left it.

Then there was the Italian with the boyfriend who ran a food stall in Elephant & Castle. He'd dated Elephant & Castle woman years ago but had fucked her around so much that she'd eventually ditched him and started seeing someone else. Which is when he decided he was in love with her. He harangued the Elephant & Castle Woman with suggestive texts and eventually coerced her into a clandestine meet in a countryside hotel for (his) birthday sex.

The day after his birthday they met for supper at Chilli's, a very cheap and very good Indian caff in London Bridge. He spilled the beans on the nookie.

— It was so good, he said. — Really messy.

— Dude, she said, pausing the spoonful of daal on its ascent to her mouth.

Later, they'd finished eating and were standing outside on the pavement, he got a touch of the birthday blues. He stood gazing towards the roundabout, bike lock in hand.

— I feel like my life is at a crossroads, he said, straightening his posture and staring wistfully at the passing traffic.

— How you mean? she said, licking a one-skinner for the walk home.

— It's, like, if this girl could just see that me and her are good together then I *know* I could sort my shit out, he said. — I can be a really good boyfriend, you know. I can commit… But it's like, if she doesn't, if it's never gonna happen, if she's gonna stay with that focking prick then, I don't know, I think it's just gonna be just this for me, forever.

What he meant by 'this' was graffiti, hating the police, prison abolition activism and more graffiti.

His shoulders sagged. Seeing him so forlorn, she stepped forward and gave him a hug.

— Don't worry, she said. — I love you. She patted him lightly on the back. — Plus 'this' is not so bad. I mean, you're not doing any damage.

— I don't know what's up with me, he said. — I never feel like this.

He rested a hand on the top of her head.

— My advice, she said, pulling out of the cuddle, — is if you love her you need to show her.

— How do I do that? he said.

— Act like her boyfriend, she said — even if you're not going out. Be there for her, don't fuck other women…

She'll notice. I mean, if she's still fucking you then she definitely feels something for you. She wouldn't be if she didn't. She probably just doesn't want to have the piss taken out of her again.

— Why wouldn't I fuck other girls if she's giving that prick shiners every night? he said.

— Mate, she said. — Come on.

— What, *mate*? he said.

— Really? she said.

The two of them looked at each other expectantly. She sighed.

— Who is fucking who, she said — has *fuck all* to do with love. Love is not transactional like that. Either it is, or it isn't.

His melancholic expression morphed into a Cheshire Cat grin.

— You know, when I'm fucking her, her pussy make these squelching noises, he said. He makes several rhythmic thrusts with his pelvis and a gross slurping sound with his mouth. — I swear, that never happens when I'm fucking anyone else.

Squelchy cunt comment aside it seemed he took her advice to heart because the next few times they met up he had no new conquests to report. But then, by the following week, things'd changed again. The first update came over the phone. Another ex-girlfriend had got in touch, they'd met up and fucked then when he called she blanked him.

— She's such a basic bitch, he said. — It's so obvious what she's doing.

— What's that? she said.

— She just wants to know that I still want to fuck her, he said. — That's it.

And two days later, when they met near Kings Cross, there was more.

— God, he said as they walked up York Way deciding where to go. — I'm *so* hungover.

— I thought you didn't drink, she said. (He was diabetic.)

— I only drink when I feel like I'm on holiday, he said.

He launched into a tale of the night before. A house party in south London with some of the Palace lot (rich kids with a skate emporium that needed shutting down).

— They got me fuuuuucked, he said.

— I hate those wankers, she said.

— Yeah, he said, — They're pricks. But fuck, it was mental… I mean, the party was whack. Full of Goldsmiths students, but there was this one chick. She starts flirting with me, like hardcore flirting. Like, 'your hands are so big' and shit like that. Then outta nowhere she's like, 'I've gotta go'. So I was like, 'cool, whatever, nice to meet you', and I guess we must've exchanged numbers but I was so pissed I don't remember doing it. But we must've cos when I decided to call it a night at, like, five in the morning, I went to order an Uber on my phone and there was this text. A picture of her arse, red, like it'd been spanked and 'wanna fuck?' But I was so wasted I couldn't remember chatting to her so I texted back like 'who is this?'. Lol. Not the kinda reply you want to a picture of your fucking butthole. So then I opened Uber to order a car but they were doing that surcharge thing and it was like forty quid back to mine, so I'm like maybe I should walk it but then this bitch texted a picture of her with one of those gimp ball things in her mouth.

— What!? she said.

— Yeah, he said. — Mental. 'Take me as you find me big boy'. That's what she wrote.

They both get the giggles.

— So I'm like 'fuck it', he said, then stopped.

— Fuck what? she said.

— She texted me her postcode, he said. — And it was literally round the corner... So, yeah, I get there and the front door's open. Anyone could've walked in. I go inside and there is this chick, naked, on her knees in the middle of the living room, tied up. Tied fucking *up*!

— Yikes, she said. — So what did you do?

— I'm a man, aren't I? he said.

He didn't divulge any more of the story than this and she didn't press him for details, assuming 'I'm a man' implied he stuck it in.

They roamed the back streets, him stopping every now and then to do his tag or add an 'A' to parking signs that said, 'CAB'. But that night in bed she thought about his sexcapade. She imagined him arriving at one of those terrifying terraced houses that make up most of south east London, imagined him naked in its living room, knees bent. She tried to picture the girl, casting a version of herself in the role but no, she couldn't imagine being the sort of person who hogtied and blindfolded herself and left the front door open in the hopes that a random would come round to fuck her. Even if she wanted to be the sort of person who hogtied and blindfolded herself and left the front door open in the hopes that a random would come round to fuck her, she wasn't sure she'd know how to go about it. It all seemed a bit extreme and she couldn't help but wonder what horribleness had happened to this anonymous woman that meant she needed to go to such lengths to get her kicks?

But because the woman was anonymous her thoughts on the matter couldn't progress beyond speculation. Something that made it easier for her to dismiss any concerns she might've had in regards to his behaviour… Not that she had a problem with fucking around, necessarily. She'd had her moments after all, working her way through entire social circles before vanishing to leave groups of bemused lads to work out what their new closeness to one another meant for themselves. No, she had no objection to casual sex or general slagginess as long as no one was getting hurt. Only in her experience, someone generally was, which is why she'd stopped doing it.

The first time she felt uncomfortable was with the Indian girl.

— Fucking fit, he said. — I made her wear a bindi while we had really naughty bum sex.

Asides from the 'made', all well and good, until they ran into said Indian girl in the street. He was right, she *was* beautiful.

An awkward hello was followed by an even more awkward silence during which the Indian girl looked at them, clearly assuming they were fucking. She looked at the Indian girl and couldn't hide the fact that she knew about the naughty bum sex. He stood back with a smile on his face.

It was a short meet. The Indian girl broke it off, walking speedily away before turning into a side street with a Dead End sign at its corner.

— Told you she was fit, he said.

— That was odd, she said.

— What was odd about it? he said.

— I mean, she was obviously upset, she said.

— What's she got to be upset about? he said.

— Did you not just see her run away? she said.

She wasn't sleeping with anyone. There was no particular reason for this other than she had started to find sex a bit grim. All the spit and sweat and spunk and silty hairs. All the straining and humping and grunting. And it wasn't just the physical act. There was the issue of what sex did to her brain. It made it soft, fat, preening, lazy, puddleduck. Satisfied by the knowledge that her body was desirable because it had just been had, her brain gave up the ghost and stopped thinking the things it was supposed to be thinking — at night all cats are grey / every act of destruction is an act of liberation / armed love means the future has no future / tactical pig symphony / up against the wall motherfucker! — and instead fixated on what the naked man wandering around her flat was thinking about: pussy, ass, Call of Duty. No, she liked her brain and preferred it in its alert, defensive, rational state to when it resembled a bowlful of jelly.

— I don't think I'm going to have sex with anyone ever again, she announced the next time they met.

— Bollocks, he said.

— I'm serious, she said.

— Why's that then? he said. — Enlighten me.

— It's just different for girls, she said. — Innit.

— Meaning? he said, sounding genuinely curious to hear what she had to say.

— We-e-ell, she said, unsure how to put it, — It's, like, if you think about the physical act of sex... Putting something inside someone is different from having something put inside you.

— Sure, he said.

— A-a-and, like, when boys cum, she said, — it's, like, getting rid of something from them and putting it onto someone else. Onto you, the girl, me.

— Are you fucking stoned? he said.

She nodded. — A bit. So what? What I'm saying is serious. When men, you, have sex, you absolve yourself of something, get rid of it, and women, we have to take it on. And then if you take that and run with it and extend it out to the way men are about women, all projection of desire, love, hate, I mean, it's all gotta come from the physical act of sex, kinda like etymologically. Cause and effect. Because women aren't the way about men that men are about women. Or maybe some of them are, but it's only because they've copied men's style because it's so seemingly successful...

But he wasn't listening anymore. He was on his phone, typing a message.

Both being self-employed ('self' being a euphemism for 'un'), it got so as they were hanging out almost every day. Late-night bike rides to nowhere places, him stopping to graffiti bus stops, shop shutters, cemetery walls... He'd write his tag and sometimes he'd write his tag and her name side by side. He urged her to have a go with the spray can on multiple occasions but each time she declined.

— I don't suffer from your addiction, she eventually said.
— And besides I don't have anything concise enough to say.

He appeared to approve of this answer and stopped bugging her about it.

When they weren't together they'd message constantly. He sent photos of his tag and lots of links to right-on Internet content, usually related to whichever current affair was making headlines in the tabloids that week. Like the video of the policeman getting his throat cut with a machete in Tottenham (so gruesome she didn't watch all the way through). He also sent a lot of petitions. Trans rights, workers' rights, justice for cleaners, defund the police, kind of stuff. She dutifully consumed all the media he sent except for the petitions. She wasn't gonna sign those. Then, one afternoon he texted a link to a petition for a boycott of the Zabludowizc Foundation, an increasingly irrelevant contemporary art gallery in Kentish Town run by Israeli arms dealers. She was aware of the Zabludowizc problem. There'd been a boycott a few years back. It made a lot of noise but, at far as she could see, had been completely ineffectual. The cunts were still cunting about and wasn't, she thought, the Al-Anon definition of insanity repeating the same behaviour again and again and expecting different results?

She clicked the link, if only to see what nonsense the so-called left were spouting this time round and was taken to a Facebook event page from 2014. It wasn't a new ineffectual boycott. It was the ineffectual boycott from before.

She messaged him: Dis page five years old yo.

She clinked a link to the Zabludowizc's website and scrolled through News and Upcoming Events. All the usual suspects: Mat Collishaw, Marina Warner, Rachel McLean and then, in a list of names for an upcoming group show, his ex-wife's name. She took a photo of the listing and texted it to him: Noooow I see ;)

One tick, two ticks. Grey ticks, blue ticks. No reply.

He called later, didn't mention the Zabludowizc faux-pas, just got her to come meet him at an Ethiopian restaurant in Vauxhall. She turned up in a naughty mood and, over shiro, started teasing him about still being hung up on his ex.

— You wish it was you with an exhibition at Zabludowizc, she said. — Is that it?

— No, he said, — I just don't see why the upper middle class get all the airspace. I mean I'm doing really good stuff, you're doing really good stuff but no one's writing articles about *you* in the fucking *Guardian*.

— Who says I want articles written about me in the fucking *Guardian*? she said. — What? 'Biracial millennial redefines rape for the social media era'? Rofl. No thanks.

He lolled. — 'Prison dude says prison sucks.'

— Exactly, she said.

She watched him tear the enjera with his grubby fingers and mop up lentils.

— But it's bullshit, he said. — 'Culture.' I'm just sick of it.

— I know you are, she said. — That's why you hang around with me.

He smiled.

— I just wish there was something we could *do*, he said. — You know, to change it up. It's like there's nothing *real* anymore.

He launched into a monologue bemoaning London's arid creative landscape and the lowly cultural statuses of themselves and people they rated.

— I mean look at Mattais, he's an amazing writer and he's what? Working on a psych ward? he said.

— At least he's working on it and not committed to it, she said.

— And your weird mate, what's she called? he said. — The music girl.

— Flora, she said.

— Yeah, he said, — I mean, she's cool, but what the fuck does she do?

— She's a freak, she said. — It's a full time job.

But he had a bee in his bonnet and wouldn't let it drop. Example followed example. The graff kid who'd had his tag stolen by Supreme for a line of t-shirts, the producer whose beat had been ripped off by Skepta, the sex blogger who'd had her account shut down by Insta. She finished eating and wiped her mouth.

— If you are so desperate to do something, she said, — why don't you just do it? We could do something. Me and you.

His face lit up. Shovelling the last of the dinner into his mouth he came up with idea after idea about what the thing they should do would be. A book? A zine! A website? A podcast! Open up a squat and run a space? All his ideas sounded fun but she couldn't help pointing out their obvious flaws: time, effort, money. In the end they settled on the most straightforward plan of action. They would put on an event. They'd both read. She could work Adobe so she'd do the flyers. He had a lot of followers and was a member of multiple WhatsApp groups so would pump it out on socials. He came up with the name: 'Reading', pronounced like 'reading a book', but using the logo for the Reading Festival from the Nineties. She suggested a couple more performers: Flora for music and Reggie Stepper, a Ghanaian she'd met peddling his self-published book, *It's On Top* in a vegan Jamaican cafe in Whitechapel. He called a friend who lived in an ex-squat, now being run as a co-op, in Bermondsey and asked if they could set up in the kitchen. A date ten days in the future was decided and by the time they paid for the food and left, the thing was on.

The event was a massive success. Way more people than she'd expected, the readings met with laughter at all the right places, and the music so ephemeral that the audience didn't notice it and (to Flora's absolute delight) talked all the way through the set.

It was over by nine but there was such a good vibe, nobody wanted to leave and so the entire unruly party strolled into the night brandishing beer cans and spray cans and spliffs, buzzing at having been at what felt like the start of something new, something genuine, something un-PR'ed. Really exciting.

The two of them felt closer than ever. This wasn't just hanging out anymore, it was business! They walked arm in arm in the middle of the crowd beaming and congratulating one another on what they'd created... Except they kept being interrupted by Reggie Stepper, who was *on* her case. Kept trying to hold her hand, calling her wifey and saying how he was gonna cook her dinner. While she was cornered by Reggie, he took out his spray can and wrote her name in massive letters on the back of a bus waiting at traffic lights.

Realising she's a dab hand at PhotoShop, the ideas came thick and fast. He suggested a poster to sell at events and through his website, a set of stickers of his graffiti, and a flyer for an activist group he was trying to ingratiate himself with. She agreed to all of the above and soon enough the two of them were churning out what he referred to as 'product' fast.

— I love working with you, he said, after she'd emailed him a few different designs for the cover of a feminist pamphlet his friend wanted doing. — Everyone else needs like three meetings and wants to email every fucking tiny change but you, you just smash it out. It's wicked.

She appreciated the compliment and liked seeing her work go out and getting likes on other people's Instagrams. On the whole, her work was put out anonymously, either under his graffiti name or one activist group or another. Until a promo postcard he asked her to design for Cape Campaign, which hashtagged his name but not hers. But then she didn't give *too* much of a shit. It was only Instagram. And she wasn't doing it for the credit. But she wasn't doing it for money either. So, why was she doing it? Because she believed in what they were campaigning for? Which was what? Prison abolition. That sounded alright, she supposed. Still, it'd clearly annoyed her because she looked at the post several times over the next few days and each time she looked felt a kick of something unpleasant.

— Oooo, that's nice, her mum, an avid Instagrammer, said, catching sight of the post on her phone. — What is it?

She locked her phone.

— It's a flyer I made, she said. — They posted it without crediting me, that's all.

— Is this for that boy you've been hanging around with? her mum said.

— Maybe, she said. — Why?

— I'll tell you straight, darling, her mum said — But you're not gonna like it. That boy has got you exactly where he wants you. He's got you running around after him, making work for him, making content in promotion of issues *he* cares about, but what is he doing for you?

— He's my friend, she said.

— Well the way I see it, her mum said, — And I know you aren't going to agree with me, is that transgressions made against private property, which is what graffiti is, which is what squatting is… he is a squatter, yes? That's one thing. People might not like it, they might not agree with it, but at the end of the day it's a wall, it's a house, it doesn't matter. But transgressions made against a person, well, that's something else entirely.

Her mother was right about her not agreeing with the opinions espoused on graffiti or squatting. *Her* attitude was, with the system as corrupt as it was, any form of opposition to it was valid. So she was able to dismiss her mother's opinion on the friendship and forgo any consideration of what her friend's hidden (possibly even to himself) intentions towards her might be.

The next time they speak he has a new proposition.

— I was thinking, he said, — you're not really a designer, you're a writer and you remember how I went to Mexico?

— Yes, she said.

— Well, I've written something about it but it's a mess and I've kinda run out of steam. I thought maybe you could have a look at it and let me know what you think. Whether it's worth doing or not.

He emailed a Word doc which she downloads to her phone. He was right, it was a mess. Text justified right, left and centre, whole paragraphs in italics for no reason, spelling mistakes highlighted eight to a line. She emailed him back.

Do you want me to go through and edit? xx

His reply arrived in her inbox in seconds.

That'd be AMAZING. I'd reaaaaally appreciate. I'm a bit worried that I come across like one of those wankers who goes in for extreme holidaying hahaha. What we saying for next event?

She replied with an attachment of a rough design for the next flyer.

Flyer already done. Just waiting for details of people/venue/ date. More soon xx

That evening she sat down to read the text properly, on her computer. It began with him arriving in Los Angeles, visiting a prison then he's in Mexico with his graffiti friend, Pear. She made light corrections as she progressed, moving commas, adding capital letters and hyphens, closing up double spaces. Then the whole thing went a bit weird and there was a massive chunk of statistics about the history of brown people in the Americas. Unsure where the information was from but not wanting to make major changes without his approval, she started to leave notes in the margins.

Clichéd. Also there are a lot of black and latino ppl who r paler than u r AND a lot of black and latino ppl who vote Republican. Best to avoid magical negro trope as a rule.

Comes across as preachy + if u extend this argument to its conclusion what ur saying is that the leftest you can get is Jeremy Corbyn. Which is not true. Also Jews got to south america b4 slavery.

WTF. You can't just cut and past from Wiki.

Also, tenses r all over the place. It's cool to switch from past to present in the same text but if u do u gotta do it u gotta go it well.

The text is just over forty thousand words so she doesn't make it to the end on first read. She works until it got dark then calls him as she makes supper. His phone goes to voicemail.

— Hi there, I rarely check my messages so if you want to get hold of me quickly send me a text.

The next morning she picks up where she left off over coffee, following his escapades from desert to *barrios*, italicising the Spanish, correcting tenses, querying repetitions. Occasionally she will take a picture of a sentence she likes and text it to him and when she reaches the end of the story, which is less of an ending and more of a stop, she calls.

— Hi there, I rarely check my....

She emails him the edit.

It's really good. Really funny. Really informative. Have tried to keep ur conversational tone but make it readable. Some suggestions re: structure also. Anyway, AWOL? Lost ur phone? Call me bitch xxx

But he doesn't call or reply to her email. She checks the messages she'd sent earlier. Delivered but not read. She assumes he is holed up with one of his women and while she has no problem with that, per se, finds herself, for the first time ever, irritated by him. She drafts a text saying how'd she'd done a helluva lotta work that she'd been happy to do but it was rude to... She remembers the Instagram post that had tagged his name and not hers. So not for the first time ever. For the second.

She doesn't hear from him for the rest of the week. Every afternoon she calls and every afternoon it's the same.
— Hi there, I rarely check my...
— Hi there...
— Hi...
And then, — This mailbox is full.
She begins to worry that her initial annoyance had been rash and maybe she should've been concerned for his safety instead. If he'd lost his phone he'd check his email. Maybe, she thinks, he's got arrested? But if he's been arrested that would mean he didn't get bail and you didn't not get bail for graffiti...

He resurfaces early Saturday morning. Calls, sounding hyper.
— Yoooo, he yells when she answers.
— Where've you *been*? she says.
— Went on a mad one didn't I? he says. — What you saying? I'm right near your house. Come meet me.
Without time for coffee she walks to where he says he is, the north side of Blackfriars Bridge, half-asleep. They set off in the direction of his but he doesn't get off his bike. He rides in wobbly circles around her, making conversation difficult.

— I was thinking, he says, — for the next event, we could get Ian Bone. He's *so* into me.

— Did you read my edit? she says.

— He emailed me, he says. — He called me comrade.

He puffed out his chest.

— Does he know you're middle class? she says.

— And then there's this graff kid. 'Ve you seen that goofy face with fangs? He's killing it. And we could get Wolfboy down from Nottingham, or wherever the fuck he lives. But we need a venue. Somewhere big this time. I was thinking you could ask your mate, what's her name, to let us use the Tin Tabernacle?

— Flora, she says. — Her name's Flora. But I don't know. I'm not sure a bunch of rowdy graffiti twats is what that place needs. If anything, it needs protecting from those kind of people. Plus Tin Tab usually rents out for £200 a night. That's how they keep the roof from falling in…

But he won't take no for an answer.

— Just text her, he says. — See what she says.

They stop while she takes out her phone and texts Flora, who responds with unusual promptness. To her surprise, Flora's answer is 'yes'.

— Sweet! he says. — That's sorted then…

— Is it? she says.

When they reach Vauxhall Bridge he gets off his bike and on his phone.

— What you doing now? he says absentmindedly.

— Nothing, she says. — Hanging out with you. Have you read the edit I sent?

He takes out his phone and writes a text.

— I think I'm gonna head, he says.

— Oh, she says. — Ok.

He puts his phone back in his pocket.

— I'll shout you tomorrow, he says. — Let's hang.

— So you get me out of bed to walk you home? she says.
— What the fuck?

— Shit, I'm sorry, he says, noticing she is miffed. — I didn't think. It's just this girl that I'm kinda seeing, she's turned up at mine… But what you doing tomorrow?

— Nothing I don't think, she says.

— Well I'll come to you, he says.

— We could look at Mexichaos, she says.

— What? he says.

— Your writing, she says.

— Oh yeah, he says, leaning over to kiss her on the cheek.
— That's a good title actually.

He gets back on his bike.

— Did you look at the version I sent you? she says

— Haven't really been checking my email, he says, pushing down on his left pedal. — Too much bollocks!

— Have a look! she shouts, jogging after him. — I mean, feel free to disregard anything, they're only suggestions…

He slows down and looks back.

— Sweet, he says, throwing a black power salute. — You're the best. I owe you one.

He drops off the pavement and into the road. She turns and walks back along the river, buying a coffee on the way home.

The next day he wants to go to the ICA where a guy he used to be friends with but now hates is hosting a zine fair. They meet out front but don't end up going in and instead sit in St. James's Park slagging off the exhibitors.

— That girl Luisa thinks she's so fit, he says. — When I was fucking her do you know what she said? She told me she thought her face was world-changing. *World-changing*. I mean, lol!

— The face that sunk a thousand chips, she says.

— Lol, he says, again.

— Anyway, did you look at what I sent you yet?

He looks blank.

— Mexico? she says.

— Ah, shit, he says. — I'm a fucking dickhead. I'll look at it tonight. Promise.

They meet the following evening at a Nigerian place in Tooting he wants to go to because he's never tried fufu. Sitting side by side under neon lights on a black faux leather sofa, they order everything on the menu.

— So, did you look at the edit or what? she says.

— Ugh, he makes a face. — Yeah I had a look but I'm not sure I can be bothered with it anymore.

— Are you serious? she says.

— What? he says, turning to face her. — What's the point? Who's even gonna publish it?

She grins.

— It's funny, she says.

— What is? he says.

— Listening to someone else get depressed about what I spend my entire life depressed about. I'm telling you, nobody else thinks like this.

— Come again, he says.

The food arrives suspiciously fast.

— I'm saying, she says, toying with the mound of fufu,

— that only writers get like this. Normal people just do their jobs and do their relationships and do their leisure time. I mean, d'you think normal people get depressed about grammar? Cos I'm telling you, they don't.

— It's not the grammar I'm depressed about, he says, pulling the shared plate towards him.

— Yes it is, she says. — You just don't know it yet.

He lifts a heaped spoonful of fufu to his mouth.

— You're being cryptic, he says, with his mouthful.

— Am I? she says. — Maybe. Either way, all you gotta do is write the thing. When it's done, something will happen. It always does. And if it doesn't, publish it yourself.

He perks up.

— Maybe we could start an imprint, he says. — You and me.

— You and Me Books, she says. — I like that.

— Hey, he says, shuffling around on the sofa, which squeaks, — why don't we go and have a look at it after this?

— I don't know, she says. — I should really get home. You know I haven't done any work for ages and it's starting to stress me out.

— This is work, he says.

— Yeah. Your work, she says. — So I don't think I should do too much more to it. It's your thing.

— I just need someone to get me going, he says. — Through the sludge. He nudges her with his elbow. — Go on. Come back to mine. Please. I'll get dinner.

He persuades her into accepting a backie to Clapham. She sits on the bicycle seat, balancing dangling legs away from the wheel while he stands and pedals. She puts her hands on his shoulders.

— Put your arms round my waist, he says. — It's easier.

153

She wraps her arms around his torso. She holds him loosely at first but then her leg muscles start to ache and she holds on tighter, leaning into him, ear pressed against his back. It's strange holding his body in her arms because although they are close and hug and kiss and touch all the time, their physical interactions are brief ('tis the English way). She's never held onto him tight for fifteen minutes with his bum rising and falling and rising and falling against her chest.

Back at his, he sets up his laptop in the kitchen. She shivers. He notices and turns on the oven with its door open for heat (more effective than you might think, although obviously a waste of energy).

— So, he says. — How we gonna do this?

— Where's what I sent you? she says.

He settles in front of the computer, opens his email and downloads it.

— I thought you said you'd read it, she says.

— Oh, he says. — Yeah, I'm just not sure where anything downloads to on this computer.

She accepts his answer but watches him closely as he opens the document.

— Shit, he says.

— What? she says, on him like a hawk.

— It's just a lot of red pen, he says.

— So you didn't read it! she says. She is triumphant.

— No, he says. — Well, I… He trails off as he scans her first edit. — That is fucking *good*. He bangs his fist on the kitchen counter and scrolls. — Yes. Agree…

He deletes his text and replaces it with her edit then scrolls some more.

— Maybe I'll just accept all changes, he says.

— No! she grabs his hand, then realising they're holding hands, takes her hand back.

— It's just there's a lot of questions and stuff that shouldn't be in the final edit.

He gets to his feet and pulls back the chair.

— Why don't you sit? he says. — You know what you're doing. It'll be quicker.

With her on the keyboard and him pacing the room listening to her reading his words aloud, they make good progress. She adds edits and deletes notes.

— What about moving this bit, how 'Russians are the only white people anyone is scared of' to before where they're laughing at the gringos? she says.

When he doesn't answer she turns to look at him and catches him shoulders hunched, mouth open, staring at her with a lascivious look on his face.

— Hello? she says.

— Shit, he says. — Sorry. I was miles away.

He comes to stand behind her to look at the extract she's highlighted, rests his hands on shoulders and leans in to look at the screen.

— Don't you think that makes more sense? she says, turning to address him without realising how close his face is to hers. They brush lips.

— Yeah, he says. — Do whatever you think's best.

She turns back to the screen, fingers on the keys. What is going on?

They work on his text for a couple of hours, stopping when they reach a natural break in the action. (The two protagonists are stranded in a railway depot in the blazing heat and will remain there for seventy-two hours). She checks the time on her phone.

— Shit, she says, realising how late it is, — I've gotta run if I'm gonna make the last tube.

— Why don't you just crash here? he says.

She hadn't thought of that.

— What's that band you like? he says, taking her place in front of the computer.

— D Block Europe, she says. — Why?

He types it into YouTube.

— Here, he says. — For you.

She smiles and raises her arms half-heartedly before being caught by an enormous yawn. He kills the music.

— Go to bed, he says. — I'll be in in a minute.

She goes through to the bedroom. Undressing to knickers and bra, the thought crosses her mind that she's never stayed round his. He'd stayed at hers and they'd slept together in the back seat of vans and at other people's houses but his bed is a first. She gets into the side of the bed that looks less slept in and smiles at how close the two of them feel and what a productive evening it'd been.

She wakes in his arms to the sound of his radio alarm clock playing Punjabi music. It's been a long time since she'd woken up in someone's arms. It's sunny and everything feels nice.

— Mornin', he says, snuggling into her before letting go and stretching. — Coffee?

They roll out of bed, don enough clothes to be decent (tops, no bottoms) then go through to the kitchen where he turns on the oven again, then they get straight back to it.

Half an hour in and they're on a roll. They're not just correcting mistakes but adding in-jokes and flourishes. They come up with the idea of adding the word 'mate' to the end of every sentence the narrator says to make him sound English and to add the word 'yo' to the end of every sentence Pear says to make him sound American and are delighted by the effect. They read chunks of direct speech at one another, hooting with laughter.

— This is so fun, he says.

— Isn't it? she says.

They work into the afternoon when they both remember they have places to be and call it a day. She goes into the bedroom to fetch the rest of her clothes then joins him in the bathroom where he hands her a toothbrush. They brush their teeth at the same time, looking at themselves and each other in the mirror. She smiles at him.

— I love brushing my teeth with people, she says.

— That's cause you're a freak, he says.

She spits, rinses the toothbrush then turns on the hot tap to wash her face. No water comes out.

— No hot water? she says.

— Waste of money, he says.

— What about soap? she says, looking around for some to wash her face.

— Don't use soap. Don't use shampoo, he says. — Waste of money.

— I stopped using shampoo too, she says, splashing her face with cold water. — I only wash my hair with conditioner but I don't think I'm ready to live without soap.

— You don't need it, he says.

— Maybe *you* don't, she says, — but if you've got a pussy, you need soap.

He walks her to the Tube wheeling his bike and bigging up the work they've done.

— Seriously, he says. — That was amazing. Really, good.

— I think if we have one more crack, we could get it done, she says.

They arrive at the station.

— How about tomorrow? he says.

— Maybe, she says. — But I might try and do some writing myself, you know?

— Ok, he says. — Well, don't forget the event Tuesday.

— I won't, she says.

He leans down to kiss her goodbye but instead of kissing her on the cheek like he usually does, he kisses half-on, half-off her mouth. He lets his lips linger on hers and squeezes her tight. She feels his chest expanding and detracting for one breath, two breath, three breath, four breath, five breath, six breath… but she can't breathe. She wriggles out of his arms and ducks into the Underground.

On the way back to hers she mulls over the events of the past twenty-four hours. The kisses, the cuddles, the highly-efficient work rate. Was there something going on or was it her imagination? It kinda seemed like they liked each other but no, that couldn't be. She's never thought of him like that and she doubts he's had any thoughts about her. No, she wasn't like the plethora of women his penis has recently been inside. She was his friend…

She makes a stab at her own work that afternoon but doesn't get far. She tries again the next morning and gets absolutely nowhere. She ends up trawling social media, clicking on the page he'd made for their last event and reads the comments.

Dream team

What a night. Restored my faith in humanity.

Best flyer ever.

He's liked them all and she wonders why he didn't bother to mention how popular her flyer was. Seventeen likes! Thinking she should text him to give him shit about not telling her about everyone loving the flyer, she unlocks her phone but before she can open messages, he calls.

— Ha, she answers. — You are so psychic.

— Why? he says. — What you doing?

An hour later she's back at door. She drop-calls him, hears his phone ringing, his footsteps on the stairs then he swings opens the front door and steps into the street in his underpants. Tight jockeys. He twangs the waistband.

— Woah, she says.

— What? he says.

— You're naked, she says,

— Oh, he says. — Yeah. I've got the oven on full blast.

He hugs her, the skin of her face meeting the hairs on his chest.

— Go up, he says. — I've got some rum. It's really good. It's like four hundred quid to buy.

He sits by the oven. He pours them a drink. She gives him a 'what are we doing?' look. He grins. She shouldn't care that he's naked, it's not like she can see anything, but it puts her a little on edge.

— Aren't we gonna look at the text? she says.

— Sure, he says.

He pulls his laptop out of a backpack on the floor and opens it.

— Oh wait, he says. — Let me play you this. He opens iTunes. — This is what we were listening to in the train yard. 'Esto es Mexico' by La Malagueña. This is what real G's listen to.

She takes a sip of her drink and sways in time to a violin. He takes her hand, lifts his arm and spins her underneath it.

— Sorry, he says, letting go of her hand. — That was so cheesy.

A woman starts to sing.

— But isn't this music nuts? he says. — Like Latino opera or something.

When the song is over they sit down in front of the computer. The Word document is open where she left it.

— Have you looked at this while I've been gone? she says.

He shakes his head and tops up the drinks.

They go through a couple of paragraphs: the train starts moving, someone nearly loses a foot…

— Fuck this, he says. — Let's go out.

— Out where? she says.

— Out nowhere, he says.

She likes the sound of that.

— Okay, she says. — But you've got to put some clothes on first.

They head to one of the Portuguese bars on the high street and order brandies. It's rowdy at the bar and a drunk Brazilian takes a shine to them, tells them they make a handsome couple and pays for their drinks. He puts his arm round her, playing up to the misconception. He winks at her.

Some more brandies and a couple of beers, then they head into the estates. He tags stairwell after stairwell with his tag and her name.

— I don't know about tagging estates, she says, drunker than she thinks she is.

— What don't you know about it? he says.

— Well it's one thing tagging a bank or a bus or a shop, she says, noticing her voice sounding like her mum's. — But here it'll never get cleaned off. And you know, people live here.

— Fuck that, he says. — Did you see what I wrote about Blaise Belleville on his house?

— Blaise who? she says.

— The guy who runs Boiler Room, he says. — What a prick. Do you know he's a fucking aristocrat? Landed gentry, no less.

They talk about this and that, nothing and everything, are kinda flirting, kinda being friends, flipping between both like it doesn't matter.

They manage to slip into one of the tower blocks behind an entering resident and ride the lift to the top floor.

— Shit, he says. — I've got the key to get up on the roof of this block but I didn't bring it. I fucked a girl up there once.

— Oh, she says. — Really?

— Maybe we should go back and get it? he says.

Was he saying what she thought he was saying?

— Okay, she says.

They take the lift back down and he takes a photo of their reflection in the mirror.

Back at his he doesn't look for the key. He pours more rum and they goof about, drunkenly setting the world to rights aka taking the piss out of people. He doesn't ask her to stay, it is assumed. They go to bed together. She strips to her underwear in front of him without giving it a second thought, shivers and gets under the duvet. He lies down beside her, rests a hand on her shoulder but remains upright, fiddling with his phone.

— What you doing? she says.

— Gotta take my insulin, he says. — I fucked it up yesterday.

She closes her eyes and listens him to take his blood sugar.

— I feel sick, she says.

He pats her head.

— Go to sleep, he says.

She listens to him self-administer the injection then pack away the kit. Lying down, he scoops her up in his arms.

— Night, one of them says.

— Night, says the other.

He kisses the back of her neck then rolls away from her. Her drunken nausea passes and she drifts off for few seconds then wakes again at the touch of his hand pawing the duvet, looking for her. It finds her and pulls her towards him. She rolls over so she is big spoon and he is little. They stay like that until she gets pins and needles in her arm. She takes it away and turns around in the sheets. He rolls after her then ever so gently rests a hand on her waist. She can feel it vibrating. He moves it slowly, sliding it onto her stomach then up her torso towards her tits. He cups them both in his palm then returns to her stomach and spreads his fingers out.

— You're shaking, he says, his voice loud in the residential quiet.

She wriggles, pushes her bum into his lap. He takes it as a signal and pops a finger under her knicker elastic. She turns her face to his and they kiss for a couple of seconds. They stop kissing at the same time.

— It'd be a disaster, one of them says.

— A total disaster, says the other.

They both giggle. He takes his arm away and they lie on their backs in the dark, both awake. His hand returns. Feels the contour of her hip, her bum. Squeezes it and they're kissing again. Surprisingly effortless for a first kiss. He rolls onto his back and pulls her on top of him, holds her hips, holds her bum then, with her straddling him, puts an index finger in her pussy. He moves his finger in and out. She makes the appropriate appreciative sound, riding up and down on top of him. She can see him looking at her intently, even in the dark. She reaches a hand between her legs in search of his willy but before she finds it, he snatches her arm away.

— No, he says, his finger still in her.

Suddenly self-conscious, she dismounts. Back on the mattress, she rolls away from him, to the other side of the bed.

— It's be a disaster, he says, sounding apologetic.

— A disaster, she says.

She tries to go back to sleep but it's impossible. Her brain is going a million miles an hour. How come he could put his finger in her pussy but she couldn't touch his dick? It didn't seem fair. Then she thought maybe he had an STD and didn't want her to get it. Or did he have a small willy and not want her to know?

He rolls over in bed again, dropping an arm heavily over her and bringing his mouth right up close to her ear.

— I just want to pull down your panties and fuck you, he says.

If the lights'd been on and they were looking at each other it would've been awkward, but in the darkness with her back to him it's only surreal. Him holding her, her not breathing until the atmosphere goes crackly.

She breaks the silence.

— Well, she says, breathing out and adopting a jovial tone to try and clear the air, — you probably will at some point but I don't think this is the moment.

He laughs. His normal, friendly, not-sexy laugh.

— Yeah, he says, — If we're gonna fuck we shouldn't do it half asleep in bed. We should do it somewhere amazing.

— Like the rooftop of a council estate? she says.

— Yeah, he says. — Exactly.

She wakes the next day feeling awful. He's next to her in bed surfing radio stations.

— You were snoring, he says.

— What's the time? she says.

— Just gone three, he says.

— Jesus, she says. — I never sleep this late. I should get home.

— Nuh-uh, he says. — We gotta be in Kilburn.

Blank.

— The event? he says. — We gotta be there in two hours to meet your friend, he says.

— Flora, she says.

Coffee makes her hangover worse but makes him eager to edit.

— Just the last few paragraphs, he says. — Then it's done.

He sits at the computer. She lies on the floor, backseat editing and eating dry granola but can't pay attention.

— Let's just leave it for another time, she says.

That's when he gets stressed.

— I just want to get it done, he says and kicks the bin.

She chuckles.

— Chill, she says. — We will.

But a bad mood has descended. They walk to the Tube in close to silence, him grunting one syllable replies to her questions. She beeps her Oyster card. He skips through the barriers behind her. She wonders whether she should say something about last night.

— You okay? she says, as a lame attempt.

He shrugs.

When they get on the train it is empty but instead of sitting beside her like he usually would, he sits two seats down. Was he being weird? Or was he just being hungover? She can't tell. She watches him for a minute, eyes shut, head nodding. But then the roaring whoosh of the train through the tunnel starts giving her a headache. Her hangover takes over and she shuts her eyes, letting the train's movement vibrate her.

They get off at Kilburn Park with him still not looking at, or talking to her, except to remind her he'll come through the gates at the same time. But then, when they get to Tin Tab, he changes tack completely. As soon as there's an audience, he comes on all touchy-feely. He gets her to sit on his lap when there isn't a chair, holds her hand, puts his arm round her shoulders, even slaps her on the bum when she says something funny.

The event goes seriously off-piste. A line up of nutters have to be prised off the mic, there's lot of drum 'n'n bass, one of his graff mates tags up the bathroom. It's fun but stressful for her because Flora is worried about the building and the neighbours. So as soon as the event is over, she does her best to coax the audience into relocating to the pub.

At the end of the night the two of them catch the Tube together. He sits beside her this time and drapes his arm round her shoulder as he goes over moments from the evening that had been particularly awkward or funny. He puts a hand on her thigh with no one around to see it. He leans his head on her shoulder, saying how he can't wait to be in bed. So she reads the signs as saying she's gonna go back to his. She wants to go back to his. But then, when the train doors open at Piccadilly Circus he turns to look at her and says, —Isn't this your stop?

— Oh, she says. — Yeah.

She grabs her jacket and jumps off the train.

— I'll call you tomorrow, they both say at the same time then laugh.

It's only when she gets outside and an alert vibrates her phone that she remembers tomorrow is the day she's supposed to fly to Berlin. A plan made time ago that being so involved in the edit and in the event, she'd completely forgotten.

Berlin is Berlin. Big scary Fraus and their big scary children, teeth-kissing Turks, British kids from the provinces posing as noise musicians, and drugs. The two of them exchange a few texts over the course of the week but their conversations are out of sync, with messages replied to hours after they are sent... But of course she thought about what was going on between them, attempting to gauge different possibilities. It seemed likely they were gonna have sex but after that would they be boyfriend and girlfriend? That seemed a bit much. Maybe something more emancipated than that. Lovers. Too schmaltzy. Fuck buddies. Too crass. Maybe just friends who love each other who sometimes have sex. She went with that one.

The day before she is due to fly back to London he messages: *When r u back?*

She types: Tomorrow... I miss Mexico.

A speech bubble pops up. It goes dot, dot dot, then disappears then pops up again. He texts: I miss you.

An unexpected development.

She smiles as she replies: Miss u too

He texts back with a link to a song on Spotify: 'Best Friend' — Vybz Kartel.

She puts her headphones in and listens.

A tight pum pum is a man's best friend, couldn't be no puppy what a load of shit. Not a rottie', not a pit, just a goodie goodie in a drawers that's it.

It's the first music with a rhythm she's heard all week.

She messages: So good xx

He replies with a photograph of Vybz Kartel in a purple suit simulating sex on a woman bent over in front of him. He texts: U and me LOL.

She laughs as she replies: Have you blacked up?

He replies: Have you?

It might be a cack-handed London version of it, but it is definitely flirting.

Fireworks Night. She wakes around ten to a text from him sent at four in the morning: Call me when u wake. Lets go fireworks xxx

She calls.

— Hey there, I rarely check my messages so if you want to get in touch with me you can send me a text.

If he was awake at four it makes sense he's sleeping now, she thinks.

She spends the morning catching up on life. Pays bills, replies to emails. He's sent her an email with a load of photos from his Mexico trip.

Thought maybe you could do a layout using these??

She downloads them and looks through. Mostly they're black and white landscape shots but one is of him completely naked on top of a moving train. His willy wasn't that small.

Running out of menial tasks mid-afternoon and too Ryanaired to do any real work, she decides to walk in the general direction of his, assuming he'll wake at some point and tell her to come over anyway. Knowing he doesn't have InDesign she takes her computer with her and since she's carrying a bag she chucks in her toothbrush and a bar of hotel soap.

She walks the usual way to his but when she gets to Westminster Bridge a protest has closed off the road. No big surprise. Society's been crumbling all year and there'd been a protest every weekend since the weather warmed up. But this protest isn't your usual demographic of the think-they're-liberal middle classes and DIY anarchos handing out risographed 'what to do if you get arrested' pamphlets. This march is entirely made up of black people, and old black people at that, dreader than dread, dressed in army fatigues. What looked like the Channel One soundsystem from carnival was playing dub on the back of a flatbed truck. She's never seen a protest like it and knows there is no way she can let it go past.

She joins the throng, walking on the pavement beside the march, partly because the road is barricaded off and partly because it is her habit to remain at the peripheries of any mass movement. Signs bob above the crowd.

'My ancestors were Kings and Queens'.

'I was stolen'.

'Reparation Day is Today!'

'Stop the Maangamizi'.

Maangamizi is a term she hasn't heard before. She takes out her phone and is about to look up what it is when an electric wheelchair speeds by, an oxygen tank on its back, driven by a man with tubes feeding the oxygen into his nose.

— Go back where you came from darkie! he yells at everyone and no one.

Her jaw drops. She was used to black fetishisation racism and racism disguised by neoliberal metaphor but it'd been a while since she'd witnessed old-fashioned, out-and-out 'darkie' shit. Was this guy serious?

A tall man wearing a Gaddafi t-shirt, with long, immaculate dreads, takes the bait.

— You piss off, he says to the disabled lunatic.

— No one wants you here wog! the disabled lunatic shouts.

Her jaw drops lower.

— You think, the tall man wearing a Gaddafi t-shirt with long, immaculate dreads turns and addresses the wheelchair, — that I am so stupid as to give you what you want? To leap over the barriers and beat you, like you deserve and then you get your footage, your precious footage to send to the papers and look: Black man attacks disabled pensioner? Well you've got the wrong man because I'm a smarter man than that.

The disabled lunatic deals out a couple more racial slurs then speeds off.

The march crosses Westminster Bridge before the crowd congregates on the lawn outside Parliament. Someone hangs the Jamaican flag over the statue of Emmeline Pankhurst, that says 'Courage calls to Courage Everywhere'. She snaps a pic of it on her phone.

Wandering through the crowd she gets a couple of dirty looks for not being black enough, but most of the protesters don't seem to mind her presence and one or two even give her a nod or a double-blink to indicate their awareness of her particular predicament. Different from theirs, but related.

A woman steps up to a mic set up on the back of the flatbed truck carrying the Channel One soundsystem.

— I am here, the woman says, — representing the Dutch West Indies and Suriname.

Not Jamaica, not Trini, not Barbados, not Martinique, not St Lucia. *Suriname*. No one *ever* talks about Suriname.

— Whoop, whoop, she whoops in excitement and throws a hand in the air to represent. It being such a rare occasion, she can't help herself.

— Too long, the woman representing the Dutch West Indies and Suriname says, throwing a hand in the air herself. The crowd echoes the words in agreement. — For too long black women have been ignored, silenced, trodden on. We have sacrificed our bodies, our minds, our children to this system without credit, without acknowledgement, without payment. How many rich people, how many famous people, how many powerful people, how many well-established people are in the places they are in because of the toil, the labour, the continuing oppression, the silencing, the invisibility of the sacrifices and efforts of black women? Four hundred years, four hundreds years! Well to those dishonourable men and women sitting in that collapsing building that houses *their* democracy I say, those four hundred years are up!

Cheers from the crowd.

— Now is the time for black women to speak and be heard, for their suffering to be recognised but also their talents, their skills, their contribution...

Her phone rings. It's him. She wants to listen so puts it on silence then changes her mind and answers.

— Hey, she says, putting a finger in her other ear so she can hear him. — I'm in Parliament Square. There's a reparations march and the speaker's from Suriname! You should come down.

— I'm fugged, he groans. — I've got dis mendal tootache. It came on lasd nighd. I was hoping id go away but id's jus fugged.

— You sound terrible, she says. — Do you want me to bring you some painkillers? I'm not far from yours. I could get some codeine.

— Nah, he says. — You're alrighd. Think I jus godda sleep id off...

— You sure? she says. — I really don't mind. Have you eaten anything? Maybe you should go to a dentist?

— Theriouthly, he says, — I'm in no fid sdade.

He sounds really bad.

— Okay, she says — Another day then. Shame... Thought we could go up on the roof of that block and watch the fireworks.

He laughs, a low throaty gurgle that sounds like he's about to expire.

— I'll led you know if da siduashion changes ad all, he says. — But righd now roofdop is off.

By the time she gets off the phone the woman representing the Dutch West Indies and Suriname has finished and the crowd is dispersing. She sets off towards home but, crossing Trafalgar Square, he calls again.

— Do you want to go to Lewes for the fireworks? he says, sounding like his usual hyper self.

She stops in her tracks, spins 180°, spins 180° back.

— Errrrr, she says. — What? When?

— ASAP, he says.

— Okay, um…, she says.

— I'm gonna jump the train, he says.

— What should I do? she says.

— Where are you now? he says.

— Victoria, she says, unsure why she lies.

— Come to mine, he says. — How quick can you be?

She calculates potential routes in her head. The 88 goes from nearby.

— Actually, scrap that he says. — Clapham Junction station. Ten minutes.

— I think it'll take me longer than that, she says.

— Okay. Twenty minutes then, he says. — Be as fast as you can, I'll be there.

She descends into Charing Cross Tube, opting for the fastest (and most expensive) route to Clapham Junction. Underground to Victoria then British Rail. A whopping £5.40. Arriving at Clapham Junction, she walks to one exit to see if he is there. He isn't. She walks to the other. No sign of him.

She texts.

— Which exit u at?

She is about to go through the ticket barriers when she realises she'll only have to come back in again and if he's going to bunk the train then she might as well bunk the train, because if he gets caught they'll both be fucked. She taps out on the 'changing journeys' machine and waits inside the barriers. Half an hour goes by, forty five minutes. She calls.

— Hi there…

She texts: Where are you?

Ten minutes later he texts back: I'm an idiot.

He calls.

— Left my phone at home, he says. — Had to come all the way back to get it so I'm only leaving now. Will be ten minutes max. Check the train times. Let me know which platform you're on.

She waits for him on Platform Six for half an hour. He appears on the stairs just as a train pulls into the station. It isn't the train to Lewes but he says they should get on anyway as it's a local train so less chance of inspectors. Rush hour commuter hell presses them against each other for several stops. She tells him about the woman from Suriname.

— I think I know her, he says. — Brenda. She's my mate.

— Brenda what? she says.

— I don't know, he says.

— I'd like to meet her, she says.

He looks worse for wear and is taking sips from an expensive-looking bottle of brandy.

— Can I have some? she says.

He hands her the bottle.

— Happy holidays, she says, raising it to her lips.

She takes a sip. It's delicious.

— I need it, he says, taking the bottle back. — It's the only thing that stops my face aching.

More people get on and they're separated so she puts her headphones in and listens to music on her phone. He messages with someone on his until the train empties out. A seat comes up.

— Sit on my lap, he says, taking the seat and patting his thigh.

She sits, taking out one headphone so she can hear him.

— What are you listening to? he says.

— DBE, she says. — Like always.

— Oh, he says, — Are they those gay boys you love so much?

He rests his hand casually on her hip, moves it inch by inch towards her bum.

— Errr, I don't think they're gay, she says and laughs. — They're completely obsessed with pussy.

— You know what I mean, he says. — Gay as in gayboys, who spend all day thinking about sex.

— Their lyrics are *so* rude, she says, putting a hand faux-coyly to her mouth.

— Tell me, he says.

She laughs. —They're too rude for rush hour.

— Whisper it then, he says, — In my ear.

She waits for the song to reach the right bit.

— That pussy drippin, I just put my tip in, my tongue in her mouth while her pussy is full up, she whisper-raps.

He gives her bum a squeeze.

At Croydon, the commuters exeunt en masse. She moves to the seat opposite, putting her feet up on the seat next to him. He's still on his phone but rests his other hand on her ankle. He closes his fingers round it. He slides his hand slowly up to her thigh.

— Check this out, he says, thrusting his phone screen in her face.

Most times she hates looking at things on people's phone but he's earned his credentials in interesting digital content over the years and so she sits forward to see. A chat is open with 'Billie'.

Hey, thanks for getting back to me so fast. I'm a REALLY big fan of your work. I'm really into crime and I think prison is bad so big up for all you're doing to try and stop it.

He scrolls back through old messages too fast for her to read them.

— What's that? she says, not understanding.

— This girl wants the D, he says and laughs.

She gets a sinking feeling. She brings her feet to the floor. Why was he touching her up at the same time as messaging Billie? Why was he messaging Billie at all? She stares out the window to hide her face from him, zones in on the reflection of a tablet belonging to a man sitting in the next compartment. She can read his email clearly. It says:

Dear Gary,

Thank you for applying for the position of Parking Lot Manager. Unfortunately, we have had a lot of applications for this position...

Poor Gary.

He's still chatting and laughing.

— What were those lyrics again? he says.

— That pussy drippin', I just put my tip in..., she says out of rhythm in a monotone.

— Billie's gonna get the tip, he says, — Just the tip, hahahaha. Nothing else.

— Who is Billie anyway? she says.

— How do I know? he says. — But I know her parents are going to the country next weekend and I'm invited.

— Her parents? she says.

The train doors open. No one moves. The train doors beep, warning they are about to close. He jumps out of his seat.

— I've been here before, he says, — There are no ticket barriers. And we can probably get a cab for like five pound or something.

He heads for the doors. She rushes after him, makes it onto the platform but her jacket gets caught in the train doors. A moment of panic. She calls his name but he's already gone. She yanks the material free and runs after him. He's right, no barriers. She spots him talking to a minicab with its engine on.

— How much to Lewes mate? he leans in the window.

— Forty pound, boss, the driver says.

— That's as much as buying tickets for the train, she says.

— You're alright boss, he says to the driver, who rolls up his window. He turns to her. — Yeah but it's the principle.

— What? she says. — The principle of supporting private enterprise over national infrastructure?

He doesn't, or pretends not to hear.

They walk to the main road, taking one last sip each of the brandy.

— I'll pay for the cab if you get some more liquor, he says. She agrees.

He orders an Uber on his phone and a few minutes later a Prius pulls up. It gets them to Lewes for £36 but when they reach the outskirts of town the turning is closed off.

— They don't want no one who isn't local coming, that's why, the Uber driver says.

The road block has caused a traffic jam, which they sit in for fifteen, twenty minutes.

— Fuck this, he says eventually. — Let's walk.

She doesn't like the sound of this and nor does the Uber driver.

— Very dangerous, he says. — Dark. No pavement.

But he is out the car and she has no choice but to follow.

At first it's fun collecting looks from people stuck in their cars but pretty soon the traffic picks up and they're walking headlong into vehicles going sixty, seventy, eighty, ninety miles per hour. He speeds ahead of her, surefooted but she's nervous and shouts for him to wait. He slows down, walking in front of her protectively, until they reach a bridge across the motorway.

— Let's go up here, he says.

She thinks they're going to climb the actual bridge.

— You're going to have to help me, she says.

— Course, he says.

He puts on builders' gloves and climbs not up the bridge but up the bank alongside it. Of course. She follows, clutching at ivy, slipping in mud. Asides from the gloves, which allow him to grip on to the slimy branches, he's wearing trainers and a tracksuit. She's in loafers that don't have any grip and a pencil skirt but she makes it without his help anyway, if only just.

She emerges from the foliage to him getting angry looks from locals as he tags a massive 'Free Palestine' tag on the sign welcoming you to town.

— You know that the PLO was set up with Nazi money? she says.

— What are you chatting about? he says, pocketing his magic marker.

— The Palestine Liberation Organisation was funded by François Genoud. Nazi banker.

— Don't tell me you're fucking pro-Israel, he says.

— No, she says, — no, but you know, most countries are founded on bloodshed and Israel has shed a lot less blood than, say England...

— You're a fucking Zionist, he says.

— I'm not a fucking anything, she says. — I'm just saying some facts.

— So what? he says.

— So I just think you should think about what you write on walls, she says.

— Where's a newsagent? he says. — You need to buy us something to drink.

They look around for a shop but can only find a pub. She buys them expensive pints for the countryside as the Proddies gather outside, oil drums burning, rockets going off.

— Let's take these and go, he says.

They hide their full pints from the bar staff and scarper, following the route of the procession. The further into town they get the busier it gets and soon the streets are rammed and they are forced in the middle of the parade, with fires burning and bangers going off. A piece of hot coal jumps out of a trailer, burns a hole in her tights and singes her leg.

— Watch out! someone shouts.

— Get back! someone shouts.

— You're not supposed to be walking. It's dangerous. You've got to wait, someone shouts.

They duck inside the barriers and push on at the back of the crowd until they come the other end of the parade where the streets empty out.

— Fuck, she says, —That was intense.

He's got his phone in his hand and is looking around.

— Yes mate, he says, high-fiving a guy who appears out of nowhere.

— Fancy bumping into you, the guy says.

— You didn't tell me we were meeting someone, she says.

He doesn't hear her.

His friend has a girlfriend and from that point forth the group arranges itself into the men conversing between themselves with the women defaulting into each other's company. The girlfriend is alright but because more preoccupied with the fact that he is, for no reason she can see, ignoring her.

They watch the bonfires, then go for a drink in a pub in town. His friend offers to drop them back to the outskirts of London on his way back to Essex.

On the drive back, the boys sit in the front seat talking shop (graffiti). The women attempt to join in the conversation but fail so the girlfriend demands control of the music.

— What shall we play? the girlfriend says, — Something good.

— D Block Europe, she says. — Outside. That's the one most people like.

His friend's girlfriend finds the song on Spotify.

— Yeah, I like this shit, the girlfriend says as it starts. — Like, what's that American group? Migos?

— Yeah, DBE are the *real* Migos, she says, cheering up.

In the front seat, he reaches forward, turns the volume down.

— Hey! she says.

— It's fucking shit, he says.

She sits forward and punches him lightly on the arm.

— What's your fucking problem? he says, nasty.

And that's her done. She takes off her seatbelt, slumps down in the seat and doesn't say anything for the rest of the journey. He carries on yammering away and doesn't notice her silence. But the friend and his girlfriend do.

When the car pulls off Blackheath roundabout she doesn't bother saying goodbye to them. She slips out, slamming the car door and runs down a side street to wee. He follows her, standing by a wall and pisses in the direction of where she is squatting.

— Well, he says, doing up his fly, — What we doing?

— Exactly what I was about to say, she mutters.

— What's that? he says.

— What are we doing? she says, wound up.

— What's your problem? he says. — Are you drunk?

— Yes, she says. — A little.

— You're acting loopy, he says, sounding irritated.

— Well? she says.

— Well what? he says.

— Well what are we doing? she says. — You and me.

— You tell me, he says.

— Don't be a goof, she says, carefully opting for a gentle jibe rather than an out-and-out insult as the mood seems electric, but he reacts as if she'd just publicly denounced him as a psychosexual rapist stalker with paedophilic inclinations anyway. He blows up.

— You should watch what you say right now, he says, gesticulating like a hard man, — I'm serious. Chose your words carefully. Because if you say some shit you don't mean right now, you won't necessarily be able to take it back.

She is shocked at his reaction, but acts nonchalant to hide it. — I always mean what I say, she says.

— Pfff, he says. — Yeah right.

They walk to a bus stop in silence. He checks his phone again and again and again.

— There's a bus in two minutes that will take us to the Walworth Road, he says.

— I'm not sure where I'm going, she says.

— Well it's all the right direction, he says. — Let's hop on this and then figure it out when we're somewhere sane.

The bus arrives. They go up to the top deck. It's empty and they take separate seats. She looks at him. He looks anywhere other than at her. She tries again.

— Don't you think, she says, — we should talk about it?

— Talk about what? he says.

— We kissed, she says.

— So what? he says.

She opens her mouth, closes it, opens it. — So nothing, she says.

They ride a couple more stops.

— All I'm trying to say, she says, — is that we are really good friends, right?

— Right, he says.

— Who tell each other we love each other all the time, right? she says.

— Right, he says.

— And now we've kissed, she says.

— Listen S... he says, then breaks off. — Fuck, I almost called you my ex-wife's name.

There is a different quality to his voice. A meanness she's not heard before.

— Okay...? she says.

— It's just that you sounded just like her then, he says.

— Sorry, she says, — but how do I sound anything like that fucking careerist Zabludowicz cunt?

She is losing control of the situation.

— It's just that she's the kind of person who makes a massive issue out of nothing, he says. — Which is what you're doing.

— So this is nothing, she says. — Is that what you're saying?

— Come on, he says. — Do we really need to have this conversation? I thought we were way past this.

— If that's how you feel, she says, — then fine. I'm not here to talk you into anything. I'm not trying to go out with you. I'm just saying that we're friends and we kissed and if that is all then it's cool but we should at least *talk* about the situation.

— We are talking about it aren't we? he says.

— Ya think? she says.

Her sarcasm seems to work.

— So, what do you want to say about 'the situation'? he says.

— Fuck, she says. — I don't know! Nothing in particular. Just maybe acknowledge there's something going on and try n' figure it out…

— One, he says, — there's no need to shout. And two, we are friends. That's it.

— Fine, she says, calming down. — Whatever you say, boss.

— Why 'boss'? he says.

— I'm just saying, she says, — that you can *say* what you want but if you look at the whole situation, I'd say it adds up to something more than just friends.

— What, he says, — do you think it is?

— Like I said, she says, — I think maybe we love each other.

— You can't love me, he says, looking directly at her.

— Why not? she says.

— Because you know the truth, he says.

He sits looking out the window, wincing and holding his bad tooth.

She feels sorry for him, decides to take it easy.

— I like the truth, she says. — I like you.

She moves seats to sit beside to him and puts her arm round his shoulders.

— I told you no, he says and shoves her hard enough for her to fall off the seat and onto the floor.

— This, she says, getting to her feet, — is exactly my point.

— What is? he says. — What is your point?

— If we are just friends, she starts to shout, — then there is no fucking reason for you to act like such a dick!

— I'm not the one making a scene, he shouts back.

— D'you wanna know what I think? she shouts louder, waggling a finger at him like a mum.

— I'm guessing I'm gonna hear it, he says, smarmy as a teenage boy.

— What I think, she says, — is that you chat a big whole load of shit and if you could put your massive ego aside for one second and actually acknowledge the way things are between us. We hang out every day, we talk every day, we work together, we say we love each other, we say we miss each other, we kiss. I just want to pull your panties down and fuck you. I just want to pull your panties down and fuck you. That's what you said. And you don't *say* shit like that to people if you don't fucking *mean* it!

— I did mean it, he says, — At the time. But after this I've changed my mind.

She eyeballs him for long enough for him to find it disconcerting.

— Look, he says, — I'm sorry if I led you on but I don't fancy you. That's just the way it is.

— Oh really? she says.

— Yes really, he says.

— Well I find that hard to believe, she says.

— Oh right, he says, meanness returning. — I forgot you think you're really fucking fit.

— What? she says, — Like I 'think' I'm black?

She's had enough. She rings the bell.

— D'you know what? Fuck this. I've never taken my clothes off in front of a man without his jaw dropping and I'm not going to act like some mincing slut where I try and prise compliments out of you to validate my beauty because I'm not that fucking insecure!

By the end of the sentence she's shrieking. She twirls round the pole onto the stairs and flounces down them.

— And I don't think I'm really fucking fit, she throws her voice up the stairwell, — I know I am, so fuck you.

She gives him the finger through the floor as the bus doors open. She steps into the street surprised to find they're already in Camberwell. He must've noticed too because he follows her out.

— Can we not just have one straight conver... she says when she sees him but he blanks her and goes into the shop.

— Fine, she shouts after him. — For. Get. It.

She walks up Peckham Road. Of all the scenarios she had in her head. This was not what was supposed to've happened. She stops. Should go back and sort it out. She turns on her heel. A couple of buses go past. She tries to see if he is on either of them, hopes he isn't, luckily or unluckily enough, when she gets to the bus stop, finds him leaning against it munching a packet of Doritos. A paper carton of coconut water pokes out his pocket. He sees her and laughs.

— Come back for more? he says.

— Can you not be an arsehole for one fucking second? she says.

— Thought of some clever way to manipulate me into fancying you? he says, pleased with his own joke.

— I came back, she says, — because if I walked off this would be a lovers' tiff and if we aren't lovers, if we are friends, then there's nothing to walk off about.

— Exactly, he says, munching crisps with his mouth open and spitting crumbs.

— I'm your friend, you know, she says. — You care about me.

He looks at her and although his features barely change she can see a sheen of something unpleasant.

— Okay then, she says. — You know what? Since this is where we've got to, let me tell you a couple of things. First, you shouldn't be going to stick the tip in to random teenage girls on the Internet you don't even know. Second, if you loved the Elephant and Castle woman, you wouldn't tell people her cunt squelches when you fuck her. Third, the gimp ball sex story is fucking atrocious, it's like who even are you anyway? And last of all the way you talk about women and the way you're talking to me is fucking bullshit and fucking hypocritical.

— Funny how you suddenly become a feminist when you know you aren't gonna get any, he says.

She is stunned into silence, unable to get her head around why he would act like this.

A bus pulls up.

— What you doing then? he says.

She is still reeling, trying to process the insult.

— I dunno, she says.

He gets on and feeling like she's lost all free will, she follows. They stay downstairs, using the driver as a chaperone. She's not sure what she should do. It wasn't going well and there was an argument to make that she should just go home. They were both hungry and tired and he was clearly in pain. She takes out her phone and Googlemaps the best way to get to hers. The quickest time is an hour and a half. His house was two stops away. She looks at him. He looks back at her with no expression. A sudden premonition: she's never gonna see him again. She doesn't want to not see him again. She panics, tries to think what she can do to remedy the situation.

— I think I'm just gonna come to yours, she says.

— Do what you want, he says.

His words smart but then she remembers all the shit they've got going on. The events, Mexico, world domination... Of course this wasn't it. This was just a bad night and a stupid misunderstanding that would figure itself out by morning.

Back at his she goes heads straight for the bedroom. She keeps her clothes on, feeling like an intruder getting into his bed and lies as far from his side as possible. He clatters about in the kitchen for ages but she's still awake when he comes in. He gets in bed and lies with his back to her, not touching. Time goes by. Maybe twenty minutes, maybe an hour. They're both awake, you can tell from their breathing but neither says a word, only moves occasionally, rustling the sheets. He'll move. She'll move. It's like a kabuki drama only without an audience to make sense of what was going on.

She wakes before he does and gets up. She considers leaving but needs his keys to unlock the door and doesn't want to go through his things so puts on coffee. Feeling grubby, she remembers the hotel soap. She finds it and washes her face then sets up her laptop on the floor in the corner of the room and for the first time in ages, writes.

There'd been plenty of opportunities…

In the ten years they'd know each other…

In the ten years they'd known each other There'd been plenty of opportunities for them to do it..

She hears him get up and a few minutes later he crashes into the kitchen.

— Hi, she says, looking up.

— Ugh, he says, kicking her bag out his way.

He stomps to the sink. She picks up her laptop, afraid he's going to step on it. He rubs his jaw.

— Tooth still giving you jip? she says, trying to use a tone of voice that'll make things seem normal.

— It's killing me, he says.

— There's an emergency dentist in Barbican that's free, she says. — For homeless people.

— Why d'you know that? he says.

— Lot of friends who are junkies, she says.

— Makes sense, he says then slams his fist on the counter. — Where's the fucking coffee pot?

— It's in the sink, she said. — I used it.

— Fuck's sake, he says.

He unscrews the coffee pot and runs the tap then grabs the edge the sink, his whole body tensing.

— Are you alright? she says.

— What the FUCK is this? he shouts but she can't see what he's shouting about.

— What is what? she says, peering round him.

He turns and presents her with the bar of hotel soap.

— I don't need this fucking BULLSHIT in my fucking house, he says.

— It's not bullshit, she says and laughs cos she's nervous but also cos it's kinda funny . — It's soap.

But even as she defends the soap she understands its implications to him. He knew that she knew he didn't have soap because they'd talked about it so having it in her bag looked like she'd planned on staying over and brought the things she needed to spend a comfortable night.

— Is it yours? he says.

— Yeah, she says. — Obviously.

He hands it to her. — Take it then.

— I don't want it, she says. — It's all wet plus I already threw away the wrapper.

— It's going in the fucking bin, he says, marching over to a half-full black bin bag slumped in the corner of the room. — Actually, fuck it, maybe I'll keep it for the next time I have some bird stay over.

She bows her head. — I think I'm gonna go, she says.

— Aren't we gonna finish the edit? he says.

— Are we? she says.

— We've only got the last bit to do, he says.

— I dunno, she says. — It doesn't feel like you want me here.

— Fine then, he says. — Whatever. We started it together

but if you want to bail that's fine. Can you at least give me the details of the emergency dentist or is that too much to ask?

— Just Google 'emergency dentist', she says. — That's it.

He takes out his phone. She goes to the bedroom to get her shoes. Why is he being such a prick? She returns to the kitchen.

— Can you let me out? she says.

— I'm leaving too, he says. — I've got an appointment. Gimme ten minutes.

She can't understand why he makes her stay considering he can barely look at her but nevertheless she waits in silence not wanting to push it. Stands by the door as he traipses round the flat downing coffee, gobbling paracetamol, getting dressed.

Twenty minutes later they leave the house. They don't speak until the Tube station comes into sight when she, not wanting to leave things badly, says — It'll be okay you know.

— What? he says.

— Between us, she says, — It'll be okay. We'll work it out.

He glowers.

— Come on, she says and jostles him. — It's not a big deal.

Still nothing.

— Fine then, she says. — If you be like that be like that.

She takes out her phone and pops in her headphones and presses shuffle. Oasis comes on. She skips ahead of him, in time to the distant guitars and when Liam comes in she sings along.

— I don't feel as if I know you, you take up all my ti-ime, she sings, thinking what a perfect sentiment it is for the moment. — The days are long and the nights will throw you away cos the sun don't shine....

— What the fuck is the matter with you? he says, snatching the headphones out of her ears. — I live here.

His face is a mask of horror.

— So what? she says.

He's got hate, actual hate, in his eyes. She can still hear the music playing out the headphones, throws out her arms and serenades him.

— We-e live in the shadows and we ha-ad the chance and threw it away. And it's never gonna be the same' here

— Fuck this, he says. — You're batshit and I'm gonna be late.

He pushes past her and breaks into a run, not a run, a sprint.

She watches him, thinking how she'd never seen anyone run away from her so fast in her life.

MARRIED TO THE STREETS

Issues of race and gender aside, anyone who knows me can vouch for the fact that I am as rude, anti-social, mistrusting and belligerent a London cunt as ever there was. The best way I can describe the relationship between me and the city I was born in is an 'inverted' psychogeography. Rather than a person or people infusing the city's lifeless bricks with meaning, the city possessed me and moulded my terrible personality into something that suited it. And not just my personality, the way I walk: swagger; the way I loiter on a street corner: Turpinesque; the way I speak: guttural; the way I think: saturated with a vindictive Victorian moralism that could not have its roots in any other location.

I have, on occasion, wondered how I might've turned out if, instead of gravitating towards western Europe in an attempt to escape their uncertain fates, my parents' parents had ended up in America. Would I have grown into a self-assured, boundary-respecting 'tragic mulatto' with my eyes on the Presidency? Or the errant Black Lives Matter activist who turned on their sponsors and firebombed McDonalds? There are myriad shoulda, woulda, could bes but one thing I'm certain of is that I wouldn't have turned out like this.

The funny thing is, is that the London I grew up in was a very different place to London as it exists today. While it must be taken into account that childhood shields a person (if they're lucky) from the uglier aspects of racism, sexism and classism that permeates every society, I would still argue that London in the 1980s was a less divided and more tolerant place. The example I always defer to, in order to exemplify the way prejudice worked back then is my friend's racist grandfather - a type of person that was so commonplace as to have become a fictional trope. My friend's racist grandfather hated black people and never missed an opportunity to make a racist remark. It was nig-nog this and darkie that and other comments that it is probably better not to put into print. But every evening without exception my friend's racist grandfather would be joined by his downstairs neighbour, a Nigerian man in his late thirties or early forties, and the pair would make their way through a bottle of whiskey or rum, shouting the odds. Having witnessed this on several occasions my friend and I worked up the courage to question her racist grandfather about this apparent inconsistency.

— We thought you hated black people grandad, my friend said.

— I do, was the racist grandfather's response.

— But what about Sadic? my friend said. — He's your friend, isn't he?

My friend's racist grandfather dismissed the question gruffly, as if having a Nigerian friend had nothing to do with thinking black people were stupid, dirty or inferior.

— Don't be ridiculous, my friend's racist grandfather said. — Sadic is a different kettle of fish altogether.

Hopefully this example makes clear what I'm trying to say but in case it doesn't, what I am saying is that, in my childish experience, London at that time was a city where people might espouse negative sentiments and prejudiced views but when confronted with a person who they might be expected to be prejudiced against, didn't put those views into practice. An aspect, I suppose, of the infamous English nimby way of thinking – that essentially whatever anyone is or does is fine as long as it's kept behind closed doors.

As a kid I lived in a kid bubble (without a thought of what might be going down in another part of town) but upon turning thirteen the streets started calling me. Suddenly the four blocks around my house, the high street and the cemetery, which had served me well up until then, lost their allure and I began to fix my sights on the furthest-flung stations the London Underground had on offer – Cockfosters, Hendon, East Ham... My first excursions into the city without my parents were as lame and pointless as can be expected but at the time seemed like the most exciting thing in the world. My friends and I would jump the Tube (sliding on our knees through the 'luggage') and take the train in one direction or another, often alighting before the official destination, at any station that's name took our fancy. I remember us finding Homerton particularly significant. We'd pile off the train, scoot back out through the luggage then bowl around checking out what the local area offer – not much, as it turned out in the case of Homerton, but that never galled us. We'd find a playground and smoke a joint or try and get people to buy us alcohol before inevitably turning towards home.

As I got older I got more clued up to the things living in London gave me access to – Soho speakeasies that sold different drugs on every floor, 24-hour south London pool halls where you could stay for whole weekends, Kings' Cross megaclubs where you could do the same and (big up) Brixton cabbies (if you know, you know) where you couldn't stay for long but was nevertheless a vital component in the mix. The world my parents and school occupied faded into irrelevance. It didn't matter how many times I was told that my GCSEs were the most important two years of my life, I never believed it.

Reaching seventeen, I quit school and left home, desperate to get into the city proper and with zero concern about how my lack of qualifications and money might affect my ability to do so. As far as I was concerned London was mine. I saw the city as my birthright, claiming every brick, no matter who actually owned it, as my own. I was in no doubt that I would find a corner of it to put myself.

To the grave concern of my parents, I spent my first independent summer like an urban Laurie Lee, 'I lived free, grubbing outside', gallivanting between friends' houses and the rooftops of Bloomsbury, where I slept out under the stars. It never occurred to me that what I was doing was odd.

When September came and it started getting chilly, I moved indoors. I was fit, I was funny and there was no shortage of boys to fuck and parties to crash and, for the in-between times, houseshares that had so many people coming and going that one more made little difference.

I moved constantly – two days here, two days there – leaving possessions strewn behind me in a trail across the city. Ladbroke Grove, Camberwell, Clapton Pond,

Stockwell, Kings Cross, Peckham, Kensal Rise, Battersea, Shepherds Bush, Vauxhall, Soho, Swiss Cottage, Deptford, World's End – always careful not to outstay my welcome in any one place, ensuring my (likely) return at a later date remained an option.

When living like this started to take its toll, I bit the bullet and went to see a few flats. After four viewings I downgraded my expectations according to budget and went to see a few rooms.

I ended up taking an industrial unit in Arnold Circus for £100 a week. A beautiful place and perfect for what I had planned, which was to write a book. A single room with whitewashed brick walls, a skylight made of that reinforced glass that has metal wires running through it and a platform with a ladder up to it, where I put my bed. There was a sink in the room and outside in the corridor were shared toilets. I signed on the dotted line as soon as I saw it, paid the landlord the deposit and first month's rent and moved in the next afternoon. I cleaned the place up a bit then unpacked. I went to the shops and bought ingredients that could be cooked on a Baby Belling. Great. It was only when I woke the next day that I realised there wasn't a bath. How could I have been so stupid? Easily, it seems.

In an attempt to remedy the situation, I walked to nearby Columbia Road flower market and found an upmarket garden shop selling Victoriana from where I purchased an old bath tub. I also bought a hose. I lugged my purchases back to my industrial unit and wasted no time in setting up the tub in the middle of the room and attaching the hose to the taps of the sink and running a bath.

Delighted by the solution I'd found, I thought having a freestanding bath in the middle of your living room incredibly decadent. It was only when I got out and dried myself off that I was confronted with the issue of there being no way to decant the wastewater. The bath was too heavy to lift and so I spent the best part of an hour decanting it mugful by mugful down the sink. It put me off washing for a while.

My time in the industrial unit was short-lived. I lasted until the first round of bills. I ignored the water bill because I already knew that the water company aren't legally allowed to cut you off; electricity I paid in full at the Post Office; but then came council tax. Except it wasn't council tax, it was business rates. *Thousands* for the first quarter. The only money I had coming in was the occasional magazine article and cash-in-hand bar work. The bill was unaffordable. I recalled the *Evening Standard* articles I'd read about people being sent to prison for outstanding council tax bills and they scared me so much that I'm not exaggerating when I say that within twenty-four hours of holding that bill in my hands, I'd packed my bags, left the keys with neighbours and scarpered. I called the landlord to tell him I had a family emergency, that I was flying to Trinidad that afternoon to never return. Adieu!

I returned to cadging favours off people, exchanging my wit and tidying skills for room and board, before landing a rich boyfriend and a job at a fashion magazine. I found myself thrust into affluence. Free rent meant all the money I earned (pittance) was 'party money' I became the sort of person that could afford holidays, so I took them. My rich boyfriend and I went to Mumbai and New York City and Sicily and the south of France. But although I loved travelling (what

London cunt doesn't?) I found I was always more excited for the return flight; bowling out of Heathrow and onto the Piccadilly line ignoring the hordes of confused tourists or, if I was in a particularly exuberant mood, stopping to give them incredibly detailed and utterly false information on how to get where they wanted to go.

I lost the rich boyfriend and the job at around the same time but by then I was savvy to ways of surviving without giving over all your time and energy to a boss: housing benefit! I rented a wicked flat in Bethnal Green where I lived happily for five years and then, when the Nasty Party cut housing benefit for under 30s, I moved to a cheaper place on the 15th floor of a pink high rise in Bow. I stayed there until the end of 2012, which was when the Nasty Party as good abolished housing benefit altogether, deciding everyone could die in a gutter. No stars.

I found myself thrown to the winds. My refusal to take part in the economic fraud that was the order of the day meant I couldn't afford anything. I tried going back to live with my parents but it was a disaster and pretty soon found myself back on the circuit, only this time it wasn't party flats and fitties, it was single parents desperate for childcare and lonely agoraphobics who needed someone to go to the shops for them. Still, I was proud of the way I lived off, or at the very least under-the-radar, operating a cashless barter system. I was convinced that my experience of London and moving round all the time was more 'real' than other people's and when people, as they often did, asked me where I lived I'd tell them that I was local, stabbing the word at them like a scalpel. I had a cornershop on every high street that knew my name! I was the member of five local libraries!

I got warm welcomes from the landlords of boozers in every Irish-Jamaican pub in Zone Two.

Even as I watched wave after wave of friends jump ship (countryside people going back to where they came from, defeated, and later as gentrification started to compost the city, whole estates left to rot before being felled one by one to make way for luxury investment storage spaces in the sky, and the next lot legged it to Hastings, Margate, Broadstairs to procreate or procrastinate, as was their persuasion) the idea of leaving London never occurred to me.

Tube fares went up even as the IQ of the population plummeted. London Living Wage was set in law at Not Quite Enough to Live On. The continual auctioning off of public space to the highest private bidder removed huge swaths of the city and introduced anti-homeless spikes outside banks and Poor Doors in new builds. A&E workers were housed in shipping containers stacked in hospital car parks, while Carillion charged £20 a pop to refill every antiseptic soap-dispenser on the wards. Double-dug basements worsened the rising damp, threatening every home from Willesden, to Barking. London Eye, Gherkin, Crossrail, Shard, Westfield, Westfield, Walkie Talkie, Olympic Village, Cheese Grater, Razor, New Spitalfields Market, Taylor Wimpey, British Land, Foxtons… Sure, I was having a terrible time. There was nowhere to go and nothing to do. Yes, everyone was annoying. But who said London was supposed to be friendly?

The worse it got the more convinced I was of the importance of staying, if only to defend the city's grimy, dead end ways against the onslaught of bougie fuckers and their unexamined Insta-lives, because if not me then who?

But resistance wasn't easy. The worse things got the more militant I became until I reached a point where having a conversation with me that wasn't about anarcho-syndicalism or the 2011 riots was impossible. My 'normal' friends, i.e. those with half-decent houses, stopped having me round. I managed a few months of cat-sitting, dog-sitting, house-sitting, flat-sitting but pretty soon it all evaporated and I ended up slinging my hook from cheap futons in dusty front rooms to damp mattresses in vegan squats to the bunkbed of a kid who'd been taken into care in a junkie's flat... It might sound exciting/romantic but in reality it was shite. The moving around I could handle. It was the calibre of people I found myself with that was the issue. Somehow, I'd ended up at the margins of society and, I'll make no secret of the fact that the marginal are my *least* favourite group of people. Sure, they might look/sound good. Smash the System? Yes mate! Damn the Man? 100%... But if you spend enough time around these fuckers to get to know them and don't come to see that their sloganeering and anti-establishmentarianism is nothing more than bravado intended to obfuscate the sad truth about themselves (which is that they are all fucking losers) then you're as much of an idiot as they are. The problem with the marginal is one, they have no understanding of nuance, and two, they have zero awareness that their dropout lifestyles are as much a part and *product* of the society we live in as any diligent careerist.

By some small miracle, amidst all this mayhem, I managed to write and publish a variety of things. The writing was as ephemeral and erratic as you would imagine the work of a person in my situation to be. Long anti-gentrification rants appeared in obscure fanzines and self-published ephemera presented largely unedited spiels about how all men were twats... I never stopped to think about what I was doing or why I was doing it.

Then, just as I was starting to crack, a flat came up. A penthouse no less, in one of the disgusting new builds on Old Street roundabout. A friend was managing the property and hadn't been able to let it out. He said I could stay there until punters were found. He couldn't say how long that might be and told me to be prepared to move out on short notice, like overnight. He gave me a code to get in the front door and left the keys with reception.

I wasted no time in going over. Couldn't wait to be alone in my own space, goof around, have a wank, whatever... But walking into the entrance I knew my time here would be brief. Just seeing my reflection in the multiple mirrors in the lobby reflected what was obvious back at me: I did not belong here. The doorman sneered at my approach and was not best pleased about the envelope containing the keys he'd been holding being for me.

I caught the lift (sleek black leather interior) up to the seventh floor, found the door number and let myself in. The cheapness of the million-pound flat was immediately apparent. The walls were flimsy, the insulation hollow, and I didn't dare step out on the balcony for fear it would drop off. Open-plan, grey textured fake-ash flooring, sliding glass doors, metallic free-standing kitchen and a giant panel of knobs and switches taking up nearly half of one wall. Hideous.

I ended up having this place for three months. I got some money work and some actual work done and then, out of the blue, a book deal. No money and a short print run but a book deal nevertheless.

For those of you who have never published a book, I'll let you in on a secret: publishing a book will change your life. Now, I'm not talking about 'changing your life' in the trashy magazine sense, where you get thrown off a horse and end up psychic, or maybe, come to think of it, I am… Either way, no matter how shit it is, no matter how unsuccessful, publishing a book is guaranteed to alter your situation. Not necessarily for the better, arguably often for the worse, never in the way you expect it.

The book was part of a series, which included five or six other titles and when I went into the publishers' office to sign the contract they gave me copies of some of the others. That night, in my Old Street pod, I read the first book and liked it so much that I looked up the author's name on the Internet. Rudimentary research revealed he had another book that had just come out in the US, so I bought it. It arrived in the post a couple of weeks later and I started reading it as soon as I opened the envelope, intending to skim the first few paragraphs then put it aside for later. Instead, I read the first third in one sitting, cackling and vehemently nodding in agreement at the things the book was saying and the way it was saying them. The author, whoever he was, was clearly an ally.

I was so impressed by the contrast between the book's snotty, know-it-all tone and the genuine altruism and desire to share information at play in the text that when I finished reading, I did something I never do. I went on Twitter and I posted a link to where the book could be bought directly from the publisher's website accompanied with a single word, 'Recommend'. Everyone that followed me ignored it, but the next afternoon, to my untold surprise, an email arrived in my inbox from the author.

He wrote that although he didn't want to come across like a stalker, he'd seen my post and it appeared so fortuitous that he couldn't not get in touch as he was at that moment reading a book *I* had written. Strange indeed. Also, he was due to arrive in London in a matter of weeks for the UK launch of his new book (the one I was reading) and although he'd been hassling his publishers to organise an event for the launch they'd failed to do so, so he had organised one himself. He was worried no one would come because no one in the UK knew who he was. He asked if I'd be up for reading at the event with him, thinking that my being there might make a few more people turn up.

I replied saying the events he described were fortuitous indeed, that I'd be happy to read, but I wasn't sure that my doing so would bring a crowd of any description. In fact, people would be more likely to avoid this. He found this funny and the deal was sealed. An event was scheduled for November 24th.

A week or so later he arrived in town. We met at Marble Arch. I was late. Very late. Sprinted up Park Lane and arrived, panting and sweating, to find him standing, hands in pockets, by the ping-pong table covered in pigeon shit. I didn't know what he looked like but recognised him immediately anyway, more from the way he was standing (looking like he was waiting for someone) than anything else.

We walked up Oxford Street, me babbling about the latest run in I'd had with the police (I'd posted a dick pic to Facebook as a *joke* but the guy'd taken it seriously resulting in me getting a caution for 'the distribution of material of a sexual nature with intent to cause distress'). My new friend wasn't fazed, in fact he found it to be hilarious and made encouraging noises about my nutter activities in a laconic pan-American accent.

— Where, I asked him, unable to place his accent, — do you live again?

— LA, he said.

Without pausing for breath I launched into an account about a trip I'd taken to LA some years before, which had entailed a trip to Britney Spears' house (sadly she wasn't there) and a brawl at Coachella before getting the fuck out of Dodge. He said that sounded about right.

I took him to Trisha's on Greek Street, where we sat in a dark corner, me drinking Camparis, him drinking vodka tonics. I can't remember what we talked about but I do know that by the time it came to leave I felt the need to apologise.

— Sorry, I said, — For being so forward. It's just that I feel like I've known you for time. I think it's cos I've read your books.

He told me I didn't have anything to be sorry about. I didn't attempt to correct him.

We met again the next afternoon. It was raining. Miserable. Even so, we walked along the Regent's Canal. Chat, chat, chat, until we got to east London and Burley Fisher, where the event was to take place. When we arrived, he ditched me to go and have a cup of tea with Iain Sinclair. I was miffed to not be invited but there was nothing I could do about it, so I popped into the bookshop to introduce myself. The men working there said hello but then went back to selling books and didn't seem to want to talk to me. I gave the bookshelves a once over then left and, The Railway Tavern being no more, took myself for a lonely pint at The Kingsland... Which turned out to be not so lonely after all because an elderly Jamaican man called Sammy bought me half a Guinness, while an equally ancient Irish man, also called Sammy, paid for a double of Jamesons. The two geriatrics sat with me, one on either side, paying me compliments and telling me how beautiful I was until my drinks were drunk, when they both disappeared into the furniture.

I returned to Burley Fisher. Audience people had arrived. The event started. I read a long, as-yet unpublished tract about my dead ex-boyfriend then my new friend got up and demolished the business model of Facebook to chuckles and guffaws from the audience. Afterwards two old women came up to me and told me I was 'brave' for 'sharing'. I needed a drink.

It was decided we (the authors, the bookshop people and the publishing people) would go for pizza. Some of the audience also tagged along. I got as many free drinks as I could and behaved in my usual, awful, drunken manner, berating the bookshop staff for the window display, criticising the publishers' business model and telling them how they should be publishing new British authors rather than buying in already-published content from America. When I paused in my monologue the publishing people's face were filled with disdain, the bookshop people's faces blanched with pity, but my new friend was grinning...

Around midnight my new friend said he had to leave. He asked whether I would walk him to the station. I agreed, hid my drink in an alcove in the window with a beer mat on top so it wouldn't be cleared away and stepped out with him, linking my arm through his thoughtlessly. The camaraderie between us so undeniable that it didn't feel weird.

I walked him to Dalston Kingsland. We stood outside the station making eyes at each other.

— Oh, I feel like I love you already, I said with what I hoped was a girlish coyness but, knowing myself better now than I did then, more likely sounded like a threat.

I kissed him on the cheek and he was gone. I went back to the bar and carried on getting wasted.

We met again the next day on the steps of the British Museum, where he wanted to see John Dee's magic tablet. I arrived before him and stood, insulated from the hordes of tourists by my hangover. I spotted him as soon as he came in through the gates. Hands in pockets again. We went inside, located the correct cabinet in the correct room and peered in at the black, reflective disc filled with a dark reflection of our faces.

— I wish I could touch it, I said.

— It's pretty amazing, my new friend said.

— Maybe we should go look at the mummies, I said.

We turned our steps towards the lift but upon reaching the Ancient Egypt section were met with a wall of shrieking, farting children. It smelt like death so we aborted the mummy mission and left.

We spent the rest of day in each other's company, with me pointing out London's charms and wonders, spilling its secrets, dispelling its myths. Then, as we were drinking our millionth cup of green tea and I was slagging off the publishers who were about to publish my book, he interrupted my art cunt rant to ask the time. When I told him it was five to eight, he jumped to his feet, saying he was supposed to be at the Leicester Square Theatre to see Stewart Lee do stand up and was late. We paid up and went outside. I took his hand and marched as fast as I could through Soho, dragging him behind me. We arrived at the theatre to find everyone had gone in but the show hadn't started and happily there was one return on the door, so I was able to join him.

We watched Stewart Lee shout about Brexit and consumerism. We didn't sit down as our seats were not together and the theatre was sold out, so we stood leaning against a pillar, shoulders touching every now and then.

In the interval we went outside.

— God, my new friend said, — He's so good.

— He's the greatest, I said.

We lapsed into silence, looking at each other.

— What do you think is happening here? I said.

— What do you mean? my new friend said.

— Well, do you think that maybe we're in love? I said.

— Ya think? he said.

After the show we walked through China Town and up Charing Cross Road, until we got to Tottenham Court Road station. The station was a building site. We stepped into the temporary doorway to the site to say goodbye to each other.

— Goodbye, I said.

— Goodbye, he said.

Nobody moved.

— Goodbye then, he said.

— Goodbye then, I said.

Stayed standing where we were.

— Put your hand in my jumper, I said.

— What? he said.

— Just do it, I said, lifting the hem.

He laid his cold hand on my stomach. I flinched.

— You should come back to mine, he said.

— Okay, I said.

— But I'm not having sex with you, he said.

— Okay, I said.

We caught the 98 back to Maida Vale, where he was staying in the spare room of a house belonging to a friend's dad's ex-wife. We crept upstairs in dark, sniggering like children. We got into bed and had a cuddle then suddenly his phone started going insane. More messages than I'd ever heard a phone get at one time. He got out of bed to see what was going on: Trump had just been voted in as President of the USA. Of course, both being of cynical persuasion, we'd each expected this to happen but wrapped up in one another as we had been, we'd forgotten about what the rest of the world was obsessing over, and so the election result came as a surprise.

We talked through the night discussing the potential NWO, kissing a bit, sleeping a bit, no sex and then, the next morning, when it was time for him to leave, had this amazingly frank discussion. We were in love, that much was obvious, and so arrangements would need to be made that would allow us to be together. What those arrangements would be were as yet unclear and would take some time to figure out.

I accompanied him to Paddington where we parted, having arrived at the incredibly adult decision not to communicate with each other by phone until we knew what we were going to do about our situation. Speaking on the phone would only be frustrating and stressful. What we would do instead was wait. Wait until we could figure out what to do.

The decision not to communicate evaporated immediately. He called two days later suggesting I join him in Amsterdam and the next morning, I was on an Easyjet flight from Stansted, excited and nervous.

Amsterdam was everything you'd expect it to be. Long walks along the canals, churning misery on behalf of the Eastern European whores writhing in Red Light District windows, weird food and filthy sex followed by a bout of boo-hooing (on my part, obvs). Then, two days later he flew back to LA and I returned to London.

Although I was glad to have gone to Amsterdam and glad to have been able to spend time with my love, the fact that we'd fucked definitely made things more difficult. When he'd left London I felt centered in my (hopefully becoming less) marginal existence, but now half of me was in a city I barely knew and didn't like on the other side of the world, and the other half of me, the physical half, was in London. Stupid, petty, horrible London with its ugly dickheads and mannerless misogynists and racist cab drivers and middle-class narcissists and depressing fake-organic shops and spineless hipsters and armchair anarchists and rapey left wingers. Could it be that I'd finally had enough?

I'd lost the penthouse by this point but managed to organise a semi-permanent, semi-affordable room in Bethnal Green. The ivy that grew in through the windows seemed to be the only thing holding the brickwork in place. Coming in and going out you'd get weird looks as if you were going into a bando or something. No front door just a metal shutter, which made a deafening clanging noise when it was pulled up and down.

The building was part of a complex that included a coach yard, another residential building and a warehouse once owned by Empress Coaches. They'd sold the complex to a developer years earlier but the developer was waiting for the nearby gasworks to be decommissioned before they started demolition and so Empress continued to operate out of the yard and rent out the residential section (officially listed as abandoned) on the cheap. Cheap enough not to complain about the mice in the kitchen, rats in the attic, hole in the roof covered with a sheet of blue tarpaulin weighed down with rocks, water that streamed down the walls when it rained, constant waft of diesel fumes from the yard or filthy conversations of the coach drivers that boomed through the floorboards.

— Ere, cunt. Watch your fucking cunting mouf.

My kind of people.

I was able to escape temporarily back into the city I knew and loved but I could tell its days were numbered. Not just because of the artisan coffee shops and supper clubs and Containerville studio complexes springing up but also (the main drawback of living in the bando), the film crews. The complex was a favourite spot with location scouts and multiple BBC dramas were shot there. They filmed a lot of *Luther* and a Joe Strummer biopic and a dramatisation of the British Black Panther movement. The film crews were made up of the kind of entitled arseholes, who would think nothing of wandering uninvited into the private bit of the house without knocking.

Having broken our promise not to communicate once, the floodgates were now open. I spoke to my love on the phone constantly (exactly what we'd been trying to avoid) batting sweet nothings, stupid jokes, and anecdotes across time zones at all hours of the day and night. The conversations were mostly pointless, covering what each of us had or hadn't done that day, people who'd annoyed us, but would always include some planning about when, where and how we'd see each other again.

The date to get thrown out of Bethnal Green was approaching and I will forgive a cynical reader for thinking that a man with a flat who loved me was the answer to all my problems. In spite of homelessness looming and in spite of my starting to resent London I still, maybe out of habit, put in a case for my love to move here. And to his credit he was up for it, but with a flat (sorry, an apartment), a cat that was obsessed with him and a successful writing career, a move for him wasn't going to be anytime soon. He needed time to pack down his life while I on the other hand (with no dependents and being largely shunned, ridiculed, and patronised (not in the good, old-fashioned way) by the 'industry' I was part of) had nothing to tie me in London beyond a book launch that was six months away. And so it was decided that I would come visit him in LA for a bit, to see how it went.

I flew to LA on Boxing Day, staying awake for the entire eleven-hour flight and peering out the window at the earth. I watched England disappear into clouds, the sea smash again Ireland's west coast, the pack ice start, the pack ice thicken, the pack ice break up again and outline what I thought might be the southern coast of Greenland, then the criss-crossed nowhere landscape of Canada, the Great Lakes, the Midwest, Nevada desert, the Rocky Mountains and into California's hazy sunshine before descending into the vomit of Los Angeles.

My love picked me up from the airport in a Zipcar and although we were both pleased to see each other we were also kinda shy. The trip felt loaded from the offset, both of us harbouring high expectations but not knowing exactly how it was gonna go.

We drove through Culver City's oil refineries, which I thought was a fucking cool thing to have in a city, then went east on the 5 before taking Sunset and then going up to Hollywood where we stopped at a red light. I looked out the window thinking how beautifully blank Los Angeles was. No history here, unless you count the hundreds of thousands of dead Native Americans.

The red light was next to a Wendy's, its neon sign glowing in the twilight. The bushes beside it were rustling. Looking closer, I saw a group of homeless people sitting in them, living in them by the looks of things. Broken plastic chairs, tarpaulins, piles of weird stuff. Then, as the lights changed, a ball shot out into the road, a dirty child minus shoes rushed out after it. The Mustangs and Hummers paid no heed to the child and revved away from their starting points. I'm glad to say my love kept his foot off the pedal and waited for the kid to grab its ball and return to the safety of the pavement. Sorry, sidewalk. The kid didn't seem the least bit affected by its brush with death and neither, I noticed, did the adults. Not one of the people in the homeless encampment so much as blinked.

— What the fuck? I said, as the car started moving. — I can't believe people *live* like that.

— Welcome to California, my love said.

The first week passed in a blur of jet lag but once I escaped GMT and shifted to PST we fell into a routine that was workable. It was a provincial existence compared to the one promised by LA's reputation. I'd wake early and sit out on the balcony and write. My love would wake around midday. We'd drink coffee. We'd cook. We'd shower. We'd fuck. We'd shower again then, because he didn't have a car, would walk or Uber somewhere. He showed me round the city, taking me to Frank Lloyd Wright houses in the hills and pointing out the scenes of mass murders and Elvis Presley's favourite spots. We walked Downtown, along the Atwood River. We caught the L to Venice. We drank cocktails at Musso & Frank's. We ate out at Clifton's. We went to dive bars and old movie theatres and then, two days before I was due to leave, we went to Beverley Hills County Court and got married.

I returned to London with, for the first time ever, absolutely no desire to do so. I flew into Gatwick, my most hated of airports, and caught the Thameslink into town. Lost in my LA dream, I hadn't bothered to sort anywhere to stay and so I was heading towards my parents' house. I can't say I was happy about it and I can't say they were either. My only reassurance was that the situation was temporary since now the plan was to move to LA.

I got off the train at Farringdon and walked up the hill then turned onto Leather Lane. The market traders were packing up for the day. The air smelt of fat. A man in white overalls stepped up to the kerb with a big bucket of slops, which he emptied into the drain. After the balminess of LA, where the streets are quiet and there is never anyone else on the pavement but you, the closeness and dirtiness of London was awful.

Arriving at my parents' house they wasted no time in sitting me down to 'discuss my situation'. I was 35, I had no money, writing was all well and good but didn't appear to be viable financially. What was I going to do? Couldn't I just get a part-time job or something? In response, I made the announcement that I'd taken a husband, he was American, we'd met two months earlier and I was moving to Los Angeles to be with him. I watched their crestfallen expressions as they realised, as they'd had done many times before, that there was fuck all they could do or say about it.

The months that followed were the most normal of my life. This was mainly because the visa application was such a paranoia-inducing process that it made me feel like I needed to behave for the duration of it. Nothing stupid, nothing illegal, act like you're being watched. I unfollowed all the old anarchists I followed on Twitter, stopped going out and getting trashed, released my book and got a couple of freelance gigs (InDesign work for a publishing company and proofreading).

Thinking I was about to leave London forever and aware that the city was changing fast, I spent the rest of my time going on long walks (or, death marches, as my love called them) in what I can only describe as a farewell tour. I didn't do it knowingly, it was more like I'd think of a place I hadn't been to in ages and think that, if I went to LA, I probably wouldn't see it again in the state it was in.

I walked round Soho to find whole blocks had been demolished. I went to Dalston to find my favourite Turkish shop gone. I went to Peckham to find trendy galleries everywhere. I went to Deptford to find that the Job Centre had shut down and been replaced by a bar called The Job Centre. I went to the King's Road to find the streets empty, Sainsbury's replaced by Waitrose and Morris Minors and Volvos by Lamborghinis and 4x4s. I went to the Earl Percy on Ladbroke Grove, my first employer, now, the Portobello Hotel, invisible behind foliage, security on the door. A craft ale and stonebaked pizza monstrosity. I went back to Bethnal to find the block I'd lived in, which had always been open to the street, now had security gates and CCTV and was inaccessible. The second hand bookshop on the corner that I'd loved was gone and in its place was an S&M lingerie boutique. The local pool had upgraded and was now a relaxation spa. I went back to Bow to find the empty warehouses full of chi-chi arseholes and the estates boarded up.

Far from prompting rosy reminisces, my trips down memory lane forced me to admit it was too late. The London I loved was gone. The city had become a parody of itself, rebranded as tourist attraction. My affectionate nostalgia went up in smoke, taking with it any belief there was something left worth fighting for. The conviction I'd held – that London needed me, that I owed it a debt – was bollocks. My experience of London wasn't more real than everyone else's. It was merely more shit. The obvious finally dawned on me: London wanted rid.

My visa came through at the end of May. I wanted to buy a one-way ticket but my love needed to be in the UK in September so I bought a return flight for the end of

August, because if I was going back I wasn't going to miss Carnival.

Because I knew I was coming back I didn't bother to say any goodbyes other than a lowkey dinner with the fam. I packed an insane amount of my possessions into two huge suitcases and left.

I don't know what it was about this trip, maybe the stress of the application process, but things did not go well. To start with my jet lag was horrendous, and combined with a dodgy flu I caught on the plane made me irritable and argumentative. Not the best frame of mind to begin what I was already thinking of as My New Life. I set out to achieve a few basic tasks, which I thought might make my living in LA a bit more realistic. I tried to open a bank account and failed. I needed a State ID. I tried to get a State ID and failed. I needed a bank account. I managed to sort a SIM card for my phone and that was about it. My love was worried about money but instead of listening to his valid concerns about our future, I took his financial musings as personal attack, thinking he was saying he couldn't afford me, as if I was a pet or something. We managed to avoid an actual fight but spent long afternoons apart or sitting in the stifling LA heat in silence. After two weeks of this I was going stir crazy and persuaded my love to rent a car and drive out of town. We drove to Lake Berryessa, where I swam. My love told me about the Zodiac killer stabbing a bunch of teenagers not twenty feet from where we stood. We debated going to a B&B but in the end drove back to LA the same night, which was lucky because I woke up the next day with the worst ear infection of my life. The pain left me incapacitated, even after a visit to the Hollywood walk-in centre, where my ear was syringed and I was given codeine. It took me a week to get over, by which point I had reached fever pitch about what a waste of a trip it'd been and how little I'd got done. Things between my love and I were quite tense and we'd stopped having sex (the ear infection had infantilised me to such a degree that it'd be hard for anyone to find me sexy). I decided to give him some time to himself and set out to explore the city on my own.

I went to Griffith Park, endeavouring to climb the mountain but ended up tumbling down a cliffside and getting cut up by prickly plants before having to wade through rubbish, sorry, trash, for half a mile.

After that I got ripped off in Venice buying weed, paying $200 for a 'licence' to buy an eighth of horrible skunk, itself another $35. From here, I took one wrong train followed by another wrong train followed by a long walk in the wrong direction. Starving hungry I bought a burger from a diner, had a terrible reaction a block later and had to shit on a street corner outside a 7-11 in front of a well-heeled Hispanic family. It was my knickers, or the floor.

And then Grenfell happened.

I was in the kitchen making supper when my love, who was sat at the kitchen table, looked up from his laptop and said, — Where in London is this tower block that's on fire?

Thinking he was (as he often did) feeding his Anglophilia by perusing the BBC's regional news section, I barely looked up from stirring the onions.

— Shepherds' Bush? he persisted.

— That's basically Notting Hill Gate, I told him, knowing that was the best point of reference he'd have.

It was only when he brought it up again a couple of minutes later, making a comment along the lines of the fire being 'really bad', that I turned down the hob and came to look over his shoulder at the screen. It must've been about 6pm in Los Angeles, so 2am in London, by which point the fire was enormous.

What to do here? The normal thing would be to describe the fire. It's the sort of sensationalist, pornographic writing that is any writer's dream. But I shan't describe it and I'll tell you why: because it is unnecessary. Because everyone saw it, everyone knows, everyone remembers what happened.

As soon as I saw the live-streamed feed, which must've been filmed from a helicopter or a drone, I freaked. Wooden spatula raised in hand, other hand gripping the back of the chair my love was sitting on, I started to shout. I couldn't believe what I was looking at. I didn't want to look at it but couldn't look away. Desperately trying to avoid looking directly at the fire itself, I scanned the background of the shot, searching the horizon for clues of which block it was that was on fire. First I thought it was White City but couldn't think of any high rises there. Then I thought it was Goldhawk Road, or Golborne but for the life of me, I couldn't place it. My head reeled. My love lowered the screen then stood to prise the wooden spatula out of my fist. He put his arms round me.

— It's okay, mate, he said.

But he was wrong. It was the furthest from okay anything had ever been.

— No, I said, pushing him away from me, wanting to say something unkind about how he couldn't possibly

understand because he was American, he wasn't London...
London, London, London.

I ran into the bedroom to retrieve my laptop. I opened
it and sat on the floor, hammering at the space bar. My love
poked his head round the door.

— What are you doing? he said, sounding concerned.

— I'm changing my ticket, I said, as if it should've been
obvious.

— Mate, he said.

— I've got to go back, I said. — I've got to be there.

I managed to open Norwegian Air's website and click
'Manage Booking' before my love lifted the laptop out of
my lap.

— What are you doing? I said.

— There's nothing you can do, he said.

— What do you mean? I said.

I started crying. Or maybe I'd been crying all along and
only just noticed.

— There's nothing you can do, he said. — Whether you're
here, whether you're there...

This time my love was right. Being there wouldn't make
any difference but even so, I felt an undeniable guilt at what
I saw as a dereliction of duty. I'd left, and this had happened.
I'm not trying to say that because I'd left it'd happened, or
that if I'd been there it wouldn't have happened, just that I'd
not been paying attention to what was happening and I felt
fucking terrible.

After Grenfell, LA disappeared for me. My heart longed for
London and so I did what any powerless person yearning
for something they cannot have does: I went on social media.

I have never spent as much time on Twitter as I spent over the last two weeks of that trip. To say I was obsessed doesn't come close. I read pages and pages of posts, following every account that had anything to say on the matter. Official news sources, left-wing commentators, right-wing commentators, the London Fire Brigade, local residents, housing activists, solidarity groups, the Royal Borough of Kensington and Chelsea...

Mimicking the future-inquiry, my investigations initially focused on the events of the night of the fire. Where it started, how quickly it spread, how long it took the fire brigade to arrive, why they didn't have ladders tall or hoses long enough to reach the top floors, how fire engines had to be sent in from out of London taking more than an hour to arrive.

I sat patiently through hour-long videos of first-person accounts from people who'd got out of the building, from people who lived close by and witnessed the whole thing, from people who had relatives that were still unaccounted for.

It soon became clear that the official narrative was not up to much and diverged hugely from the thousands of unverifiable (but tempting to believe) personal accounts.

When I wasn't on Twitter I lectured my love on the culture of corruption that defined the UK construction industry and the strategy of managed decline employed by London's inner-city councils in spite of budgets running a surplus.

The body count went up and up. Lily Allen went on *Channel 4 News* and said it was a cover-up and that hundreds of people, rather than official number of 72 that was eventually reached, were dead. I, like any person of even meagre calibre, was not of the disposition to take Lily Allen as reputable news source but I found myself (for the first time ever) empathising with her and (also for the first time ever) despairing of *Channel 4 News*. I understood Lily's desire to speak out because it was exactly what I was feeling but watching her sticking it to the man, I found that I was glad that in spite of wanting to speak, I didn't have a platform. Because if I'd had a platform I would've used it but the reality was that I, like Lily, didn't know what I was talking about. I thought it tragic that in a moment where there were so many aspects to discuss and so many persons qualified to discuss them, that *Channel 4 News* should give the space to a Bedales kid with a waning pop career, however well-intentioned. It wasn't as if there was a lack of space for speculation and rumour. Blogs sprung up left, right and centre with stories about babies being thrown out of windows and surviving, recorded messages of people's last tearful phone calls, of letters sent months in advance warning RBKC of disaster. I was shocked that *Channel 4 News*, until-then my most trusted of all national news broadcasters, had chosen to peddle distractions over and above a proper investigation of events.

My initial reaction of not wanting to look gave way to the desire to find out as much as I could. But the coverage hard to swallow. I couldn't believe that people were reacting the way they were, the same way they always reacted to everything. Couldn't they see that the normal way of doing things was exactly what had led, both directly and indirectly, to this happening? The deferral of responsibility built-in to privatisation, which made it impossible to follow the chain of command to expose any culprit, was identical to the way spokespersons and pundits presented issues – paying lip service without examination beyond how best to deflect attention from their own culpability and with no regards for the facts. The way it was starting to look to me was that they *all* had blood on their hands. The system was corrupt and anyone who profited from it in *any* way should at this point realise it was time to shut the fuck up.

I was just getting to the point of disengaging in disgust (they could talk if they wanted to but I wasn't going to listen) when RBKC finally got it together to release an official statement. I decided to watch, not for information per se, but just to hear the official spin.

I lay in bed with the live feed open on my computer. The camera showed the empty forecourt and entrance to RBKC town hall. A door opened. A man came out. His name flashed up at the bottom of the screen. 'Rock Feilding-Mellen, RBKC Deputy Leader and Councillor for Housing'. Before he opened his mouth I was squawking like a chicken.

— Oh my god, oh my god, oh my god! I squawked, bringing my love into the bedroom. — I know him. I know him! Oh my god.

If you cast your mind back to the beginning of this 'story' to recall me speaking of my 'wild' years when I had no home of my own and gallivanted round the place with all sorts of weirdoes, well that was when I first met Rock Feilding-Mellen. And when I say weirdoes, I mean *weir*does. As his name would suggest, Rock Feilding-Mellen was a member of the aristocracy. And not just the aristocracy, the landed gentry no less. Most people's impression of the aristocracy is way below par. When they think of posh people they cannot think beyond what they can see, people with a big house in west London, people with penthouses by the river, people with two cars, people with trust funds, but none of that shit comes close. That's just the upper middle class. They might be more comfortable or appear to be more secure than people who don't own property or have savings but that aside, their lives are not hugely different from everyone else's. They walk the same streets, they visit the same shops, they go to the same pubs, etc., but the *actual* aristocracy is on another level, a level which very few people who are not part of it get to see. But I, and I don't know how, had stumbled upon it.

I met Rock Feilding-Mellen when I was seventeen. I was in a nightclub with my friends when someone, not Rock, approached our table with an envelope and handed it to me. Inside the envelope was an invitation to a party for the Millennium at Stanway House. The deliverer of the envelope pointed Rock out and said the invitation was from him. Being a skanky teenager with fuck all social life beyond my circle of skanky teenage friends the idea of going to a swanky party in the countryside was thrilling.

The party was my introduction to how the other side live. Arriving at Stanway House I was amazed – I'd never seen a stately home of this scale that someone actually lived in, but my incredulity at the house was soon overshadowed by the behaviour of its inhabitants. People lounged on Edwardian day beds openly smoking crack cocaine out of specially-crafted glass pipes, others wandered hallucinating through the rose garden shedding clothes and singing, people in yoga pants downed urine, there was an elderly man in a corner on all fours barking like a dog.

At some point in the night I ended up in conversation with a woman who, I was told, was the lady of the house – those were the actual words used to introduce her and I couldn't help imagining my mum or anyone's mum introducing themselves as the lady of the house when the house was a whitewash semi-detached. Ridiculous. Anyway, this woman spoke in one of those posh voices that are so posh it makes it impossible to understand, barely opening her mouth to talk, pronouncing 'clothes' as 'cleeves', for example. She seemed nice enough even if I didn't have the faintest clue what she was on about. It was only when she left to bemuse the next guest that someone, I forget who as I never saw or spoke to them again, informed me that the woman had a hole in her head. I wasn't sure what they were getting at and asked for clarification, which is when I was informed that 'they all did', they were trepanners. They had drilled holes in their skulls to remain permanently high. Apparently it felt like always being on the beginning of an acid trip, before you start hallucinating completely and when you just have that cold shivery feeling and your senses are heightened — colours, sounds (but not smells so much) going up.

Being as young as I was, I was too overwhelmed by the newness and the extremeness of the reality I had entered to be capable of making a value judgement. I had no context in which to place these people and no reason, at this stage, to judge them, so I didn't.

I can't say Rock Feilding-Mellen and I were close but I was on the guestlist for his parties and outside of that would run in to him from time to time. We were always civil. I liked talking to him because he was such a freak and also because at that time I held anyone who broke the law (even if it was only by taking drugs) in esteem. As long as you weren't doing what you were supposed to, you were okay with me.

That changed a couple of years later when Rock Feilding-Mellen decided he wanted to become a Tory MP. I can't remember who told me the news but I remember my reaction, which was that he was obviously an idiot because a mad aristocrat who smokes crack cocaine clearly belongs in the Labour Party; the class defector, crossing over to the other side. All his potential weakness become strengths. But the Tories? Pah.

The next time I ran into him I expressed my thoughts on the matter. I was starting to know myself better by this point and opened the conversation in no uncertain terms.

— If you join the Conservative party, I said, — then I will no longer be able to talk to you.

He smirked. We argued, him lauding his Classics degree from Oxford over me, me insisting his Classics degree from Oxford was bollocks, him talking down to me telling me I was naïve because the way he did things was the way the world actually worked and that the way I did things wasn't.

Amicably drunk, I said we would agree to disagree and as a decider cheersed my full pint of Guinness against his glass of whiskey with gusto. The glass he was holding shattered in his hand, shards flying everywhere. There was blood but the blood wasn't mine.

Although unintentional, the glass smashing and bloodied fingers were symbolic enough for us not to speak further.

Over the next few years the aristo set started to shun me. Some of them married each other and left the city to have kids while random acts of violence on my part edged the general consensus among those who remained in town to my being a 'psycho' and a 'loser'. I stopped getting invited to the kind of places where Rock might be. I hadn't seen, spoken or thought about Rock for years except, as coincidence so often has it, I'd run into him the night before I flew to LA. For reasons I can't fathom, I'd gone to a Fat White Family gig. I've never been a Fat White Family fan, in fact I fucking hated the Fat White Family and their horrible swastika scene. I had no time for the referential and derivative garage rock they played or their macho version of heroin chic. And so while the Flat Whites played upstairs, I stayed downstairs by the bar. I was, as it goes, thinking about leaving when Rock appeared.

— Hello you, he said, in his patronising manner.

Considering we had not seen or spoken to one another in over a decade, I found the greeting overfamiliar and considered picking things up where we'd left them, giving him shit about being a Tory but then, remembering I was about to leave for good, thought 'fuck it, who gives a shit?'. I didn't care what this acid casualty did with his time and maybe, if I wasn't rude to him, he might buy me a drink.

We spoke for as long as it took to neck the white wine he bought me. He told me he'd heard I'd got married, which surprised me as I didn't realise I was still a topic of conversation in the circles he moved in. I told him yes, that I was leaving for LA the next day to never return! Well no, that was a slight exaggeration but I was done with London and its fat white muppets. Rock, it seemed, felt the same way. His life, he said, was boring. He had a wife and two kids (possibly twins but I can't remember as I wasn't really listening) but hadn't got far in his attempt to become Prime Minister and was instead languishing in a council role where there was 'fuck all to do'. I asked him what he wanted to do instead and he told me he had already started a housing development company with two of his friends, which was making him 'a lot of money'. He wanted to concentrate on that.

In five short minutes he mentioned enough things I disapproved of for me to decide to call it a night. I left and thought no more of it or him until seeing him appear on the steps of the town hall. He looked like a ghost. Lots of new grey hairs.

He started blathering apologetic nonsense that wasn't up to much considering the four days it'd taken the council to get it together. Fully compliant with regulations. Followed guidelines. Not resigning.

I spent the next hour yelling at my love.

— They've got holes in their head, *holes* in their goddam *heads*! He smokes crack every day. Every *day*! He was named after a rock of crack, for fuck's sake! How did he even get into this position? He doesn't know anything about building or construction. He studied Classics!.

For once, my love let me yell. When I was done he said, — They're gonna crucify that guy.

— They should crucify him! I yelled.

— No, but seriously. When the press get their hands on this they're gonna go nuts. It's a perfect scandal.

But this was one of the rare instances where my love was not right.

A week passed and no news story appeared to mention crack cocaine or trepanning. Then, to add insult to injury, the *Times* ran a soft power piece, interviewing Rock's mother about her drug legislation lobbying and research group. She banged on about the healing properties of psychedelics for two thousand words. The article made no mention of Rock or Grenfell. I was appalled.

— Why aren't they reporting it? I asked my love. — I don't understand.

He couldn't understand it either. However bad contemporary journalists might be at their jobs surely this story was one they could find and follow. There was something dodgy going on.

A few days later, still on Grenfell (it was all I thought or spoke about) I posed a question to my love. I was imagining being back in London and running in to Rock and couldn't work out what I should do. Should I speak to him? Should I blank him? If I spoke to him, what would I say? Would I mentioned Grenfell? Would I not? I asked my love what he would do if he knew someone who had done what this guy had done and ran into them. My love considered the question, then said he couldn't answer it, even theoretically, because he would never be in a situation where he would know someone responsible for the deaths of hundreds of Muslims. (At this point in time the body count was unclear.)

The day of my departure arrived. My love rented a Zipcar and drove me to the airport. We had the sad conversation, which to some degree we'd been avoiding but had also been swept aside by Grenfell: the trip hadn't been great, I clearly wanted to be back in London, he couldn't leave LA. We parted ways with things feeling like they had when we'd parted in Amsterdam, uncertain of what the future would look like, only now we were also married.

Arriving in London I went back to my parents again. I didn't tell them the trip had been a disaster and that I'd changed my mind and was going to stay. They didn't need to know. All they would do with the information was weaponise it, use it as further evidence for my insanity, my loserdom, reinforcing the narrative they (and almost everyone else I know) has always held about me. A narrative which does little else besides setting me up to fail.

I had planned on going to see Grenfell as soon as I got back but couldn't bring myself. A trip made specifically to ogle at the ashes seemed crass and I decided that I'd just see it when I saw it, rather than joining the misery-tourism parade.

I stayed with my parents for a week. All I talked about was Grenfell, but since I'd consumed so much information on the subject and was borderline stalking Rock online, I was no longer interested in the body count or the cover-up, I was obsessed with the completely corrupt way society was set up. A rottenness that not only directly caused the fire (putting a man like Rock, with no qualifications or experience relevant to the field, in the position he was in, as well as countless other examples) but was still at play ensuring there would never be any truth, never be any justice. It was a travesty. My parents didn't see it that way. They agreed that there was an aspect of things that were corrupt, but being homeowners, were more of the persuasion to accept Grenfell as a tragic accident, a sad thing that'd happened by mistake. I found their take offensive. The conversation got personal. Of course they saw it like that because they were getting something out of the system. And if you buy in, you're gonna make excuses. We argued about generational unfairness and austerity and neoliberalism and the property market until it was clear there was nothing else for it. I had to get out.

I went to stay in Maida Vale with my old friend, JD. He had a spare box room in a spacious two-floor maisonette in a wonderful old flat, which he'd lived in since the Seventies. His landlord had tried to evict him countless times but because he moved in before Thatcher's Shorthold Tenancy Agreements came in, it meant that try as they might his landlords couldn't get rid of him and the most they could put his rent up by per year was 10%.

In spite of being back in the hood I stuck to my guns about not making a specific trip to go and see Grenfell. The first sighting I had of it was at Carnival. Walking in with my sister we turned into whatever the name of that street is that runs towards Portobello. On the horizon was a tower block shining in the sunlight.

— Oh my god, I said, wrapping my fingers round my sister's upper arm. Is that it? I felt cold to my bones. Then, — No, it can't be.

The block in front of us looked odd but it wasn't black like in the photos. It was glowing. A beacon of light. A pillar of gold. I couldn't figure it out. I felt uneasy. I couldn't stop staring. Neither of us could. Then slowly it became clear. The light was not the sun reflecting off windows, it was the sun shining right through the building from the other side. Every blasted-out window, every burnt out floor, bursting with light. Aside from the basic concrete and metal structure, there was nothing left.

I put my hands to my head. It was obvious my sister and I realised what we were looking at at the same time because we stood still. When we turned to look at each other we were both in tears.

— Oh fuck, my sister said.

I took her hand and we started walking. We turned onto All Saints Road, arriving at the first soundsystem and I'm telling you I'd never before, not once in my entire life, arrived at Carnival in silence. It was so fucking heavy, so fucking horrendous, so fucking deep, so fucking fucked, so fucking wrong on so many fucking levels. The first bassline of the weekend licked us and I don't think there is anything on God's earth that could've kept me away from that speaker.

Carnival is always wild, but that Carnival under the auspices of Grenfell was something else entirely. No crime, no violence, just an outpouring of the kind of love and solidarity (actual solidarity, which by the following Carnival had gone again, battlelines redrawn) that instead of pretending like everything is okay and making nice, acknowledges all the pain, heartache, misery and unfairness of life. That year was a death carnival, which is what carnival is supposed to be. It was as if all the bullshit everyone'd had to put up with for last three decades was laid bare and what was exposed behind it was the old London, unchanged, untouched, unrivalled, brimful of crims, a poltergeist at every corner.

VICTIM BLAMING

I have had more than my fair share of run-ins with the police. I've been arrested for singing, I've been arrested for shouting, I've been arrested for stealing, I've been arrested for fighting, I've been arrested for texting, I've been arrested for posting stuff on Facebook, I've been arrested for throwing a chair, I've been arrested for 'destroying' a hat, I've even been arrested for giving someone the finger.

Though plentiful, my crimes are, without exception, petty and asides from a couple of cautions (accepted under duress, with the police confiscating my phone and laptop and telling me if I didn't confess they had the power to keep them for up to three months) no charges have been upheld.

Getting arrested by the Metropolitan Police is never pleasant. It's an unnecessarily long, drawn-out process, boringly bureaucratic, and having to deal with the sort of donuts who become policemen sucks. But like any dose of bad luck, getting arrested does have a few things going for it. First is that it is very instructive, providing a rare glimpse (or maybe not so rare, depending who you are) of England's nanny state without her make-up on. That bitch ain't no Mary Poppins. Nanny reminds, with a withering look, the fundamental fact that everyone prefers to ignore: freedom is at best conditional, at worst illusory. An unfathomably important life lesson.

Most unfathomably important life lessons are imparted on the fly, putting in an appearance during highly-charged emotional moments like romantic break-ups or having taken too many drugs. These unfathomably important life lessons are often too much to take in *in the moment* and are instead pieced together in the aftermath, upon reflection. However, the thing with getting arrested and locked in a cell is that it gives you time to think about what's happening *while it is happening*.

Nine times out of ten 'arrested thinking' will kick off with the same question: why am I locked in this cell? The simple answer is whatever you've done, your crime. This is what the police want you to be thinking about. It's why they leave you in there for hours while they pretend to do paperwork. They want you to make the connection between your actions and your situation. If you hadn't punched Jerry Hall's niece on the nose, if you hadn't posted a blurry photo of the son of the head of Goldman Sachs' penis to Reddit, if you hadn't graffitied 'fuck you' on a prolific graffiti writer's front door, then you wouldn't be here. If you don't do anything, you can't get caught.

If you're guilty of the crime you've been accused of then you're likely to begrudgingly accept this as true, but it's a harder rationale to swallow if you haven't done what you're accused of and are locked in a cell all the same.

Next up for dissection is how the matter came to the attention of the police. If you've been caught red-handed, apprehended mid-crime, then there's not a great deal to consider. It's your own silly fault and you should've planned it better. But if (as is the case with every single instance of *me* being arrested) someone has made a call, an allegation against you, collated a file of evidence, provided your name, your number, your address and email addresses, well then, there's plenty of meat…

Knowing you are incarcerated at someone else's whim spins the whole situation 180. Just think how many bops have landed on schnozzes, the levels of mindless vandalism and all the limp-dicked nonsense that exists online without warranting police attention. No, viewed through this prism of desire, whatever crime you have (or haven't) committed pales into insignificance; when someone you know brings the police to your door, the one thing you can be sure of is that it is always, always personal. Personal meaning it has less to do with *what you've done* than *who you are*.

Bizarre as it may sound, it wasn't until I started getting arrested on a semi-regular basis that I gave any thought whatsoever to the matter of 'who' I was. I'd never been in any doubt. I was me. Dur.

Luckily for me, the police didn't give it any thought either. The desk sergeant who booked me on my first arrest took one look at me and didn't even bother to query before marking the 'SOUTHEUROWHITE' box. And why should I have corrected him?

Upon release, I did allow myself a quiet chuckle imagining how differently the arrest might've played out if he'd marked the 'MIXEDOTHER' option, but my laughter was accompanied by another, less comfortable sensation I found impossible to place. The closest thing I can describe to it is guilt but not the kind of guilt you feel when you've done something wrong, the kind of guilt you feel you feel when you know you've got away with something that someone else wouldn't't've.

The reason I'd never thought about who I was comes down to one simple fact: my parents never told me. Insofar as there was any conversation on the topic of where we were from, my dad was Dutch and my mum was English. *The End.* I doubt my parents' reticence was intentional. I can't imagine them sitting down to discuss what to tell or not to tell 'the kids', whereas I can picture them making the optimistic assumption that there was no need to talk to their children about things like race because race didn't matter anymore. This was a widely-held social convention in the 1980s, where pointing out racial differences was considered racist, unlike now, when it's racist not to. But propping up that social convention was a past compromised by many painful and difficult-to-explain things, as well as plenty of ominous inexplicables.

Any conversation that might've taken place wasn't the sort of conversation anyone in their right mind would have with children, their own or anyone else's. There's no point explaining famous violences like slavery or the Holocaust to a five-year-old. It's too confusing, too upsetting, and in a world of bike rides and learning to read, hardly matters. So my childhood began, like so many first-world childhoods before it, in a utopian bubble where I was no different to the Sophies and Lauras surrounding me. But as with any attempt – however well-intentioned – to repress and deny reality, my parents' blinkered decision to shut their mouths and hope that their mulatto children would default to 'white' backfired. The foundations were too shallow, the fault lines too deep.

A good place to begin is a story my dad still occasionally tells from before my sisters were born. He was holding baby-me in his arms when I peed on him. A childhood event so common in normal circumstance it would barely merit a mention, but in this instance my dad freaked out. Even with a total absence of statistics to go on I'm going to take the bet that the majority of babies over the millennia have peed on their fathers. To most fathers it's no big deal, sweet even. The way my dad tells it is that he found it challenging. He wasn't challenged by the realness of it, this was no test sent by the gods. He was being challenged by me. He read it as a throw-down, a gauntlet, me attempting to assert my infantile dominance over him. An insane reaction that it took me years to understand: the reaction of a man who feels like the world is taking the piss.

The precedent was set.

It has to be said that, for the most part, my early childhood was pretty groovy. My parents were clever, attractive, in love, lived in a nice flat in a good part of town, had a car. My dad had a job and my mum looked after my sisters and me. We were sent to good schools and went on faraway holidays, with evenings and weekends packed with ballet and swimming and parties and trips. The only fly in the ointment was that every now and then my dad (who, like a lot of little girls, I thought of as my best friend in the world, coveting his approval far more than I did my mother's) would lose his temper. Never with my mum or my sisters, only with me. I didn't understand why my dad got so mad at me but then I didn't really try to, I accepted his bad moods in the way all little children accept the more unpleasant aspects of their parents' personalities, because they don't know any different.

Parallel to my treacherous home life, which I accepted unquestioningly, was school, which I did not accept unquestioningly but where I was nonetheless sent. School did exactly what it was supposed to do: gave little-me a wide range of little people against which to compare myself.

My first memory of noticing a difference between my family and other people's was revealed in Art. Our art teacher told the class to draw a picture of their 'entire family'. She wrote the words on the board. I got straight to it, drawing my parents, drawing my sisters, drawing me. But when it came to Show & Tell I found that while everyone had drawn parents and siblings, they'd also drawn cousins, grandparents, great-grandparents, aunties, uncles… This would've been 1987 or '88, when both of my dad's parents were alive, as were his sisters and their children and although I had met them, they all lived 'somewhere else' and for one reason or another didn't figure in my kiddy-world in any real way. My mum's parents died before I was born but I'm unable to say if I was aware of that by this stage, it being hard to notice the absence of something that's never been there. There was an uncle, my mum's brother, who I was vaguely aware of, but I didn't think of him as my uncle, only as my mum's brother. The only person who was really around was Kinnie, a big, blonde Austrian woman who I knew was something to do with my mum but they weren't related. You only had to look at them to know that.

I don't remember bringing up my Art class experience with my parents but I do remember a brief obsession with cousins. An obsession which manifested as a short-lived imaginary cousin called Maggie (named, terrifyingly enough, after Margaret Thatcher).

My next reality check went down in the swimming pool changing rooms — the scene of many a rude childhood awakening. Mindlessly stripping before donning my swimsuit and racing to the pool (swimming was my favourite), one of the four Sophies in my class loud-whispered to one of the three Lauras about me being a funny colour. I remember looking down at my tiny torso under the strip lights and, sure enough where everyone else was pink or brown, I was green.

And then there was the Christmas party I went to at Nat the Bat's. Ten or twenty kids high on e-numbers, the grown-ups drinking, when who should arrive but Santa, with a sack full of plastic tat. The other kids crowded round to receive their presents but I hung back, fixated by the sight of Santa's hands, knowing this couldn't be Santa because I'd seen pictures of Santa and Santa's hands were fat and pink but this Santa's fingers were flat and brown. Hands I'd recognise anywhere: my dad's.

In the 1990 recession my dad lost his job. One of the first people at his firm do so. We, the kids, only understood this wasn't good because when we raced into my parents' room at 6am to demand the toys being advertised on telly, we were told we couldn't afford them. Other than that, our new financial status didn't mean anything to us. We still lived in the same flat and ate the same food and went to the same schools. The only palpable difference was that there were no more holidays and my dad stayed home all the time, under the impression that he'd be re-hired by his old job when things got better. But he wasn't re-hired, despite them keeping a photograph of him on the company website long after his departure.

My dad's unemployment eventually became self-employment. He started his own due diligence company, which proved to be a task suited to his unique and peculiar way of thinking. What had been the dining room became his office, which we, the kids would make a massive deal out of pantomime-tiptoeing past, loudly telling each other to be quiet.

Any problems that existed between my parents were kept out of earshot from the kids until I was nine or ten, when my dad had an affair. The affair didn't last long but when he came clean, as might be expected, shit went haywire. It's hard for me to get a time scale on the fallout. It could've been a single day or it could've been weeks but there was a lot of shouting, slamming doors, storming off and coming back to shout some more. It was the first time I'd ever seen any shouting in my family home that wasn't my dad shouting at me and although I was doubtless distressed on some level, I do remember enjoying it being him being shouted at for once.

Things were touch and go for a while but eventually my mum forgave my dad. The forgiveness was frosty at first but soon a new normal descended. The new normal resembled the old normal with one discrepancy: the fracas had undoubtedly been my dad's fault, it was (as far as the kids were concerned) my mum who got the blame. We weren't reacting to what had happened because we didn't understand what'd happened, or the first thing about gender relations and how women are physically tied to their children in a way which men are not. We were reacting to my mum's reaction. Her outpouring of vitriol and upset at my dad's betrayal and, worse than that, the prospect of the only family she had left falling to pieces.

This unconscious siding with my dad created friction between me, as the eldest of the children and spokesperson, and my mum. I stopped listening to her when she asked me to do things and started answering back. Early warning signs of my imminent teenage rebellion. Instead of confronting me over my bad behaviour, my mum simply relayed word to my dad. A fight I'd got in, a scribble I'd done on a wall, the tantrum I'd had when I was caught. It wouldn't take much to rile my dad, who was on tenterhooks and spinning out about his life choices as it was. He'd march into whatever room I was in, demand an explanation, wouldn't get one, and then explode.

Where, as a young child, I'd accepted my dad's divine authority, outbursts and all, my new go-to was to challenge it. Safe in the knowledge that my dad would never really hurt me, while knowing that he himself had done something 'bad' and was 'in trouble', I began to square up to him, shouting back, refusing to accept his version or my mother's version of events of what I'd done, calling them both hypocrites. They screamed and shouted and threw things at each other so who were they to tell me how to behave?

My escalating naughtiness made my parents decide I needed therapy. So to therapy I was sent.

I hated therapy. Boring hours sat in a beige room, being stared at by a long-skirted, cloying woman who spoke in the patronising tone of voice that adults who don't remember being children use on them. I was less than forthcoming, often refusing to speak for whole 'sessions' – the word still makes me barf.

The therapist tried to get me to draw, hoping I might spin off a few doodles of a sacrificial lamb with its innards out or a house with my family in it on fire. No such luck.

Every few months my parents would meet the therapist to discuss my 'progress'. I'm telling you I would've paid good money (which in those days, on pocket money of £10 a week, would've been maybe £100) to have sat in on those meetings and hear their resentments refashioned into concern as they tried to figure out what to do with me.

Although I hated therapy, the idea of not going never occurred to me. My parents would drop me off at Chelsea & Westminster Hospital for the appointments, but I was always made to go in alone (part of the 'treatment') and because I was at my core a good girl who did what she was told, it was months before it occurred to me to ditch the dreaded session, to go in the front entrance and then skip out the back to goof around the Embankment for an hour.

Teenagehood kicked in. I started going out, dying my hair, going to parties, getting drunk, kissing boys, falling in swimming pools, shaving my head, smoking hash, going to gigs, huffing cans of Lynx Africa through a sock. My bog-standard rebellion sent my parents into panic mode. New rules were plucked out of thin air. Things I couldn't do, people I couldn't see, times I had to be home by, all without explanation.

Appalled by the arbitrariness of the new rules, bored by playing dress up with my sisters, embarrassed by how lame my parents were and raging with hormones that convinced me that I was right about everything, my confrontations with my dad went up a notch. Knowing the answer was gonna be no to whatever I was asking, I began starting fights pre-emptively going for my dad before he could get a look-in and leading him in cat-and-mouse scrambles round the flat. It was during one of these early teenage fights that I had the police called on me for the first time. I must've been around fourteen-years-old because I was already into Nirvana (Kurt two years dead). I can't remember what the initial disagreement was, but I do remember the aftermath. Me sitting on the balcony outside my room in my underwear boo-hooing and bashing out Nirvana's version of 'In the Pines' on my acoustic guitar. My refusal to come in or shut up for several hours summoned two uniformed police officers into my bedroom, the only sanctuary I had in the world. Walkie-talkies blaring, handcuffs clinking. I remember how big they looked against a backdrop of Oasis posters and I remember their hot, clammy trotters pawing at my naked upper arms and thighs as they dragged me and my guitar inside.

Being manhandled by the police, who were gruff and yelled at me to 'calm down' with a threat of arrest, shut me up, but once the policemen had gone and the shock and embarrassment faded, the only thing I was left with was disgust. It is hard to convey quite how appalled I was by my first taste of state authority and just how low my parents fell in my estimation. The era where my dad switched between being my best friend and confidant to my worst enemy was over. He'd called the police on me and I could scarcely stand to look at him. And by the look on his face when he looked at me, the feeling was mutual. He bristled with rage and resentment at the way I was turning out, as if my character, my behaviour, my very appearance (which at this point was pretty ridiculous) revealed something he didn't want the world to know. Something that needed to be corrected, fixed, reconditioned.

From this point, shit unravelled. There was fight after fight after fight. Fights about me going out, fights about me not eating my dinner, fights about things my parents had found in my pockets, fights about playing music too loud, fights about what I was wearing, fights about where I'd been, fights about getting kicked out of school, fights about stealing my sister's pocket money. But by this stage I was hip to the fact that there was a world outside home and outside school where my parents had no jurisdiction. I took to the streets.

The first time I left after a fight all I did was prowl the local area until I was sure everyone was in bed, but the worse the arguments got the further afield I ventured. I'd go to friend's houses and stay multiple nights without calling my parents to let them know where I was. Or, if things were really bad and I couldn't find a friend's house to go to, I'd sleep with tramps in Oxford Street doorways, choosing Oxford Street for its proximity to school, which for some insane reason I still attending, even if what they were teaching seemed more and more convoluted and less and less relevant to the very pressing issues I was facing in day-to-day life. I'm all for Katherine Mansfield but I could've done with a little Artaud.

Some days I'd arrive at school without books, and on one particularly memorable occasion, without shoes, having run out of the house in a state without time to get my things in order. When my friends asked me why I'd come to school with no shoes I told them I'd had a fight with my dad but I felt stupid saying it because I didn't have any injuries to show. When I thought of parents who hit their children, I thought of the Childline ad that ran on breaks between cartoons, of a kid in a vest chained to a radiator but that wasn't what my fights with my dad were like. My fights were like fights between equals. Mano a mano. Or at least that's what I told myself when I was feeling brave. When a little less puffed up, the truth was that I found it all really confusing and couldn't for the life of me figure out what it was about me that wound my dad up so much.

From the age of sixteen I left home so many times it's hard for me to pinpoint exactly when I left for good, if ever. Disavowing my family, I'd march off, determined never to return. Not having any money and being utterly disinterested in getting a job, I dived headlong into a series of abusive relationships with men who were significantly older and/or richer than me in order to survive. My abuse of these men was using them to live off, theirs was fucking a half-crazed child. But I wasn't the easiest paedophilic lay. Bubbling with mistrust and used to being fucked over, I was always testing, always wanting to find out what these men were made of, and as it turns out they weren't made of much. These men weren't my dad – who might have been an abusive weirdo but his abusive weirdness was rooted in love: the men I was fucking didn't give two shits. There was no substance to it. All these relationships ended the same way. With me feeling betrayed. One insignificant sleight and I was off, throwing phones out of windows and tagging front doors like a deranged Wee Willie Winkie. I (unsurprisingly) found myself ostracised, broke and homeless again and again but worse than being billy-no-mates, I was also getting arrested all the time. Criminal damage, harassment, common assault, the charges piled up. What was it about me that made everyone so eager to call the cops? I'd seen much worse behaviour, sometimes by the people who did the calling, sometimes by their friends but I was the only person who ever seemed to have the police show up.

I'd return to my parents house, tail between legs. I didn't want to but what choice did I have? I had no other back up in the world. My parents welcomed me with semi-open arms. Yes, I could stay, yes, they had missed me but no, they hadn't kicked me out, I'd chosen to leave and what were my long-terms plans? They tried to coax me back into education, suggesting I sit the A Levels I'd walked out on, or apply for University but I found their simpering respect for qualifications immensely irritating and bourgeois. What use was knowing History, English or Chemistry in a world where all it took was one call to undermine someone completely?

Although my parents didn't have the full picture, they could tell from the bizarro anarcho theories I was starting to spout that I was struggling. They tried to get me to open up about what was going but I didn't want to talk to them about what I was gonna do with my life. If I was going to talk to them about anything, it was gonna be about what they'd done to it. Didn't they understand that I'd slept on the streets? Didn't they understand the danger they'd put me in? Didn't they understand how much they fucked me up in terms of understanding love and relationships? These conversations went in circles, with my parents eventually getting fed up and falling back on the same tropes everyone was applying to me: I was lazy, crazy, a liar, a thief, wouldn't know the truth if it hit me over the head with a skateboard...

It was after one especially humiliating arrest, where I was dragged out of party in front of crowds of cheering toffs, that I finally dropped my guard enough to share an edited version of the current unfolding disaster with my dad.

I told him about the cheating ex-boyfriend who had started the whole thing, about the cheating ex-boyfriend's brother who'd hanged himself, about being frozen out by everyone after the funeral. My dad knew exactly what I was talking about without me needing to go on. I was amazed how good it felt to be confiding in him again, like the old, old days, when I'd confided in him about my sticker collection or my favourite beetle. It wasn't like talking to other people, where I needed to reexplain things several times until they understood it, it was like talking to my people.

It was during this conversation that, in response to my list of woes, my dad came back with something typically left-field but surprisingly insightful. He said, 'The thing these people don't understand is that the more a person ignores or denies something in life, the more ruled by it he becomes. By cutting you out, these people simply create a boundary, which will go on to shape and inform their lives, arguably giving you far greater influence over them than if you'd simply been friends.'

The complicated truth of what my dad was saying (essentially a psychoanalytical version of 'denial ain't just a river in Egypt, honey') settled upon my thoughts with a strangely calming effect. I turned the concept over in my head: by saying no to me, by cutting me out, by silencing and disallowing me, 'these people' would have to silence a whole load of other things too. Things that reminded them of me, things that looked like me, things that sounded like me, things that acted like me. The idea slotted so gracefully into my thoughts that it was impossible to deny it. It was if my brain had been a messy desk, piled high with random papers and suddenly a filing cupboard ready-filled with pre-labelled folders had appeared, as if by magic, providing a place for everything. Once it was tidy, another thought occurred to me, which was this: what if 'these people' weren't responding to me at all? What if it was that I reminded them of something they were already trying to suppress? Someone else they'd wronged, someone else they'd fucked over, someone who just happened to look and sound and act like me.

Delighted with my epiphany, which allowed me to dismiss anyone who didn't like me as racist, I spent a couple of days enjoyably applying my dad's words to every neg-out situation I could think of: ex-boyfriends, ex-bosses, ex-teachers, ex-friends. Dirty, naughty racists. Hateful, old deniers. It was only when I ran out of *other* people to apply my dad's wisdom to that I finally (actually by accident) applied it to myself. The unwelcome thought popped up into my brain on a walk through Fitzrovia: I had just spent the last decade doing my utmost to live as if I didn't have any parents. I'd put *all* my energy into trying to get away from them, to shut them up, to silence them, just like the world was doing to me. Had the world done the same to them? I wondered. I had no idea. I tried to collate what little I did know into some kind of order and found it severely lacking. I knew my mum was born in Australia and that her parents were maybe Russian, maybe Polish, maybe Ukrainian, definitely Jews, who'd gone to Oz after the war before coming to England. I knew my dad was born in Holland and that his parents were from Suriname, but I'm not sure I could've located Suriname on a map and definitely couldn't tell you the name of the capital. I knew my mum's parents had died when she was small. Her mum when she was maybe nine, maybe ten, her dad when she was twelve or thirteen, and that she had a brother. I knew my dad had three sisters, one who'd converted to Islam. I might've been able to conjure up a couple more random factoids but that was essentially it. Standing on an Oxford Street corner, outside the Boots where I'd slept for a few nights during my GCSEs, the spectres of my parents and my parents' parents and all their parents before them loomed large. Where were all these lost people and what were they to me?

My initial attempts at trying to find out about The Family were not particularly successful. My mum divulged various titbits in a frustratingly roundabout manner, acting surprised when I claimed to not have been told about her dad being a law professor at Lvov before the war, or her mum being a disc jockey in Paris and a magazine journalist in Oz and at some point ending up in Hollywood. I lapped up everything she said but the thing that stuck with me most from these first exploratory steps into my mum's family was hearing my mum calling her mum and dad 'mummy' and 'daddy'.

Pulling the same number on my dad, it has to be said, my dad knew shockingly little. He told me his parents had gone to Holland because his mum had TB and the drugs to cure it weren't available in Suriname at the time (the

Fifties, I guess). And about an uncle, his dad's brother, who had been a sailor and paid for the trip. He said his parents had initially intended to return to Suriname but ending up staying in Holland for the rest of their lives, returning only once, in their eighties. Without much else to say, my dad reminded me of a song that his dad had sung him when he was small and which he'd sung to me and my sisters as babies, 'Konoe Oloisi Lassie'.

— Konoe oloisi lassi a mi era bogo take-eh, yes bananci, yes a mi take-eh, Yes banaci yes.

Watching my dad as he sung in his soft, funny accent, hands skiffling from side to side, told me more than any anecdote he could come up with. It was, I thought, like watching a Sam Cooke, or a Nat King Cole from another dimension. A fantasy world in which the English hadn't traded Paramaribo for New York with the Dutch.

It took a long time but bit by bit my parents opened up and shared what they knew about their parents with me and my sisters. My mum revealed a suitcase she had full of fake passports and old photos. Going through them told of how her mum had ended up being in Paris at the outbreak of the war after being sent there from Kiev as a little girl for deciding that the ruling Communist party wasn't Communist enough and distributing flyers at school. She'd been hurried off to the train station by her mother, tipped off by a teacher, before the authorities could get involved. My mum told me about her dad, who didn't have papers, arriving in Paris and hiding under her mum's bed for months after the Nazis invaded. But that was easily a decade later and there were no stories from in between. She told me about that her parents travelled together from Paris to Warsaw to rescue my mum's mum from the Warsaw Ghetto but how they achieved it she didn't know. She thought they might have lived in the forest outside Warsaw over a winter or two, but that was information got from an old lady in New York, who had been with her mum when she died. This old lady had another story about my mum's mum being on a train to Auschwitz, of the train stopping, of it being hot, of the prisoners forcing the train door open, of my mum's mum and one other woman being the only people brave enough to make run for it, of them hiding in a barn, of them being found by the farmer, of the farmer hiding them, then the story is cut short.

My dad also caught the bug and began extensive emailing with distant family members and an amateur Surinamese anthropologist he found in Canada, using the skills he'd developed in his job to turn up what little info there was. Old addresses in dodgy Paramaribo districts, notorious for prostitutes. A great-grandfather who was a policeman, known for his use of excessive violence. A great-aunt and her mother who died on a leper colony. A lot of writers, journalists mostly, but writers nevertheless. His mother being adopted. Whispers of a rape or violence, a shameful event that hadn't ever been talked about and no one knew what exactly it was. And the plantation 'we' were from, called Rac à Rac, deep in the Surinamese interior.

I took the things my parents told me and used them to do my own research online, attempting to fill in gaps of which there were far more than there were stories.

At first, I revelled in each new discovery I made. Stories of one-way boat trips and one-way train rides seemed to explain my obsession with packing. Stories of slave uprisings where slave drivers were killed made my hotheadedness and violent dislike of authority a noble tradition. Stories of distributing print ephemera and unachievable political idealism explained my mode of writing and perverse desire to publish.

The more I learned about my grandparents and their parents and brothers and sisters and aunts and uncles, the more I felt love for, and an affinity with, my lost relatives and their kin... But then something funny happened. The love and affinity I felt made me realise that what I was doing was selfish. I was cherry-picking anecdotes I liked the sound of, or felt reflected some aspect of me, which, in actual fact, was a massive betrayal of the very people I claimed to care about and wanted to represent. It was like some distant relative of mine in the future finding out a half-truth about me and instead of trying to understand and empathise, just using it to cudgel other people over the head with.

The more I learned, the more I cared and the more I cared, the more the uncomfortable reality reared its simple, ugly head. People in chains, people being hunted, people in hiding, people as cargo, cargo thrown overboard halfway across the Atlantic, people in exile, people in bondage. It was a miracle that any of us survived at all! It was, I realised, nothing short of a miracle that I was alive, and not just alive, but alive at the flourishing heart of empire. There was no one chasing me, there was no one coming to kill me, there was no one coming to tie me up and force me into servitude or make me sleep under the stairs or out on the porch or under the bed.

The uncomfortable conclusion I finally arrived at was that while it is tempting to point the finger and accuse everyone of being racist, the personal horrors my family (or the stand-ins I had to find for them where there were no stories) lived through at the hands of racists and genocidal maniacs, bore little resemblance to my happy-go-lucky life. Sure I've been arrested a few times and thrown in a cell, sure I've had people ridicule my big lips and my gappy teeth, sure I've been homeless, sure I'd been broke, sure I'd never been properly re-numerated for a job, but having to tolerate the bizarre form racism has morphed into in the UK today (where my ancestors probably would've liked to get away from the fact that they were black or the fact they were Jewish, I find myself constantly having to persuade people that I'm not of their stocky island descent, that my hands are clean) is nothing compared to the misfortune that characterised my ancestors' lives.

What I realised is that the enjoyment I took in romanticising the lives of my parents' parents and all their parents before them, and the relevance I choose to take from it, was a privilege and like any privilege taken, it left little space for the real tragedy of just how painful and just how unfair these lives had been. Sure, there are echoes, hangovers, hang-ups, inherited trauma where I desperately try and chase sufferation, without being sure why, but how can I, in good faith, stand up and represent on matters I understand so little?

It's impossible to know what to say. Violence is wrong? Slavery was bad? The Holocaust shouldn't have happened? Only there is no alternate dimension, no other happy universe where a Surinameer (which, if slavery hadn't happened, wouldn't be a place) and a lapsed Ashkenazi Jew could meet in a revolving door at Manchester University and go on to procreate. Without the Holocaust, without slavery, without violence, without prejudice, without all the shit that all the people in my family went through, there wouldn't be me. I wouldn't exist. All there would be instead was a couple of weirdoes rolling round Ukraine or Russia or France or Angola or Sierra Leone or Ghana or The Gambia or Senegal or maybe even Indonesia, who had eyes or a temperament or a physique or preferences or talents or tastes vaguely similar to mine.

About The Author

Iphgenia Baal is a writer who lives and works in London. She is the author of several fiction books, including *The Hardy Tree* (Trolley Books, 2011) and *Death & Facebook* (We Heard You Like Books, 2017).

Her unique prose style, once cited as a 'marrying of politics and ass', has been likened to writers as varied as James Joyce, Manuel Puig and Dodie Bellamy, and appeared in publications including *AQNB*, *Nervemeter*, *Schizm* and *The White Review*, among others.

Home
Decorating

Home
Decorating
Tony Wilkins

Newnes Technical Books

The Butterworth Group

UNITED KINGDOM

Butterworth & Co (Publishers) Ltd
London: 88 Kingsway, WC2B 6 AB

AUSTRALIA

Butterworths Pty Ltd
Sydney: 586 Pacific Highway, Chatswood NSW 2067
Also at Melbourne, Brisbane, Adelaide and Perth

CANADA

Butterworth & Co (Canada) Ltd
Toronto: 2265 Midland Avenue, Scarborough,
Ontario, M1P 4S1

NEW ZEALAND

Butterworths of New Zealand Ltd
Wellington: 26—28 Waring Taylor Street, 1

SOUTH AFRICA

Butterworth & Co (South Africa) (Pty) Ltd
Durban: 152—154 Gale Street

USA

Butterworth (Publishers) Inc
Boston: 19 Cummings Park, Woburn Mass 01801, USA

First published 1977 by Newnes Technical Books
a Butterworth imprint

© Butterworth & Co (Publishers) Ltd, 1977

ISBN 0 408 00243 3

Typeset by Butterworths Litho Preparation Department

Printed in England by Butler & Tanner Ltd.,
Frome and London

Preface

The term do-it-yourself encompasses a very wide field of activity, and there is much to learn. It is not always easy, but once new skills have been mastered d-i-y becomes rewarding and satisfying. The books in this series which as well as decorating, cover subjects ranging from Plumbing and electric wiring to heating, are designed to help you acquire the necessary skills. All you need to add is practice.

They are written by people with very considerable practical experience in the d-i-y field, and all have been involved in feature-writing for DIY magazine over the years.

A home will not look after itself, and as the occupant you must be prepared to do battle with damp, rust and corrosion, fading, peeling, wormholes, leaks, blown fuses as well as redecorating inside and outside when necessary.

Interior decorating is well within the scope of the average householder, but the outside may be more of a problem. The tips given in this book should assist you in both respects.

Of course you can call in a man, but with so much of the work labour-intensive in areas where costs are now so very high-you will have to delve deep into your pocket to keep up with the bills. By doing the work yourself you can reduce costs to materials only, and this will have two immediate effects. First, you will have money to do more and, second, you may have money available with which to buy better quality materials and add the frills.

May I wish you success in all you undertake.

Tony Wilkins
Editor, 'Do-It-Yourself' Magazine

Contents

Introduction

There is nothing new in the desire to decorate our homes. It dates back to our cave-man ancestors and their very descriptive wall paintings. What is relatively new is the vast industry that has grown up to supply tools and materials to the home owner. This has made decorating easier, faster and more attractive.

There are really two main reasons for decorating. One is to make the place look nice and the other is the need to preserve the fabric and prevent deterioration by the elements. The second reason is the more important as, given a chance, damp in many forms will cause endless trouble. So, whatever you plan to do, bear in mind that one needs to preserve as well as beautify.

This book assumes that your home is in a reasonable state of repair. If it is not, you will need to study another book in this series *'Home Repair and Maintenance'*.

Choice of decor is a very personal matter, and we are in the main far too cautious. Do not be afraid to experiment

Accurate records and advance planning will bring a sense of order to your decorating programme

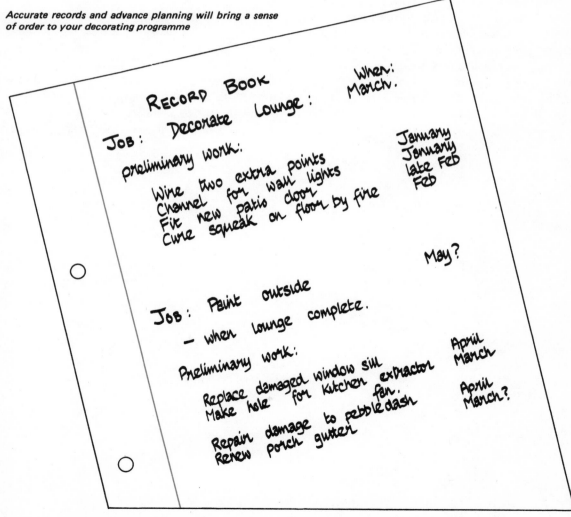

RECORD BOOK

JOB: Decorate Lounge: When: March.

Preliminary work:

Wire two extra points   January
Channel for wall lights   January
Fit new patio door   late Feb
Cure squeak on floor by fire   Feb

May?

JOB: Paint outside
— when lounge complete.

Preliminary work:

Replace damaged window sill   April
Make hole for kitchen extractor   March
fan.
Repair damage to pebble dash   April
Renew porch gutter   March?

with new colours, textures, patterns and materials. It is useful to find a showroom where room sets incorporate these new materials. It always pays to experiment in a small way first, so that you can gauge what the overall effect will look like. In this way you will not spend a lot of money on something that you may not enjoy living with.

Modern materials make change far easier than in earlier times, so one can think of redecorating a room such as the lounge after two or three years. For example, easy-strip vinyls enable you to strip a whole room in a matter of minutes, and you are ready to hang a pre-pasted alternative, or give the remaining lining paper a couple of coats of quick drying water-based paint. The job is easier, far quicker, and a lot less messy than it was in the past.

Whatever you intend doing, work to a plan. A record book is invaluable, for in it you can set out what has to be done, with a rough working timetable. Your schedule can of course be varied as necessary, but at least you have something to work to. Big jobs, like decorating the outside, need holiday periods if the work is to be completed in reasonable time. Small jobs, like decorating the spare bedroom can be fitted into odd days and evenings without causing too much disruption. Kitchens and bathrooms need a short concerted effort, or the family routine will grind to a very strained halt!

Painting window frames means the windows must be left open while the paint hardens. Paint dries far faster in the late spring and summer but, when painting the exteriors remember that mid-summer is also the time of dust and flying insects. Late spring and early autumn offer less problems.

These points are made only to illustrate the kind of factors which can influence your timetable. Having decided what to do—roll up our sleeves and make a start!

Chapter 1
Colour and pattern

Choice of colour is of course a very personal matter, but even so there is a psychological significance which affects us all whatever our taste. It is certainly worth keeping some basic ideas in mind when choosing colour schemes.

Grey is a very much neglected colour, but it can give a feeling of spaciousness, and it is a very good foil for splashes of brighter colours. As it is neutral, it makes a good background for colour changes as it blends with most colours. It is also a very practical colour where grubby fingers are involved, and it goes well with very modern furniture with chrome frames and black seats.

Blue is looked upon as a cool colour, and again it has the ability to make small spaces look larger. It is restful and relaxing and will have the effect of calming down busy living areas. Dark blue can look most effective, though, like most bold colours, it is best used in small areas—such as one wall dark blue and three white.

Green, and particularly the warmer greens, is a very satisfying summery colour conjuring up pictures of the countryside. A lime green has far more sharpness to it and goes well with a modern lifestyle. It is a restful colour too and is ideal as a base colour for the lounge.

Orange is a lively colour, and is one of those colours which close in a room rather than extend it. It is not particularly restful on its own, but it combines well with browns and rusts. This is the colour that will brighten a north facing bedroom, or add warmth to a cold basement area.

Yellow can be cool or warm, according to the tone chosen, and those colours nearer the orange end will bring sunshine into the colder north facing rooms. It combines well with the rusts, browns and green to give a feeling of security and warmth.

Pink and red. Pink is a pretty colour which will warm a cheerless area, and which is unbeatable as a base colour in a girl's bedroom. Reds are far from restful, but which can, in small quantities, add zest to the decorating. Red will go well in the nursery—but not as the main colour in the kitchen where it can become overpowering when considerable time is spent looking at it. Red will also make the larger room look smaller. or lower a high ceiling.

Mauve and lilac. These are gracious, elegant colours and give an air of spaciousness which goes well with traditional furniture and furnishings. Add a little vibrant colour, if you wish to wake the place up.

Patterns

Apart from colour, pattern has its effect too. Heavy bold stripes may look good in a pattern book, but they may give you a restless feeling in large quantities. Then there is the practical problem in that if walls are out of true, stripes will quickly highlight the trouble. Watch out for patterns which, in small areas, seem to have no stripe, but when a whole wall is covered, a definite stripe pattern is clearly seen.

Vertical stripes will make a room look taller, and tend to shorten it. Horizontal stripes have the reverse effect. Bold patterns with very large designs are best kept for large rooms. In a small area they can be stifling, making the walls close in on you. They can also be quite wasteful if a very large repeat is involved. If you are looking

3

for something restful avoid large patterns with a sense of movement. Sailing ships on a very rough sea, for example, are not necessarily ideal at breakfast-time in the dining room!

At the other extreme, examine fine detail bright patterns at a distance. What may appear at close quarters as a bright pattern of summer flowers can appear as a khaki mess at a range of 5 m (16 ft).

First, decide how you will allocate pattern, for you can over-do things. A floral paper may call for a plain carpet; or you may prefer floral curtains and carpet and a very plain paper. Bear in mind the colour of the furniture covers; for best effect it is worth making up a very simple model out of an old shoe box, painting in the colours and patterns, to see how it all goes together. There are few of us who can really visualise what a complete room will look like unless it is presented to us in some visual form.

Do not forget to include smallish items like cushions and lampshades. These can add a wonderful splash of colour to an otherwise lifeless room.

Textures have a part to play too, particularly where a plain colour is required. It can be plain yet attractively textured, and if wall lights or spotlights are used carefully, the whole surface can be made to live.

Finally, as you plan, keep your lighting in mind. For example, darkish shades of brown and rust may be very restful, but they absorb light very readily. So, for those occasions when one may wish to read, write or do hobbies, you will need perhaps more light available in the form of standard lamp, table lamps and wall lights. At the other end of the scale, a particularly pale colour scheme with lots of pastels and whites do not need masses of light overall or it will look like a hospital operating theatre. It needs areas of lighting which can be subdued— perhaps by dimmer switches—for those occasions when a restful atmosphere is required.

Lighting is covered in detail in a companion volume in this series—*Home Electrics*.

Chapter 2
Tools

The quality of your decorating will be influenced by three main factors. The right tools; the time you give to preparation of surfaces, and the use of good quality materials.

In this chapter we will deal with the tools, then devote separate chapters to materials and preparation.

The gathering together of a first class

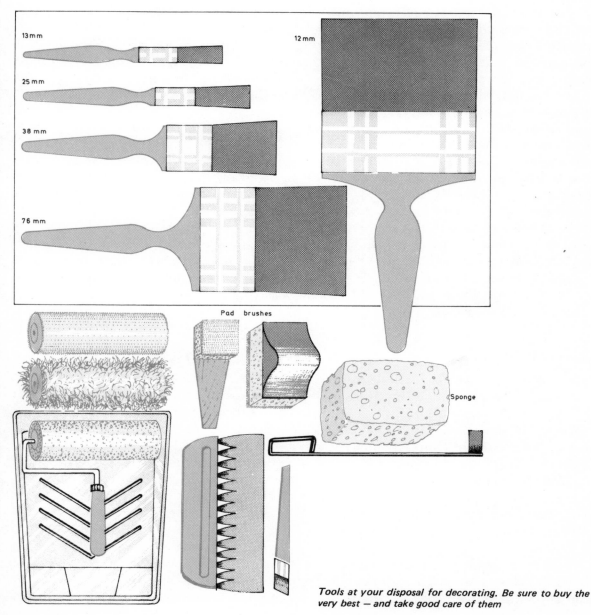

Tools at your disposal for decorating. Be sure to buy the very best — and take good care of them

kit of tools is always a problem for the couple just making a start, and there is a temptation to buy cheap so you can get more things. Avoid this at all costs and buy the very best—even if in the meantime you have to borrow certain items from members of your family. Poor quality tools produce poor finishes, and it does not take long to recognise the difference.

For example, a cheap brush will contain a minimum of bristle, it will be poorly shaped, and the bristle may be poorly anchored so that as you use it bristles are pulled out and deposited on your work. Some brushes will be bulked with artificial fibres which have not the qualities of a natural bristle, so the holding power of the brush is impaired. On some brushes the metal ferrule may be a poor fit on the handle. All these faults add up to a poor finish.

A good brush, properly cared for, will give almost endless service. Even when its bristles have worn short, it will still serve for applying primers and, perhaps finally, as your favourite dusting brush.

Some of the tools you will need for decorating are as follows.

Brushes

There is a wide size range of brushes, but for most jobs a 13 mm (½ in), 25 mm (1 in) and 38 mm (1½ in) will do for frames. For larger areas like flush doors, use at least a 50 mm (2 in) and preferably a 76 mm (3 in), brush so that you cover quickly. A smaller brush will lead to ugly dry edges which are impossible to disguise. For wall surfaces use a 100 mm (4 in) or 127 mm (5 in) brush so that you cover quickly.

You also need a dusting brush for removing dust after rubbing down. This can either be brought specially, or an old well worn brush can be kept just for this job. Never use a dusting brush for painting!

For smoothing paper in place you need a smoothing brush, which needs to be kept dry and clean; for modern vinyls, a sponge is better than a brush. For applying paste to wallcoverings you will need a pasting brush, and here again, it is wise to keep a brush just for this use.

Obviously it is wise to have more than one of each type of brush. For example, when painting, use a newish brush for priming and undercoating so that if it sheds a few bristles they can be rubbed off. After a few careful uses, the brush can be promoted to finishing coats.

Paint pads

Although the pad has been available for very many years, it has had very slow acceptance, perhaps because of its unusual design. Basically the paint pad consists of a fine mohair pad mounted on a layer of foam, which in turn is stuck to a handle. Only the mohair is loaded with paint, which is then applied to the surface to be painted.

Paint pads are best for large areas of work and will quickly coat walls and ceilings, whether textured or plain. A wide range of sizes is available. Small pads on short handles for frames, and larger ones on longer handles for walls and ceilings. Some have a hollow handle which will take a broom handle to extend your reach. With all pad work it is wise to have a small paintbrush handy to touch in small areas where the pad does not reach properly.

Pads should be kept for use only with water-based paint materials—emulsions, acrylic gloss and water-based vinyls. This means the pads can be cleaned in water. Oil-based materials involving the use of chemical cleaners can mean damage to the

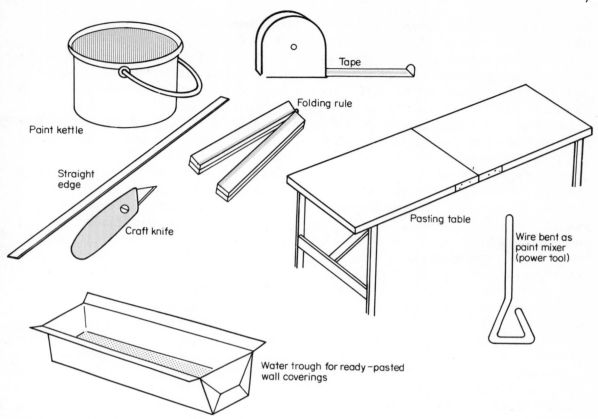

Paint kettle

Tape

Folding rule

Straight edge

Craft knife

Pasting table

Wire bent as paint mixer (power tool)

Water trough for ready–pasted wall coverings

Tools you will need. A pasting table is not necessary when using pre-pasted wallcoverings

adhesive bond between pad and foam or foam and handle, causing the pad to curl away. In other words, they will handle gloss paints very well—but the resultant cleaning of the pad brush is hard.

With the pads will come a tray in which to hold paint; though a flat baking tin is a good substitute. Some pads come with a deep trough, used as a reservoir, and a plastic drum which picks paint from the trough and transfers it to the roller. This gives an accurate measure of paint, ensuring the pad does not pick up too much.

It is unwise to leave pads loaded with paint after use. The mohair is so fine that it soon hardens. Make a habit of washing out your pads after each session; this saves a great deal of trouble subsequently.

Paint rollers

The paint roller is now a well established tool in the field, and incidentally developed especially for it. There are three basic types available.

Foam. Among the cheaper tools, the foam roller gives a reasonable finish, though it does tend to spatter due to its cellular structure. It is better for emulsions than for use with oil-based paints. Because the sleeve slips off the central core, cleaning is easy, and replacement of a worn sleeve equally simple.

Mohair. This type of roller has a hard central core with a fine mohair pile stuck to it. This makes it ideal for applying thin coats to flat surfaces, and it will give a good finish to gloss coats. It is not much use on textured surfaces, as the short pile will not reach into hollows. The pile is not easy to clean as the sleeve cannot be removed; because of the delicate nature of the pile, never leave a mohair roller loaded with paint. Clean the roller as soon as work stops.

Lambswool or nylon pile. This is the most popular type of roller, and it comes in a number of varieties. A short pile will give a good finish on plain or textured surfaces, but from a cleaning point of view it is best to keep it to water-based paints. A long, shaggy, pile roller is ideal for highly textured surfaces such as pebbledash or textured ceiling finishes, though it will not give such a smooth coating. If you need a roller for outdoor use, buy one designed for this purpose; it will have a tougher, more durable pile.

Paint trays are usually supplied with a roller kit. The tray is designed to combine a paint well with a sloping area where the roller can be run to spread the paint and discard any surplus. The thinner the paint, the easier it is to transfer to the roller.

Apart from standard decorating rollers, special thin versions are available for getting at awkward spots, such as behind pipes and radiators. These may only be stocked by the larger decorator's suppliers.

Aerosol paints

These are classed as tools, as you really buy a miniature paint sprayer along with your paint. The aerosol is best suited to small, intricate jobs such as painting a wicker chair or a wrought iron gate.

The can has a limited capacity, and the paint has to be extra-thin to come out of the very fine nozzle, so it is not suited to larger areas such as doors. (see also paint spray guns later in this chapter).

Scrapers

These fall into two main categories. There is the very sharp bladed variety designed for rapid paint stripping without the use of chemical stripper. It can be rather harsh, but on surfaces like banister rails it is very effective if care is taken not to tear the wood. It certainly saves on chemical stripper and it avoids the possible scorching by blowtorch. Replaceable blades are available, but be careful when checking whether a blade is sharp! Do not use your fingers!

The second type of scraper has a flexible blade designed to ease wallpaper from the wall after softening. It can also be used for scraping cellulose filler smooth once set, and for removing scraps of paper remaining on the wall after stripping. Do not sharpen the blade; a square edge is preferable.

The shave-hook is really of the same family, though it is not flexible. Two main types are available; pear shaped, for tackling mouldings, and triangular for flat surfaces. Again, a sharp square edge is preferable to a sharpened edge.

Filling knife

This is really a thin bladed scraper, designed to flex well. It is made for spreading and levelling filler used for hiding cracks and gaps in wood and plaster.

Plumb bob

This is merely a weight fixed to the end of a length of twine, it is designed to give a true vertical when marking to hang the first length of wallcovering. Types vary from a simple pear-shaped bob to one fitted with scriber or pencil.

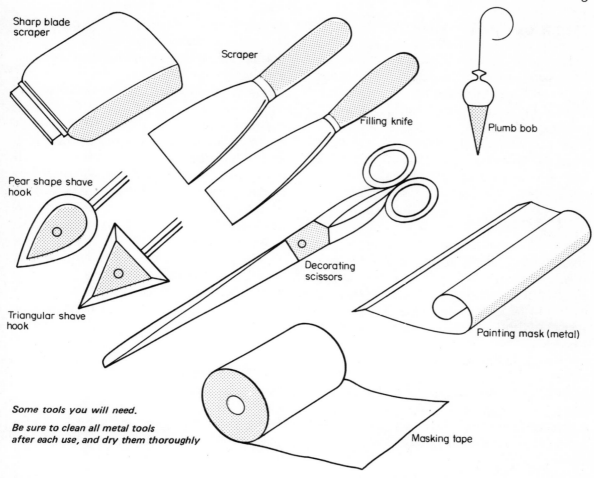

Sharp blade scraper

Scraper

Filling knife

Plumb bob

Pear shape shave hook

Triangular shave hook

Decorating scissors

Painting mask (metal)

Masking tape

Some tools you will need.

Be sure to clean all metal tools after each use, and dry them thoroughly

Scissors

A good pair of decorators' scissors is essential when papering. They are used for pre-cutting to length and trimming after hanging. One of the principal uses was for removing the selvedge. or protective edge, from rolls of wallpaper, but now, almost without exception, this selvedge is already cut off. Even so, a good pair of scissors ensures a neat finish.

A smaller pair of scissors may be added to deal with the small fiddling jobs, such as cutting around ceiling roses and light switches. Decorating scissors should not be used for any other cutting jobs, or their edges will soon become dulled and they will tear rather than cut—especially when paper is wet.

Painting mask

This is useful for keeping paint where it belongs, the mask being laid on the area not to be painted. A typical use is on the glass of a window while the frame is painted—allowing just a few millimetres of paint on the glass to seal the gap between glass and putty.

Special masking tape is also available for masking long runs, such as between a cove cornice and a wall being painted. The adhesive used is a special quick release one which will not pull a decorative surface, or leave adhesive behind. Transparent adhesive tape should never be used for masking. It will probably pull off paint—or in some cases leave it's adhesive behind.

Tack or tacky rag

This is a special duster impregnated with resin, making the rag tacky but not sticky. It is ideal to use when fine finishing, to pick up traces of dust and dirt prior to painting.

However the rag should only be used after dusting with a dusting brush, or it will clog up too quickly.

Glasspaper

You will need a selection of grades of glasspaper, ranging from coarse to very fine, or flour grade. For fine finishing you can get a waterproof type which, if used with a little water, will give a very smooth surface without creating a lot of dust. Known as 'wet or dry', it is often found in shops supplying materials for car body repair.

You will need a sanding block around which to wrap the glasspaper; a cork block is ideal and there are also blocks available which grip the paper.

Power tools

Power tools can be used for sanding, and you will encounter three basic methods.

Disc sander. A simple rubber disc designed to hold a sheet of abrasive. It is suitable for rubbing down timber where appearance does not matter too much for, however used, it tends to scratch across the wood grain. When used on painted surfaces the disc will very quickly clog, as the friction produces heat, which in turn melts the paint. There are variations on the disc but the same basic problems remain.

Orbital sander. An attachment which holds an abrasive pad, but which works with a very fine reciprocal movement. It produces a fine finish with scratches of such fine proportions as to be invisible in normal use. It is designed for fine finishing, and it is not intended for removal of material in quantity. It is not ideal for paint removal.

Drum sander. As the name applies, it is based upon a foam plastic drum to which is fitted a belt of abrasive, held in place by a heat-melted wax. A variety of grades of abrasive are available, and because of the direction of rotation the drum can be directed along the grain of the wood so that no scratches are visible. With a coarse abrasive, it will remove paint, where, because of the drum size, the abrasive is not overheated. So, it does not clog like the disc. This is by far the best tool for smoothing.

Paint kettle

This is a good old traditional tool, but with a very sensible use. It is merely a container with carrying handle, for a quantity of paint for immediate application. It makes carrying easy especially when working from a ladder, and it ensures that should anything contaminate the paint—masonry dust or falling leaves—it only affects the paint in use.

If you only have one paint kettle and you plan to change colours, lining the kettle with foil will make it easy to clean. In fact no cleaning should be necessary.

The traditional kettle was metal, but a plastic one is perfectly acceptable.

Rags

These are hardly a tool, but plenty of clean, lint-free rag is necessary when painting—particularly for wiping up splashes as they occur. Wet paint is easily removed; dry paint is not.

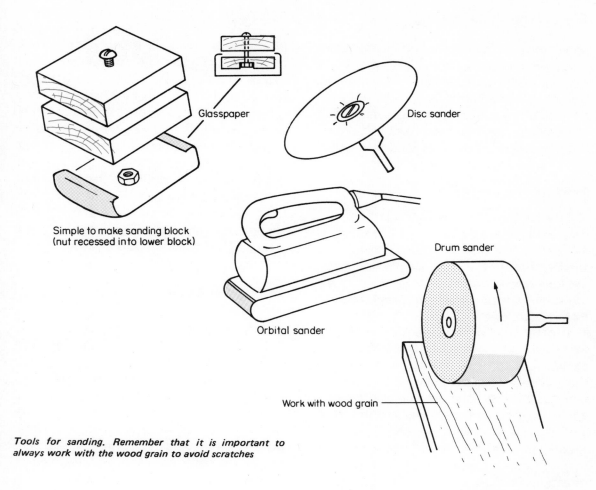

Glasspaper

Disc sander

Simple to make sanding block
(nut recessed into lower block)

Drum sander

Orbital sander

Work with wood grain

Tools for sanding. Remember that it is important to always work with the wood grain to avoid scratches

Chalk line

You can buy a chalk line stored in a special container, but for home use a simple length of string rubbed with a piece of coloured chalk is usually adequate.

It is used for snapping a mark on a ceiling to indicate where the first length goes, or similarly on a floor to mark a centre line for floor tiles.

You need a tack one end to hold the line to a measured mark or marks on the ceiling; pull it taut with one hand, and snap it smartly with the other.

Tape measure

For decorating, choose the longest measure you can get. It saves double or treble measurements, when error can creep in. Use metal or reinforced plastic tape—not the cotton tape type measure used for dressmaking.

A folding boxwood rule will also be useful for measuring shorter distances, such as marking measurements on a piece of wallcovering. If you have to use a tape, one with a little lock on it which stops the tape retracting will make work easier.

Pasting table

Some form of table is essential if you are using the traditional papering system. Good folding tables are available which makes storage easier when the table is not required. If one is not available, a flush door with the door furniture removed and rested over a couple of stout boxes is a good alternative.

Paint stirrers

It is vital that paint is thoroughly mixed before use, especially if it has been standing for any length of time. You can buy paint stirring rods, but a flat piece of stick, or an old long-bladed knife will do. For small tins use lolly sticks, washed and dried, rescued from the children.

A power tool may be used for stirring, in which case you need to buy a stirring rod, or you can bend a piece of stiff wire to shape. Always ensure the rod is in the paint before the tool is started, and make sure it comes to rest before the stirrer is withdrawn!

The exception to the above is with thixotropic, or jelly paints; these need no mixing before use. If in doubt, read the directions on the can.

Paint strainer

Certain hardware or painters' supply shops will supply paint strainers for removing skin and bits from paint, but for normal home use, a piece of well washed nylon stocking stretched over a tin will do.

Alternatively, make the piece big enough to push down into the paint, then secure around the tin with elastic bands. You can then pick up paint from within the piece of stocking.

Do not strain your paint until it has been thoroughly mixed. Often, oils gather under a paint skin—and this oil is a necessary ingredient.

Safety goggles

For jobs like wire brushing rusted areas, rubbing down walls, or applying chemicals like paint strippers, it pays to wear protective glasses. These can be purchased from tool shops in two types. A small variety which fit close to the eyes, and larger models designed to go over existing glasses if you happen to wear them.

Do not rely on ordinary glasses for jobs like cutting paving slabs. Flying pieces can badly chip glass, even if they do not actually break it. For jobs such as applying chemicals, motorcycling goggles could be used.

Dust sheets

Often it is not possible to remove all furniture from a room when decorating. In this case cover the remaining items with dust sheets. The best type is the cotton sheet as it is absorbent enough to hold light splashing.

Polythene sheets are available, but remember water will run down and gather on the sheet, and wet polythene is very slippery. Dust sheets can also be used to protect tiles on porches, or flower borders, when working on the exterior.

Blowlamps/blowtorches

The standard blowlamp which burns paraffin and needs regular refilling, has gone out of favour in recent years, though it still offers an economical method of paint stripping. Its main problem was getting it lit after filling—especially in cold, windy conditions. Nowadays the bottled gas blowtorch is favoured, though one has to pay for the privilege of extra convenience.

The simplest type is lit by a match or gas lighter, but the latest types have a built-in crystal igniter operated by a simple trigger.

Traditional blowlamp

Blowtorch

Choose a ladder which extends
3 rungs above gutter level

This ladder has rubber suction
cups to prevent slipping

Step ladder with
hand rail

Combined ladder/steps

Ladder platform

*Safe access to the job is vital. Do not skimp on tools;
particularly where safety is involved. Having a ladder of
the correct length is vital. When erecting the ladder ensure
that it is safely anchored at top and bottom before
venturing on to it.*

This makes the tool ideal for outside use,
on ladder or scaffold. The torch can be
lit, then switched off as soon as necessary,
with no problem of re-ignition when
required.

When buying blowtorches, check which
types of refills will fit as the different
makes are rarely interchangeable.

Paint spray gun

While ideal for car re-sprays and large
areas like a garage door, there are few
other jobs of a decorating nature where
the spray gun will help. It can be used
for painting window and door frames,
but the time spent in masking surrounding
areas to avoid over-spray can soon out-
weigh the advantages.

For small jobs, such as wickerwork,
wrought iron and small whitewood items,
an aerosol paint can will prove adequate.

Sponge

This is the ideal accessory for smoothing vinyl wallcoverings in place and is better than a smoothing brush.

It is necessary to have at least two sponges. One sponge for general mopping up and washing down and one kept specially as a smoother for wallcoverings.

Water trough

This item is fairly new on the decorating scene, for it comes with rolls of pre-pasted wallcoverings.

It is supplied flat but pre-creased and is made of waxed card. It is merely folded into shape, the flaps tucked in, and you have a waterproof trough.

Craft knife

A stout knife with interchangeable blades will be needed for cutting stouter decorating materials, such as vinyl floorcovering or carpet. Special blades are available—hooked for carpet cutting, and shaped for laminate scoring.

A steel straight-edge is useful when using the knife. Be sure at all times to keep your hand behind the direction of cut. These knives are very sharp!

Ladders

For exterior work, a sound ladder which will extend at least three rungs above the highest point you wish to reach is essential. It can be of timber or alloy and, with the price of timber having climbed, there is now little to choose as far as price is concerned. Timber feels warmer in cold weather but alloy is far lighter making the ladder easier to move and position.

A two-extension ladder is usually adequate. If you go for the three-extension, bear in mind it is that much harder to raise on your own.

Choose a ladder with wide treads which give reasonable support for your feet. Working from a ladder can be very tiring. Ladder platforms are available which, if fitted at the height you wish to work, will give a bigger platform on which to stand. For hints on ladder safety see Chapter 11.

Steps

For interior decorating, you will need at least one pair of wide tread steps, preferably with a hand rail to grip when working high or overhead. Two pairs are even better, for by using a strong scaffold board between them, you have a safe working platform.

One pair of steps and a strong timber box is an alternative arrangement as a board support, but you are stuck for height by the size of the box. Never work from kitchen stools or an old chair.

If you live in a bungalow, ladders are now available which very simply convert from ladder to wide base steps. 'Three ladders in one' if you also look upon such as arrangement as also offering access to the loft.

Roof ladder

Most homes do not need to invest in a roof ladder as it is not required that often. If you do buy one, see that it is designed for the job. Wheels make it easy to move up the roof tiles, and a large specially shaped section is designed to hook over the ridge.

The roof ladder must be used in conjunction with a well-anchored extension ladder so you can move from one to the other easily. If you feel unsafe at roof height, call in expert help. Never take risks!

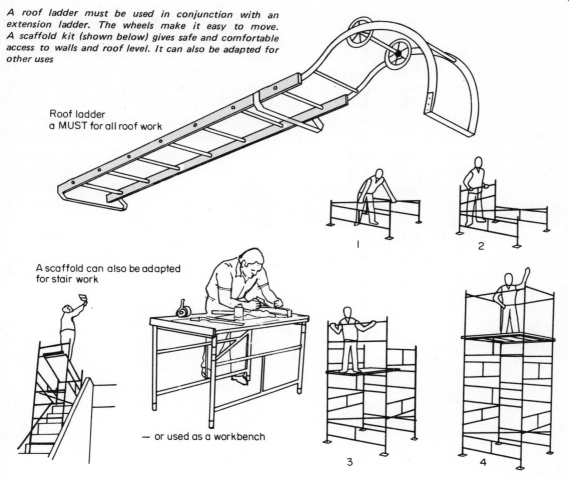

A roof ladder must be used in conjunction with an extension ladder. The wheels make it easy to move. A scaffold kit (shown below) gives safe and comfortable access to walls and roof level. It can also be adapted for other uses

Roof ladder
a MUST for all roof work

A scaffold can also be adapted
for stair work

— or used as a workbench

1

2

3

4

Hiring equipment

There are many jobs about the house where a piece of specialist equipment would make the work much easier. In the past, such equipment has been for the professional, but with the introduction of chains of specialist hire shops, many items are now available to the home owner.

Obviously it does not pay to buy specialised items, but being able to hire these either by the day or week has completely transformed the situation.

It is not only large items which can be hired. If you need to decorate before you have tools of your own, then most decorating tools are available but, of course, you must pay for the privilege.

Collecting and returning items yourself will help reduce charges, while careful planning can reduce the period of hire. For example, a floor sander will make short work of a dirty parquet floor. If you remove furniture, check for nails and other possible obstructions that could damage a sanding belt prior to hiring the sander, you can then put it to use as soon as you get it home.

Before tackling decorating, get hold of a current catalogue of a local hire firm and check to see what they stock. There may be something there which could save you at lot of unpleasant work as well as hours of your time.

Two examples are given below. *Steam wallpaper stripping machine*. If you encounter a really tough paper that is bonded to the wall, days can be wasted in cleaning it off. The steam stripper will do the job in hours.

Water in a special container is heated by bottled gas or electricity until it becomes steam and this is fed to a special plate which is held against the wall.

The effect of the combined heat and water is to dissolve the adhesive, allowing the paper to be pulled away by the sheet.

Ladders. Perhaps your own ladder will not reach a particular spot such as a chimney stack. The hire of a longer ladder can solve the problem. Alternatively you may wish to add another ladder to the one you already have, then add a pair of cripples to form a platform for scaffold boards. The boards and cripples can also be hired from your local hire shop.

A roof ladder will give you safe access to the loose tiles or missing ridge tile, and a scaffold kit of the type designed for handyman use can give you comfortable working platforms when painting large wall areas.

Chapter 3
Materials

There is a wide selection of materials available today, to the point that it can be very confusing when trying to choose. This is particularly true of the paint field, where technology has encouraged the introduction of many new additives. Modern paints tend to get fancy names which help very little when it comes to choosing what you need, so the first job is to establish which family the paint belongs to, and whether it is designed for interior use, exterior use, or perhaps both.

When choosing paint, ask at the same time just what materials back it up. Is there a special primer or undercoat? Is the material oil-based, needing special thinners and brush cleaners? Is it water-based, where brushes can be rinsed under the tap?

Choosing your colour can be equally confusing as the colour mixing machine is being extensively used. The machine has base colours into which a practically limitless variation of tints and combinations of tints can be added. If you are choosing a colour scheme, it will pay to take any samples you have—pieces of carpet, curtain, wallcovering—so that you can match the colour.

Alternatively ask for a detailed colour card, or for colour chips which can be taken home and examined at leisure. Bear in mind that small samples give a very false picture of what a large area of colour will look like. A large area will tend to look darker than the small sample.

As a general rule, pastels can be chosen from a mixing machine, though it is wise to buy as much as you require right away in case of slight variations in any further mix. Strong, bold colours are best chosen from a ready-mixed range of paints.

Now let us look at some of the materials currently available, starting with paints.

Alkyd resin paint

There is nothing new about alkyd resin gloss paint, it has been around for many years and is the standard good quality gloss which replaced the old lead-based paints. Materials painted need to be primed to seal the surface, undercoated to give body and obliterate any under-colour, then top coated. Alkyd paint is mainly used for high gloss work, though sheen and matt finishes are also available.

Up to now, the British market has always demanded a high gloss, but many countries accept a sheen or semi-gloss for surfaces such as doors and woodwork. While semi-gloss paint may collect dust or dirt more readily out of doors, for interior work it is much kinder where blemishes or irregular surfaces are encountered.

Acrylic paint

This is a material of the same family as the emulsion paints we have been using for years—though with more sheen. It is water-based, which makes it very easy to handle. It has virtually no smell; a boon to those who suffer from chest complaints or who just dislike the lingering smell of drying paint. In addition, the painting tools can be rinsed out in water.

Remember to protect water-based paints from frost, and not to store them in containers which could rust from the effect of the water content. Drying time is much faster than with oil-based materials, so if you are willing to accept less gloss on your work, the acrylic paint is ideal for a quick re-paint.

Stemming from the acrylics, come a whole range of water-based materials with additives such as vinyl and polyurethane to give a more durable finish and change the surface reflection. Some are soluble in water, while others need the addition of some form of solvent, such as washing up liquid, added to the water. As these products cannot possibly be classified, it is advisable to check carefully when choosing to see just what you are buying.

Emulsion paint

This water-based material has been well established for many years now, and fortunately the characteristics of peeling and flaking which gave the early emulsions such a bad name have gone forever. Distemper has now been replaced by emulsion paint but can still give considerable trouble in older homes, where its chalky, unstable surface must be either completely removed or sealed with a special sealing material before anything new is put over the top.

Emulsion paint, being water-based, makes the ideal material for large wall surfaces. It is quick drying, leaves no brush marks, and it has no unpleasant smell. It is best not applied direct to bare wood, as the water content will raise the wood grain. Brushes can be rinsed with water.

Thixotropic paints

Here again, another advance in paint technology has made it possible to produce a jelly-like paint which thins only when stirred or spread. The principle has been adapted for both emulsion and gloss paints, producing paints well suited to the beginner. They can be applied thicker without sagging; do not drip easily, and the paint stays on the brush. In the main these 'jelly' paints do not appeal to the experienced painter as they cannot be brushed out to a very fine finish.

Because of the extra thickness which can be applied, a new one-coat paint system was introduced with these paints, where the undercoat is incorporated in the top coat. On new work this system can be adequate, but where a change of colour is necessary, often there is insufficient pigment to obliterate an under-colour without applying two coats. A standard undercoat and top coat would be more effective. The one-coat system best suits the beginner. It has not replaced the standard painting system but rather has supplemented it.

Polyurethane paint

This has all the characteristics of a high gloss paint, but with an exceptional toughness built in. The coating is hard and is perhaps a little more prone to chipping than standard gloss, but it is able to withstand abrasion in a way not found in most other paints.

It is ideal for painting metal surfaces, such as garage doors, where it will give good protection. Because of its hardness, the instructions concerning applying second coats should be read very carefully. If too long is left in between coats, the under-coat will be so hard that the top one will not adhere well.

Enamels

These are high quality paints where the ingredients are ground very fine to give a dense, high gloss. Drying time can be controlled during manufacture according to use; the fastest drying enamels are those supplied for car body touch-up work.

As far as decorating is concerned, enamels are best suited to smaller jobs such as small items of whitewood furniture in nurseries, coathangers, door knobs and toys.

When used on such surfaces, as long as the wood is smooth, no primer or undercoat is necessary.

Aerosol paints

With aerosols the paint has to be ejected through a very fine nozzle under pressure. It has to be an extremely thinned-down material, and this is the main problem. The very thinnest of coats is applied, so a new technique must be adopted.

The surface must be covered by applying one thin coat upon another until the required density is achieved, allowing each coat to dry. As drying time is measured in minutes, this is no real hardship. Applying too thick a coat at one go merely results in drips and runs.

Aerosols are not cheap because of the sophisticated packaging and, as the paint is inside a sealed container, it is difficult to gauge easily how much paint you have. The aerosol is best used on smallish difficult surfaces such as wrought ironwork, perforated materials such as pegboard, and woven materials such as wicker furniture. Aerosols are not really suitable for large areas such as doors. One aerosol may not cover, and the next can may differ very slightly in colour, particularly if the can comes from a different batch. You will find a batch number of the base.

Masking is essential to avoid spray getting on other surfaces. Never use an aerosol out of doors where the wind could carry spray on to the surfaces such as your neighbour's car! If you work out of doors you need to make a spray booth from hardboard or cardboard.

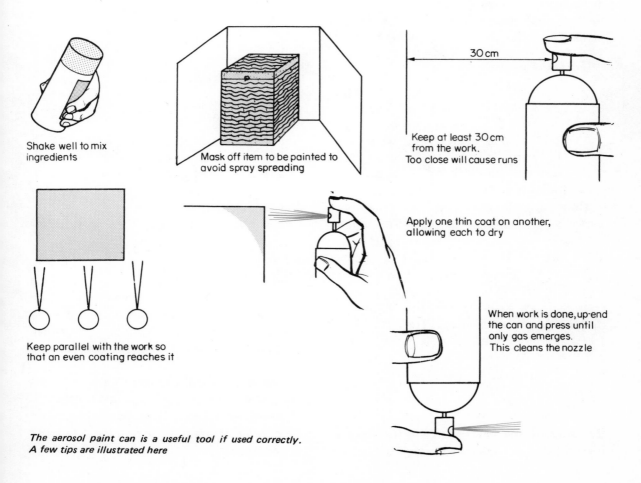

Shake well to mix ingredients

Mask off item to be painted to avoid spray spreading

Keep at least 30 cm from the work. Too close will cause runs

Keep parallel with the work so that an even coating reaches it

Apply one thin coat on another, allowing each to dry

When work is done, up-end the can and press until only gas emerges. This cleans the nozzle

The aerosol paint can is a useful tool if used correctly. A few tips are illustrated here

Anti-condensation paint

This is an emulsion specially developed for use in areas where condensation is a problem. It has the ability to absorb a certain amount of moisture, which can evaporate when conditions are dry. This paint contains a fungicide which discourages the growth of mould. It is a very useful material in bathrooms and kitchens.

Fire retardant paint

Such materials have been widely used industrially for many years, but they are finding their way into the d-i-y market as people become more aware of the danger of fire in the home.

The paint looks very similar to a normal emulsion, but when exposed to severe heat it expands to form an insulating crust. It can be used on timbers, and also on expanded polystyrene tiles for kitchens.

Texture coatings

These should be classed as compounds, for they are supplied, in the main, as ready-mixed coatings in tubes and are far thicker than a paint. Their main advantage is their ability to hide irregular surfaces, so they have been widely used for ceilings where there are joins to hide or nail heads to lose.

Once applied by brush or roller, the material is textured by patterning or pulling up the compound, after which it sets hard. Once dry, it is painted, using a shaggy lambswool or nylon roller.

This material can also be used for wall coating, and again it has the ability to disguise poor wall surfaces. The main point to bear in mind is that it is designed as a permanent decoration, and it is hard to remove. You cannot paper over it.

Masonry paints

Basically, these are paints with durable ingredients or additives, well able to withstand external weathering. They can be cement-based, stone-based or emulsion-based, to which bulk may be added in the form of nylon fibre or silica.

A material like nylon is a very efficient binding agent, and it acts as a filler, hiding minor hair cracks and gaps.

When purchasing, ask about back-up products such as stabilising solutions to prepare a surface for painting, and fungicides to kill off any mould growth on the external walls.

Materials for preparation

The paints and compounds we have looked at so far are classified as decorative coatings. There is, however, a whole range of materials which are necessary in the preparation of surfaces. Some of these materials are described in the following paragraphs and include products used for knot sealing, primers, fillers, mastics, pastes, paint strippers, brush cleaners, etc.

Knotting

Knotting-compound is a shellac-based material designed to seal off knots in wood. This is most important on external work for knots may bleed resin, which will ruin any decoration.

The compound will prevent resin escaping, and it need only be applied to the actual knot area.

Primers

A priming paint is designed to seal off the material being painted from the decorative coating, and it is important to see you use the correct one.

There are metal primers, plaster primers and wood primers, in the main, sold as separate items. Multi-purpose primers can be bought which are suitable for a number of materials.

Fillers

While a primer has the ability to seal off a surface, it cannot seal holes, cracks and gaps. This is the job of a fillers. Various types are available as follows.

Cellulose filler. This will tackle cracks and holes in plaster and any timberwork which is not exposed to damp. It may be supplied by the packet to be mixed with water, or in a tub ready-mixed. Where large areas are involved, a material such as Keene's cement will be more economical. Deep cracks should be built up layer by layer, keying each by scratching the surface before it sets.

Fine surface fillers. This is a further development of the cellulose filler. It comes ready-mixed, has adhesive properties and will not be affected by damp. It should be worked well into the surface with a flexible filling knife and rubbed smooth when hard.

Wood stopping. A very well established form of adhesive filler which is ideal for timberwork. Supplied as a fine paste, it is worked well into the wood and allowed to set hard before rubbing smooth. It is available in a number of wood colours so that clear varnish finishes can be used after filling. Two grades are supplied: internal and external. The external grade should be used wherever damp conditions are likely to be encountered.

Epoxy resin based filler. This is supplied as a grey paste in a large tube. The material is activated by the addition of a hardener supplied in a smaller tube. Once mixed, setting is by chemical action, and nothing will stop it. This type of material is ideal for repairs to gutters and downpipes where cracks and gaps in metalwork need to be filled. Once set it can be filed or sanded smooth.

Mastics

A mastic differs from a filler in that it is designed to remain flexible even though it hardens on the surface. So you would use a mastic to fill any gap where there is likely to be movement, either through shrinkage of timber or through temperature variations. This makes mastics particularly suitable for outdoor work, especially window frames and other areas where cracks need filling.

Mastic is available either in strip form, rather like rolled out Plasticine, or in tubes with a special dispenser nozzle, or in cartridges to be fitted in a mastic gun. The strips are adequate for most small jobs, whereas a gun would be ideal if, say, all the window frames of the house were to be treated.

For gutter work and for sealing gaps in surfaces, such as flat roofs, there is a bituminous mastic available in tins. This would be applied by a small trowel. To strengthen an area, such as a tear in roofing felt, the mastic can be reinforced by using jute scrim or glass fibre bandage.

Keene's cement

A plaster-like material which is more economical to use for larger filling jobs. Pinkish in colour, it is fast drying, so no more should be mixed than can be used in about five minutes. For deep holes, build it up coat on coat, keying the previous one by scratching it with a trowel point before it sets.

Perhaps it should be mentioned here that plaster of paris is not really suitable for repair work. It sets far too quickly to be manageable. The most it could be used for is filling a deep hole to within 25 mm of the surface, then finishing with a standard filler. To give a stronger key, tap galvanised clout nails into the first coat, going well below the plaster surface.

Wallcovering pastes

There are several types of pastes and the correct one should be chosen according to the job in hand.

Cellulose paste. Ideal for lightweight wallpapers where there is a chance of staining. It has high water content, so makes a wallcovering very wet. A heavy duty cellulose is available for heavier materials.

Cold water paste. A traditional flour paste which is very full bodied, making it ideal for heavier materials such as ceiling papers and Anaglyptas. Because it has less water content, it has less tendency to expand heavier papers than a cellulose paste. It would be used in conjunction with a glue size, which is applied to the wall prior to decorating.

The size adds 'slip', making a paper easier to position, and it increases the adhesion of the paste. It shouldn't be applied too thickly or there may be a chance of surplus size coming up through joints when papering.

Vinyl wallcovering paste. This is a special paste to which is added a fungicide, because the vinyl film is impervious and will not allow moisture to evaporate off. Always use the paste recommended by the manufacturer when hanging vinyls.

Fungicide

When mould growth is encountered on walls or paintwork, it must be killed off with a fungicide prior to redecorating. This is available in bottles or in 'one use' sachets.

The fungicide cannot be applied over wallcoverings. You must strip off the decoration, then apply the fungicide to the clean wall. Household bleach is often used to kill mould growths, but experience shows it has no lasting effect. It is far better to use a proprietary fungicide. However, keep it away from children!

Chemical stripper

This is a thick liquid designed to attack and break down a paint film so that it can be removed with shave hooks and scrapers. Types vary considerably, so the instructions on the container should be followed very carefully, both with regard to application and neutralising after use.

Eyes and hands should be protected when using these materials. Most strippers will also soften hard paintbrushes if the brushes are suspended in the material until soft.

Brush cleaners

Proprietary materials designed for the easy cleaning of brushes after use with oil-based paints. An alternative is to use paraffin in a jar to loosen and remove the paint, then thoroughly rinse the brush with soap and water to remove the paraffin. This is a cheaper process than using a brush cleaner, but it does take longer.

To conserve proprietary brush cleaner, let it settle after use, then pour off the still useable material into another container, only throwing away the dregs. An economical way of using cleaner is to pour a little into a polythene bag, insert the brush, seal the bag with an elastic band and work the brush bristles through the plastic.

Damp sealers

These are special liquids designed to form a thin skin of the surface of a wall to prevent damp coming through.

While they can be effective, they are best used after the cause of the damp has been treated. If the damp is persistent, it will tend to move elsewhere and come through in a new place which has not been sealed.

Silicone water repellant

This is a transparent liquid designed to coat brickwork of rendering so that water cannot penetrate. The seal does not stop the wall 'breathing' so vapour in the wall surface can still get out.

Stains and varnishes

These are described in Chapter 10 'Wood-finishing'.

Wallpapers

These fall into four main categories: plain where a pattern is printed on to a roll of paper; duplex, where two papers are bonded together during manufacture, adding texture and strength; wipable, where superficial marks can be wiped away without spoiling the surface, and washable, where a protective film is added over the pattern so that it can be cleaned.

As a general rule, the heavier the paper, the easier it is to handle. It is false economy to start with a very cheap paper, for in inexpert hands it will tear and mark very easily.

Also, the heavier the material, the longer it should be given to soak, prior to hanging, to avoid bubbling. The continued expansion while on the wall can cause bubbles, and very often the paste will get a grip before the paper has dried out—so the bubbles remain.

Wall coverings

These include wallpapers in various categories and comprise winyls, heavily-embossed paper-backed coverings (for instance, Lincrusta), hessians and grass cloths. All these are described in the following paragraphs.

Vinyls

Printing on plastics and the texturing of sheet plastics has improved tremendously in recent years, making the vinyl wallcovering a most attractive proposition. True they still cost more than papers, but they have many advantages. Vinyls are easy to cut and handle; the surface is unaffected by water, paste and fingermarks.

Apart from the standard one, you can now buy pre-pasted vinyls, where the adhesive on the back merely needs activating by dipping the vinyl in a water trough. There is ample adhesive for any surface, and in some cases a surplus may squeeze out at the joints. This is quite normal, and the surplus can be wiped away. The only difficulty you may encounter is at points where vinyl overlaps vinyl. The joints need special treatment and this subject is dealt with in Chapter 5.

Another advantage of most vinyls is that they are easy to strip. Lift a corner and pull the whole vinyl sheet away from the backing paper. The paper is left in place and is used as a lining paper for the next vinyl. This is a great advance on the old methods of wallpaper stripping.

Anaglypta, Supaglypta and Vynaglypta

These are heavy embossed materials adding a pleasant texture to a wall surface. A whole range of patterns is available, from simple plaster swirl effects through to basket weaves and contemporary designs.

They are ideal for use on ceilings and walls where the surfaces are not really smooth, for the textured surface will hide defects very well. The material can be emulsion coated to form an attractive and tough wallcovering.

Lincrusta

This is a traditional wallcovering material very much resembling putty stuck to a paper backing. It is available in very many effects, from coiled rope designs through to imitation panelling, and it gives a very deep pattern.

A special adhesive must be used to apply it, and the material should be looked upon as permanent.

Woodchip paper

In this case a plain paper is coated with wood chips, then covered by another sheet of paper so that the chips are sealed in. The effect is a pleasing texture which, when painted, produces a very durable wall-covering.

Too much of this material tends to cheapen the effect, so it looks at its best as a feature wall or in alcoves. It is not ideal for children's rooms because it feels rough if you fall against it.

A similar effect is probably available in Anaglypta which is much smoother to the touch.

Cork-faced wallcovering

This rather luxurious finish consists of a paper backing with a paint finish, to which is stuck very thin veneers of natural cork so the colour shows through.

It gives a very warm, luxurious effect and, because of its structure, it does tend to be expensive.

Hessians

These have become popular in recent years, despite the fact they are at the dearer end of the market. Those for d-i-y use are paper backed, and are stuck to the wall by means of a special heavy adhesive.

As they are merely woven panels, no matching between pieces is possible. You must accept that you will see every join quite clearly.

An interesting range of colours is available.

Grass cloths

These were primarily designed as a feature material. The wallcovering is woven from natural grasses, giving a very pleasant texture.

It is best kept for feature walls and alcoves where it will not be subject to wear and tear. Again, as it is a natural product, no matching of panels is possible.

Imitation effects

Apart from the normal run of decoration, you will now find a steadily growing range of imitation effects for your walls. These range from special effect papers first used in photographic studios, through to panels of imitation stone, brick and timber panelling.

The masonry and stone wall effects look most realistic. Panelling tends to look a bit like wallpaper through obvious repetitions of grain patterns and knots.

Wall panelling

Moving away from thinner sheet materials, real wall panelling has become very popular. It comes in various forms, the cheapest being sheets of thin plywood scored to represent panelling and perhaps faced with a thin veneer of high quality wood. At the other end of the scale are timber strips which are designed to be fixed individually. These look most effective, but are expensive.

An alternative is to use tongued and grooved boarding, choosing the boards for their grain pattern and knots. These may be stained and sealed to suit any décor.

Fixing is by· means of special adhesive, or by battening the walls and pinning the timber to the battens. Obviously the adhesive offers the simplest way, and it cuts out the cost of battening.

Colour should be borne in mind when choosing panelling. A dark colour may look fine in a big old study, but it can be very overpowering and make the room feel enclosed in our smaller homes. Perhaps a dark feature wall may be sufficient, or it may be better to choose a light colour, like pine, if a room is on the small side. Once sealed correctly, panelling is very easy to maintain.

For those who want the real thing, brick, stone and slate are available in very thin sheets to use rather like tiles. Stuck in place, these can give very pleasing effects, especially where a period effect is required. Very often a feature wall is all that is needed, or perhaps a chimney breast incorporating a ledge and seat.

Floor and ceiling coverings

For details of floor and ceiling materials, see Chapter 8 and 9.

Chapter 4 Preparation

With any decorating job, adequate preparation is 90 per cent of the battle. Practically all faults and failures which are blamed on materials can be traced back to the fact that the surface upon which the material was placed had been poorly prepared. Let us take just one example which highlights the problem. A ceiling which has been distempered.

If all the old material is not removed or neutralised, any subsequent coating, say an emulsion paint, is not in contact with the ceiling at all. It is resting on what for all intents and purposes is a layer of chalk. Is it surprising that before long the emulsion will pull away?

So we must face the fact that a lot of groundwork has to be done before any new materials are applied—however much we hate waiting to see what the finished effect will be!

Planning the job

The very first stage is planning. Work out how much time you have at your disposal. Will it be a number of evenings? Weekends? Or perhaps a week's holiday? Will it be winter, when night comes on quickly and there are no evenings; when the cold weather will prevent drying of damp surfaces and wet paint. Or will there be long summer evenings with dry weather and faster drying times for materials?

Having decided how much time you have, work out how best to divide the work up to fit it. Out of doors, you should plan so that at the end of a day no timber or metal is ever left without the protection of at least a priming coat. This may mean doing only one frame at a time. You may decide that the weekend will only allow one face of the house to be treated, in which case plan to do just one face of the house at a time, completing all the work on that face before moving round.

Having decided on a plan of campaign, measure up for materials. Assuming you have chosen the type of paint you require, the colour card will detail coverage. I have found the simplest way for windows is to treat the window as if it were a flat area equal to window height times width. This would be for a timber frame with a fair amount of mouldings. Obviously, a modern picture window with metal frame would need considerably less.

Simple scale plans of the various elevations will help in calculating wall areas where perhaps a masonry paint is needed. Check to see whether two full coats are recommended, or whether the first is a thinned coat. Are you covering an existing colour? If so you may need an extra undercoat to obliterate the under-colour. Remember that top coat has not the obliterative power of undercoat. It is merely decorative and protective.

Try to order paint in the biggest batches possible, and see that batch numbers are the same, especially where colours are used. With wallcoverings, it pays to order an extra roll or two if there is any doubt as to how much you really need. Most stores will take back an unopened roll, but few can guarantee to order one more roll with the same batch number! If you have to accept different batches, open the rolls and check for colour and shading. If you find variations you will have to plan to lose the discrepancy in a corner or behind furniture.

Ordering materials

Order your materials well in advance if they are not in stock. We are all very prone to ordering on a Friday, telling the poor shopkeeper we hope to use it next day!

If materials are delivered, check them through before signing the vanman's docket. If it says you have received the materials ordered in good condition and you sign to that effect, you cannot expect the shopkeeper to be sympathetic when you discover that some items are missing.

Apart from the obvious materials like paint and paper, check through your stocks of items like brush cleaner, filler, refills for the blowtorch. These are so often the kind of thing which bring everything to a grinding halt on Saturday evening when all the shops are shut. This is where your record book mentioned earlier would come in useful. A list of tools and materials for any given job would be invaluable. When it is written down you will be amazed just how many items are needed for even the most simple task.

First of the preparatory jobs may involve tackling projects which are best done when it does not matter if you spoil the decoration in the process. Thinking of new windows? It would be that much less of a worry if the room were empty. New doors? A change of decoration could well include a new door. Perhaps a nice panelled front door, or a glass door to the kitchen to let in more light, or a stable-type back door so that the top could be opened during the summer months. Perhaps just pulling off that hardboard panel which covers an attractive panelled interior door. It is not as hard to paint panelled doors as it used to be!

There may also be floor repairs. Damaged or worn boards to turn or replace. Damp or rot to treat, uneven boards to sand smooth. Perhaps you have to re-wire and this can involve lifting floorboards to route new cable. Central heating also involves lifting boards to run pipes under the floor. Perhaps you would like the picture rail down to make the walls look higher. This is a messy job (see chapter 5).

How about a hatch between kitchen and dining area? This involves bashing a hole through the wall—never a clean job at the best of times. Or perhaps you want to put up cove-cornice, which has to be fixed to wall plaster, not wallpaper.

Then again you may be planning to fit wall lights. This will involve channelling the walls, with the resultant mess. Perhaps you have plans to put in a new fireplace; build one in stone, or merely resurrect the existing one now that fuel prices have gone so high. You may like to fit a back boiler to utilise heat from a fire that is in use—or replace an open fire with an enclosed stove. All these jobs may involve more than just moving a new unit in place. There can be cutting, widening and altering, the fitting of a flue liner or the relining of a flue.

Badly damaged ceilings may need cutting away; walls may have loose areas of plaster; there may be structural damp to treat, or cold walls to insulate.

When you really sit down to think about it, actual decorating may seem light years away! But it is far better than seeing someone cutting away the decorations you have just completed.

Preparing the room

Now what sort of work is involved in preparation? let us look at the interior first.

Assuming a room has to be completely decorated, it first needs emptying of furniture as far as is possible. Lift rugs and carpets, underlays and carpet holding strips.

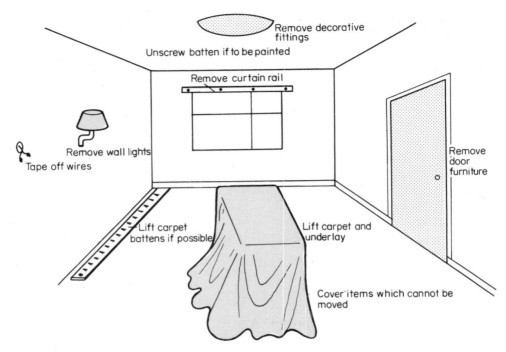

Remove decorative fittings

Unscrew batten if to be painted

Remove curtain rail

Remove wall lights

Tape off wires

Remove door furniture

Lift carpet battens if possible

Lift carpet and underlay

Cover items which cannot be moved

Preparing the room. The more a room can be cleared, the easier will be the job of decorating it

Take down light fittings; disconnect wall lights if possible (having cut off the power at the fuse box or consumer unit first!) Take down curtain rails and remove door furniture. If any furniture has to stay in the room, place it in the centre and cover with dust sheets.

The ceiling

Now have a look at the ceiling. If there is work to be done, cover the floor with newspaper to prevent the floorboards getting dirty and the gaps between them filling with dust.

If the ceiling paper is sound but just dirty and you plan to paint, merely wash the ceiling using warm water to which sugar soap has been added. A roughish cloth, such as an old towel, will do ideally. Rinse with clean water. Check to see that the paper hasn't bubbled up through being wet. If it has, see if it dries out. If not, slit any

bubbles, tear the paper back, paste and press back. Such treatment rarely shows when re-painted.

If there were signs of bubbling; when you apply emulsion paint see that the room is not heated. If the emulsion dries faster than the paper contracts, you can end up with permanent blisters.

If the paper is in poor shape and is pulling away, soak it with water and pull it off. A scraper may be needed to remove stubborn areas, but be careful not to dig the ceiling plaster. Check the ceiling by rubbing wet fingers over the plaster. If your fingers come away white, there is distemper on the ceiling and this probably caused the paper to lose its grip. Use a coarse cloth and plenty of water to rub it off.

If the distemper is really thick, never tackle it dry. It will make a dreadful mess. Wet it thoroughly, then use a scraper to remove it. Hold a dustpan under the scraper to collect the distemper as it falls away. This will save a lot of mess on the floor. Then finish off with your coarse rag and plenty of warm water.

Where a ceiling is paint on plaster, washing down should be sufficient. If it is flaking away, suspect distemper underneath, and treat as already described for the removal of distemper. Where paint is sound, you can apply new paint, or, if you wish, paper over the old paint. Before papering, it is wise to roughen the surface to afford a better key.

It is quite in order to redecorate the ceiling before removing wallpaper from the walls. Dirty splashes or paint splashed on to the walls will come off when the paper is stripped.

The only ceiling decorating job that can be left until later is perhaps tiling. If tiles are left until the room has been decorated,

be sure to paint them before putting them up! Apart from being the simplest method, it will ensure that paint is not splashed on new decoration.

Stripping wallcovering

The wallcovering can come next. Assuming it is to be stripped, soften it with warm water to which has been added some washing-up liquid. This acts as a wetting agent, and it will speed up the stripping process. On thicker papers, the addition of a handful of cellulose wallpaper paste to the stripping water will help. The paste keeps water on the wall where normally it would just run down.

With varnished papers, wipables and washables, you will have to break down the surface so the water can get through. Use a wire brush or an abrasive pad, but

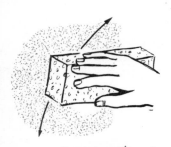
Collect thick distemper in a dustpan

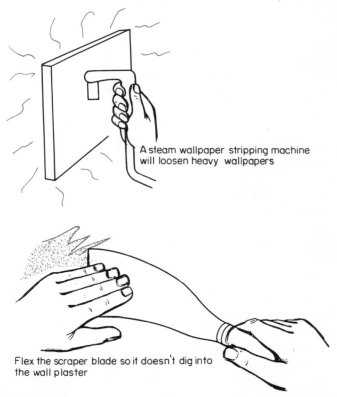
A steam wallpaper stripping machine will loosen heavy wallpapers

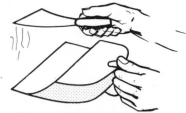
Break down the surface of washable papers to let water soak in

Flex the scraper blade so it doesn't dig into the wall plaster

Some ways of removing wall finishes. Remember that dampened surfaces make far less dust than dry surfaces

Dry scraping

Blowtorch and scraper

Keep a bucket of water handy in which to drop smouldering paint

Chemical stripper and scraper

NO paper on the floor

Three ways of removing paint. Take creat care when using a blowtorch as there is a fire risk

take care not to damage the plaster beneath.

If you encounter a really tough paper, or layers of paper, it is worth hiring a steam wallpaper stripper. This will speed up the job considerably, and paper can be pulled from the wall by the sheet. This process is also ideal where surface plaster is weak and would pull away with the paper. The only snag with a steam stripper is that unless you are very careful you will strip the ceiling as well!

If you are fortunate to find a room where a relatively new wallcovering has been used, you may be lucky. It could be one of the easy-to-strip range. Peel back a corner of one length and see if the patterned surface

will pull away. If it is an easy strip, the whole piece will pull from its backing, leaving a lining sheet behind. This need not be removed as you can decorate over it. Obviously, such papers save an enormous amount of time when it somes to redecorating.

Woodwork

Next, examine the woodwork. If paint is in good condition it may only be necessary to rub it down and re-paint. There is no point in stripping off a good coating, unless it is so thick that it is interfering with the opening of doors or windows. Full details of repainting are given in Chapter 5.

Removing old paint

If the paint is damaged in places, perhaps through items having been knocked against it, you may be able to rub down these areas with fine glasspaper, and dust clean. If there is quite a deep hole, apply undercoat with a fine camel hair brush, keeping it within the confines of the damage. When this is dry, you can apply top coat to bring the surface level with the surrounding area.

Once the repairs are really hard, say after a week, you can flat down the whole area with a pumice stripping block to remove surface gloss; wipe clean and re-paint.

If the damage goes right through to bare wood, it will be necessary to apply primer to the bare patches prior to putting on the undercoat. This seals the wood pores.

Where paint is badly worn, or is flaking away, it will need to be stripped to bare wood. There are three ways you can do this.

Paint scraper. A special sharp bladed scraper will pull paint away from many areas, though care should be taken not to dig into the wood. It is a help when you encounter several coats of paint for, by pulling most of the paint away dry, you will save a little on cost of fuel or chemical stripper. You would be wise to protect your eyes when doing this job as pieces fly off in all directions.

Blowlamp or blowtorch. This is a quick way of removing paint, but it does need a little practice before you can coordinate one hand holding the torch and the other wielding a scraper. The torch must be kept on the move to avoid scorching the wood and the heat should be withdrawn as soon as the paint blisters up. It should not catch fire intentionally. Be sure to hold your scraper at an angle so that very hot paint doesn't drop on to your hand.

A blowtorch and scraper offers an economical way of stripping paint

If you use a chemical stripper, allow ample time for it to soften the paint before scraping

A shave hook will get into the awkward areas like mouldings and decorative beadings

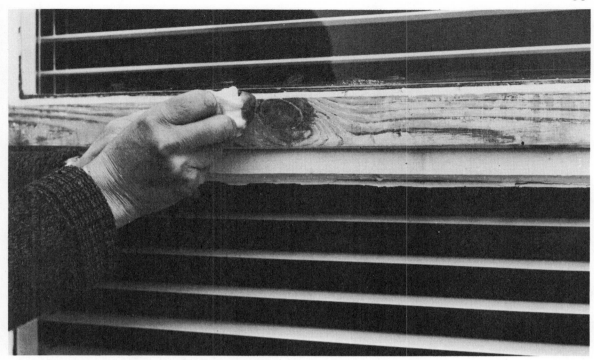

Use patent knotting to seal knots before applying a coat of wood primer

It is a wise precaution to have a bucket of water nearby into which you can drop any burning paint. Never let the paint drop on the floor and never have newspapers down when burning off. Good ventilation is wise too, or the smell of burned paint will hang in the house for days.

When burning off on window frames, never work with curtains in place (and people have!) and do not play the lamp on the glass. You may crack it, and add another job to your list. Be particularly careful when working in sunlight as it makes a bottled gas flame invisible where it is hottest.

Chemical strippers. If you are at all worried about using a blowtorch, a chemical stripper can be used instead. This is designed to break down the paint structure, making it blister and crack. You need to be patient, for where a number of coats of paint are involved, it can take time and will need

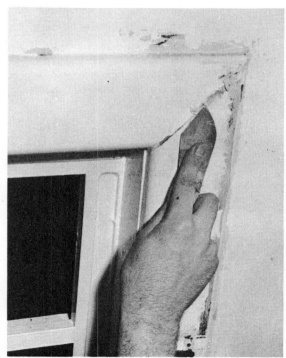

Fill cracks and gaps with putty or with a proprietary filler. Rub smooth when set

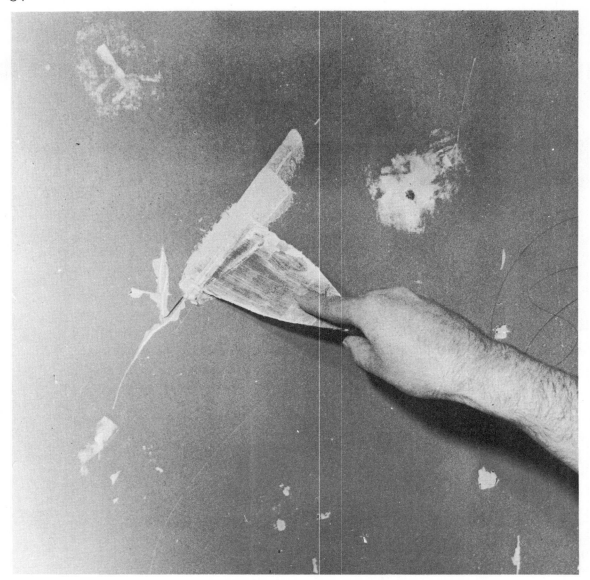

Fill wall cracks with cellulose filler. Take proud of the surface then rub smooth when hard

more than one coat to really soften the paint. Do not try to strip the paint until it is soft enough to be scraped away. You will merely waste the stripper.

Once soft, use a shave hook and scraper to remove the paint down to bare wood. For difficult areas, wear a rubber glove and use wire wool to rub the area, always working with the wood grain. When applying stripper with a brush, it is also wise to wear protective glasses. If you should get stripper in your eye, wash it with plenty of water as soon as possible.

The instructions on the container will give advice on neutralising any stripper left on the wood after stripping. In some cases it may mean a rinse with clean water, after which the wood is left to dry. Then it can be rubbed smooth with fine glass-paper working with the wood grain, and the surface is ready for filling and priming.

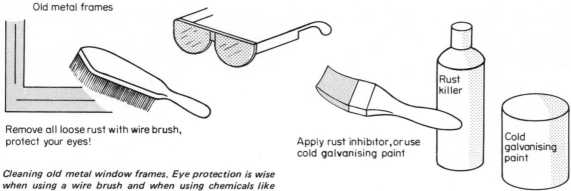

Old metal frames

Remove all loose rust with wire brush, protect your eyes!

Apply rust inhibitor, or use cold galvanising paint

Rust killer

Cold galvanising paint

Cleaning old metal window frames. Eye protection is wise when using a wire brush and when using chemicals like rust killer

Cracks in woodwork

Cracks and gaps in timber must be filled prior to painting, for paint cannot be expected to hide them. While ordinary cellulose filler can be used, it is far better to use a more durable material such as fine surface filler or wood stopping. This must be pressed well into cracks, left to set, then rubbed smooth. Where damp may be encountered, such as on a window sill where condensation may gather, fill with a waterproof wood stopping. Ordinary cellulose filler would dissolve in moisture.

Where knots are encountered, coat them with patent knotting to seal the resin in the knot. If this is not done the knot may bleed at some later date, and the resin

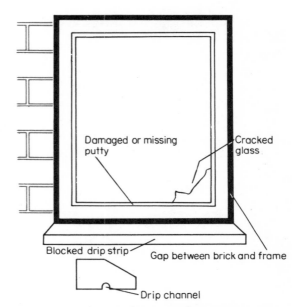

Damaged or missing putty

Cracked glass

Blocked drip strip

Gap between brick and frame

Drip channel

Points where damp may get in around a window frame. Use mastic for sealing gaps as in previous illustration

Mastics for gaps and cracks

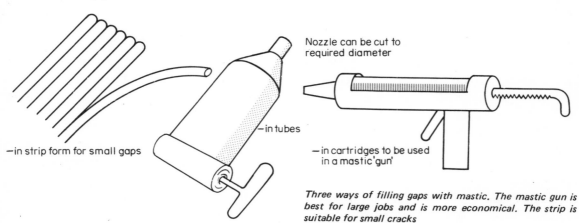

—in strip form for small gaps

—in tubes

Nozzle can be cut to required diameter

—in cartridges to be used in a mastic 'gun'

Three ways of filling gaps with mastic. The mastic gun is best for large jobs and is more economical. The strip is suitable for small cracks

will push its way through your paint coating. This applies particularly to areas of paintwork exposed to the heat of the sun.

If you encounter soft areas of wood (the effects of wet rot) you need to cut out the damaged wood then build up with new wood. If the area is only small, a repair filler may be used. Take the filler a little proud of the surrounding area, then sand it to shape when hard.

Metal window frames

With old metal window frames, look for signs of rust. Rusted areas must be rubbed free of all loose scale then treated with a rust killing liquid prior to repainting. Make sure that *all* rust is removed, even if it means scraping off an area of seemingly sound paint. Hidden rust may well start up a new attack.

Modern metal frames will be heavily galvanised and should not rust, In my opinion, however, galvanising is very often not a very stable base for paint, and you may find paint peeling away from it. All flaking paint must be stripped to bare frame, then you need to prime and under-coat the galvanised surface.

Where paint is sound on metal frames, leave it there. Merely use the pumice block to remove the gloss from the paint, and re-paint.

Window furniture often looks a mess, mainly because most people try to paint this in place. For best results, remove window stays and handles and decorate them separately. With many metal frames, it is not possible to remove handles—in which case you need to mask the sur-rounding area while you do the best you can. Leave the window furniture as long as possible before closing windows, or you will find all your new paint has been rubbed away by friction against the frame.

Smoothing-down plaster walls

Plaster walls need to be examined for flaws. Bulging areas which give a hollow sound may need to be cut away and re-plastered. The same goes for areas of crumbling plaster. Cellulose filler can be used to fill minor gaps and cracks, but for larger areas, a material such as Keene's cement is more economical. It is fairly fast drying, so do not mix too much at a time. If holes are quite deep, build layer upon layer, scratching the surface of each layer to afford a key for the next. If you try to fill in one go, you will find the filler slumps out of the hole.

Remember not to fill plugged holes if that is where fittings go! It is a good idea to push a matchstick in such holes so that when you re-paper, the matchstick will push through the paper. Otherwise you may find it very difficult to find the holes again.

Full details of repair work can be found in the companion book in this series *'Home Repair and Maintenance'*, which deals solely with repair work.

Exterior preparation

Now let us move to the exterior of the house. Obviously we will be looking for similar problems on exterior joinery as were encountered indoors, but the exterior is more prone to damage due to exposure to the weather.

Where paintwork is sound, leave it alone and merely rub down with a stripping block to remove grime and to take the gloss from the paint surface. If you are keeping to the same colour, you could apply two coats of new exterior gloss over the prepared old coat, but if you are changing colour, always use an undercoat to obliterate the old colour. A top coat is relatively thin and it has little obliterative power.

Where paintwork is chipped, the treatment described for interior paintwork can be carried out. Make sure to prime any bare patches of wood prior to undercoating.

Badly damaged paint must be stripped away to bare wood, and cracks and gaps in the wood filled with waterproof stopping or fine surface filler. Sills made of oak present a particular problem, for the open grain of oak makes it hard to fill. Air trapped in the wood grain tends to expand in the heat of the sun, and this will push off a paint coating however well applied the paint may be. Some people overcome this by leaving the oak unpainted and treating it with a clear or pigmented preservative. Alternatively you can paint it with a clear exterior grade varnish.

If you really wish to paint the oak to match the rest of the house, strip it clean, then rub fine surface filler deep into the grain with a piece of lint-free rag. Rub over the whole wood surface, then when set, rub it smooth with fine glasspaper, working only with the wood grain. You can then prime and undercoat as normal.

Outside windows and doors

Metal frames need the same kind of examination as we gave internally, paying particular attention to areas of rust. If this creeps under the glass, the pressure is sufficient to crack a pane of glass. This is very often the explanation for mysterious cracks which seem to appear without reason.

Look for loose or cracking putty on frames, and be ruthless. Dig it out; clean the area and prime the bare wood before putting in new putty. Make sure there is a seal between glass and putty, for this is where water creeps in, rotting the frame beneath. On metal frames damaged putty must be replaced by special metal case-ment putty. Ordinary putty does not set, as the oil cannot soak in as with timber frames.

The same examination applies to glazed doors, for a bad seal between glass and putty or beadings will allow water into the door, causing wet rot. If it is not checked, you will soon need a new door, or some pretty extensive repairs. If the glass in the door is fluted or otherwise textured, make sure that the flutes are on the inside. If they are outside, this may result in a bad seal between glass and door.

Look for cracks around window and door frames. This is quite a common fault due to slight shrinkage of timber frames. These cracks should be filled with a flexible mastic; never use putty or cement mortar. The latter set hard and you soon have a new crack appear. A mastic remains flexible throughout its life, even if it does dry on the surface.

Pipes and gutters

Check the rainwater gutters for signs of damage. Down pipes give little trouble as they do not hold water, but gutters can rust and rot away if neglected. An accumulation of debris in the gutter may trap water, adding to the problem, so the first job is to clean out gutters, flush through with water, then examine for damage. Dead leaves are particularly troublesome if left.

Rusted areas should be wirebrushed to remove scale, then treated with a rust killer. Holes can be filled with bituminous mastic applied with a trowel, or with one of the epoxy repair materials. Be sure to make the inside of the gutter smooth, otherwise the projection may trap debris.

Where gutters are in poor shape, it may be wise to remove them and replace with plastic ones. You will need help to lift down the metal ones, but you may be able to manage the lightweight plastic gutters on your own.

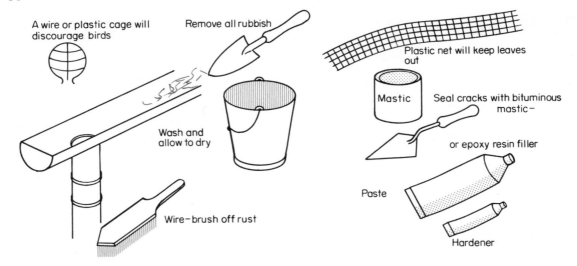

A wire or plastic cage will discourage birds

Remove all rubbish

Wash and allow to dry

Wire-brush off rust

Plastic net will keep leaves out

Mastic

Seal cracks with bituminous mastic –

or epoxy resin filler

Paste

Hardener

Cleaning gutters. Regular maintenance of gutters, to remove rubbish and treat rust, is advisable. It is sensible to do this job after the leaves have fallen

Outside walls

Walls need examining for faults prior to decorating. The most a decorative brick needs is a thorough wash with clean water. Do not be tempted to add chemicals or detergents to the water as you may end up with a whitish residue which is difficult to remove. If the bricks are grubby, find a piece of brick of the same type and colour, and use this as a pumice block. A brisk rub, plus an application of clean water can do wonders.

Examine the pointing between bricks. If it is loose and crumbling, dig it out to a depth of 12 mm (½ in) and re-point with a dryish mortar mix. A wet mix will slop on to your brickwork and then be very hard to clean off.

To make decorative bricks stand out, you can use white cement for the pointing mortar. This merely adds more contrast in colour between pointing and brickwork.

Walls rendered with cement will need a thorough wash down to remove grime, plus a rub with a coarse floor scrubbing brush to loosen persistent dirt. Areas of mould should be treated with a fungicide, for if the mould is not killed off, it could discolour any new paint you apply. Holes and cracks should be filled with a mortar mix. Do not rely on a new coat of paint to hide cracks, masonry paint will cover fine hair cracks, but no more.

Pebble dash and spar dash can present problems if the surface is crumbling or if areas are bulging away from the wall. Loose material is best brushed away with a stiff brush, and hollow areas need cutting out and rebuilding, using a mortar mix to which some pva adhesive has been added to improve adhesion. Keep the stones that are taken off, as these will give the best match when doing repairs.

If you have to buy new stones, try to mix in some darker ones so the repaired areas are not too obvious. Stones are best thrown on to a wet mortar surface, using a coal shovel. You need sacking or polythene sheeting at the base to catch any stones which do not stick first time.

Painted walls may need a thorough wash down to remove grime, using a scrubbing brush to loosen obstinate dirt. Once clean, cracks can be filled with mortar mix.

Cladding

Many homes now have an area of cladding as part of the exterior decoration. This may be of timber, either painted or treated with preservative, or it may be of plastic and, in a few cases, aluminium. Timber needs examining and treating as for any other timber surface, filling cracks and gaps with a waterproof stopping. If the wood is stained and sealed, choose a stopping which matches in colour. For painted work, any colour will 'of course' do.

Plastic cladding needs little attention apart from a thorough wash with water and detergent or household cleaner. Do not use abrasive materials, or let dirty water run down the decorative brickwork. This leaves the whitish stains mentioned earlier.

Exterior repairs

Obviously, this is also the time for effecting any exterior repairs which need attention. In fact any of those jobs which, if left until later, could spoil new decorations.

Amongst the jobs may be replacing damaged slates or tiles, dealing with faulty damp proof courses, fitting an extractor fan through the wall, cleaning glass or plastic roofing to outhouses or extensions, removing damaged trellis, cutting back climbing plants, on building a porch to the back door.

Chapter 5
Paintwork

Having looked at the tools, materials and general preparation necessary for decorating, let us consider the more exciting aspect —actually applying our new finishes. We will start indoors.

There is no general rule as to which comes first, walls or woodwork. The author's preference is that if walls are to be papered, do all the paintwork first, taking the paint just on to the walls so that if there are any slight gaps where paper does not meet wood, no wall will show through. If walls are to be painted, it may be preferable to do these first followed by the woodwork, having primed all the wood prior to painting walls. The reason is that it is harder to control large brushes than small, so there is more chance of wall paint straying on to woodwork.

Painting walls

So, let us start with the walls. Assuming they are clean, dry and filled where necessary—is the plaster smooth enough to take a coat of paint? If there are irregularities, the paint could highlight them, making the job look very cheap.

Assuming the wall plaster is good, what paint should we use? An oil-based gloss paint can be used, but it must be preceded by a plaster primer and preferably an undercoat. Once applied, it would be durable, but a high gloss does tend to highlight faults in the surface, and as the paint is an impervious coating, it can encourage condensation if walls are on the cold side.

Then there is the problem of brush or roller cleaning, using some form of proprietary cleaner. As I mentioned earlier, some cleaners affect pads and some others may affect paint rollers.

There are enough discouragements here to rule out the use of gloss paints in favour of one of the more easy to handle emulsion coatings. Apart from the standard emulsion paint with which we are all familiar, you could use a water-based acrylic gloss if you wanted more sheen, or a vinyl for real durability. No special undercoat is required, and painting tools can be cleaned in water. Check to see whether you use plain water or whether detergent needs to be added to the cleaning water. This information should appear on the can.

If the wall is bare plaster, make up a dilute coat of emulsion, half paint and half water, and prime the wall with this. If it has been previously painted, the priming is not necessary.

Now to choice of tools. A wide paint brush, preferably 127 mm, (5 in) is the traditional tool, and it gives a good finish once you have mastered its use. Only dip a third of the depth of bristle in the paint; do not overload the brush or it will drip. Starting at the top of one wall, nearest the corner, apply paint in vertical strokes, then brush out horizontally, and finally stroke off vertically again, spreading the paint as far as it will go without skimping. Try not to cover too large an area, imagine the wall divided into squares, and do one at a time.

Work down the wall, but if there are signs that the paint is drying quickly, extend your work a little sideways as well so that you keep all edges 'wet'. This is to avoid join marks between sections. For ease of working, keep the room temperature low so that drying is prolonged. You will still find your first coat is touch-dry in about 20 minutes. If you find it hard to work a large brush into corners, keep a smaller brush handy for touching in.

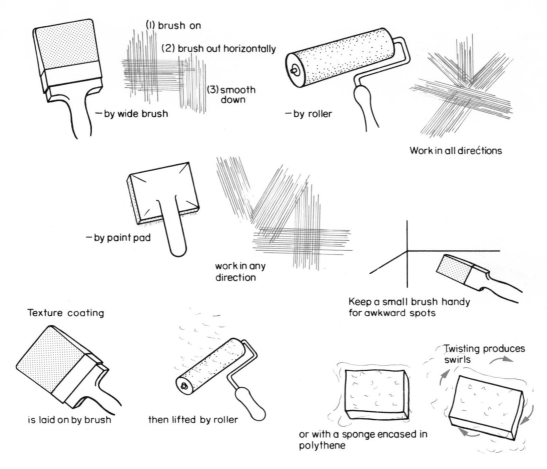

(1) brush on

(2) brush out horizontally

(3) smooth down

—by wide brush

—by roller

Work in all directions

—by paint pad

work in any direction

Keep a small brush handy for awkward spots

Texture coating

is laid on by brush

then lifted by roller

or with a sponge encased in polythene

Twisting produces swirls

If you are not happy with a brush, you can use a roller. For a plaster wall it is preferable to choose a short pile lambswool or nylon roller, but you could use a foam one.

Roller technique is entirely different from using a brush. You merely work out from a point, and it does not matter much in which direction you roll as long as you cover every part of the wall. Again it is important to keep edges wet so that no joins show, but as working with a roller is faster than brush work, this is not such a problem. Make sure you do not over-charge the roller, and do not spin it too rapidly or paint will be thrown off.

If your paint does not cover well in one coat, do not try to put the paint on thicker. Be content to apply a thinner coat, then

The three basic tools for wall painting are seen here. Brush, paint roller and paint pad. Note especially the different painting methods for brush and roller application

put another over the top when the first is dry.

Alternatively, you may care to experiment with a paint pad, which I have used almost exclusively for walls over very many years. Again the technique is different. The direction of stroke really does not matter as long as all your sections overlap. Using a large pad, you can work quite fast, with little fear of drips or splashes. Do not overcharge a pad, or paint may squeeze out of the foam backing. You may find it easier to finish in corners with a small paintbrush, but a little experimenting will soon show you how best to work.

When the first coat is dry, check to see there are no bits of dust spoiling the surface, and check also that you have not missed any patches of wall. If you paint at night, it pays to save the second coat until daylight. You will be amazed what so often shows up.

Dealing with rough walls

So far we have dealt with a smooth wall, but what if the surface is rather irregular—perhaps due to rather poor plastering? Unfortunately a coat of paint tends to highlight such faults, so it would be wise to disguise the fault by adding a new texture. The Anaglypta range of papers has some interesting effects, ranging from a simple plaster daub through to quite intricate basket weave patterns. You can read how to hang this material in Chapter 6.

With an Anaglypta paper in place, you can emulsion coat as for a plaster wall, using any of the tools already mentioned. A couple of coats of paint is advisable, however well it seems to cover, to ensure that you get into all the surface texture.

Some of the patterned effects are also available as coloured wallpaper, so it is possible to combine paper and paint to good effect.

In a cottage setting, you may prefer to amplify an irregular wall surface to make a real feature of it. In which case there is a special texturing compound which is applied to the wall as a thick plastic coating. It may then be patterned by running a roller over it or by pulling up the surface with a sponge covered in polythene. With a little practice, some interesting daub patterns can be reproduced, after which the material sets hard.

The best tool to paint such a surface is a long pile lambswool or nylon roller. A foam roller would be damaged, and pads will not get into the deep texture. The brush could be used if handled with a dabbing motion rather than the usual painting strokes.

Painting woodwork

Now let us look at the woodwork. Assuming that it is in a good state of repair, and that all cracks and gaps have been filled as recommended in Chapter 4, work to be painted should be given a final smoothing over with fine glasspaper. Dust off carefully and apply your tack rag to gather up any remaining bits.

Bare wood must be primed with primer, and this should be worked well into the wood grain. A thick coating is not necessary as long as the wood is completely covered. This clogs the pores of the wood so that subsequent coats do not soak into the surface. It also acts as a key for the undercoat.

When the primer is dry, check to see if there are any nibs in the surface. If there are, give only the lightest rub with fine glasspaper, rub too hard, and you will be back to bare wood! Dust off, and the surface is ready for undercoat.

The purpose of the undercoat is to add body to the surface and to obliterate any under-colour. If a medium coat of undercoat does not hide an under-colour, you must apply another when the first is dry. Do not rely on a top coat to hide anything.

A top coat is purely protective, and most gloss paints are quite thin, with little real covering power. Before it is applied, give the undercoat a light rub over to remove any nibs, dust off, use the tack rag, then the surface is ready for its next coat.

The tool most likely to be used here is the standard paint-brush, and you should choose a width to suit the job in hand. For frame work, the 12 mm (½ in) will get more use, backed by the 25 mm (1 in) for wider sections. Switch to the 50 mm (2 in)

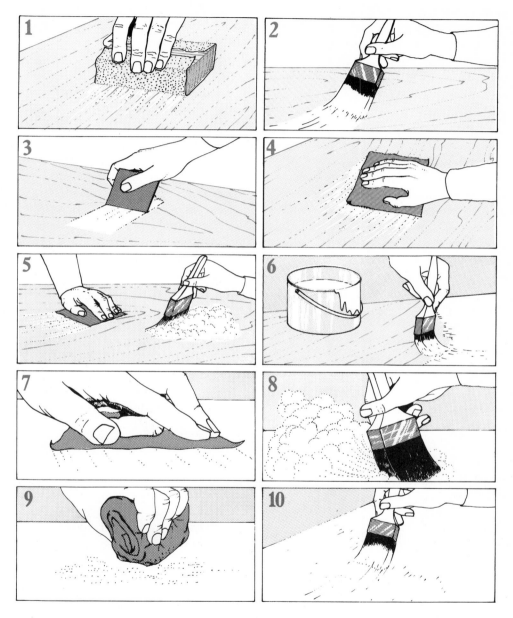

for window ledges, and back to the 12 mm (½ in) for edges. As a general rule, work with brush strokes in the direction of the wood grain, or along the length of the wood. Try to ensure that an adequate layer of paint is deposited on edges where, unless you watch it, the brush tends to wipe paint off.

Steps in painting a timber surface: 1, rub smooth, working with the wood grain. 2, apply patent knotting to wood knots. 3, work filler into cracks and gaps. 4, when set, rub smooth. 5, then dust off with a dusting brush or lint-free rag. 6, apply wood primer, then undercoat. 7, lightly sand to remove any nibs. 8, use the dusting brush to clean the surface. 9, then pick up any remaining dust on a tacky rag. 10, apply your top coat

Avoid overloading your brush, particularly when dealing with mouldings. Paint may gather and run down to form tears which will spoil the general appearance of your work. The same rule applies for larger panels, for too much paint may form sags and runs. It is far better to apply two thin coats than one heavy one.

The only exception to this rule is when using the thixotropic or jelly paints. Often referred to as 'one-coat paints', these combine undercoat and top coat in a jelly-like consistency which should not be over-stirred. The effect of dipping in the brush is to liquefy the paint, after which it starts to 'gel' again. When applied to the wood, it is laid on rather than brushed out, so you get a much thicker coating than with standard paint. Despite the name 'one-coat', when changing colour, particularly from dark to light, you may well need two coats to cover adequately.

The order of painting window frames and doors is purely a matter of convenience and common sense. While the illustrations show suggested orders, do not feel bound by regulations!

Gloss paint is still widely used for internal woodwork, but there is a trend towards using acrylic gloss finishes as an alternative. True you do not get a very high gloss—but is it really necessary anyway? A high gloss will highlight any faults in joinery and it can make a job look cheap.

A nice sheen makes an attractive alternative, and you have the benefits of fast drying and ease of brush cleaning. For those who suffer from chest troubles, there is the added bonus that you do not get the smell as with gloss paints. In other words, you are using glossy emulsion paint.

A suggested order for painting doors and windows. Always brush out along the length of each panel

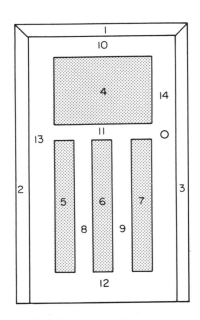

Painting a panelled door

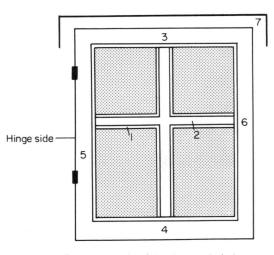

The handle side of the door and window is done last

Painting metalwork

Painting metal differs little from timber once the preparation is done except, perhaps, that you have no grain to follow. Edges are even more important on metal frames as they will be thinner and that much harder to paint. Again, be careful not to overload a surface or you will end up with runs.

Radiators present little problem. Most come ready-primed, and once you have removed any grease from plumbing work, plus the inevitable grubby finger marks using turps substitute, you can apply gloss coat. If you have chosen a strong colour, then an undercoat may be advisable just to give depth to the colour.

Copper pipes can be painted without priming as long as they are free from grease and dirt. It is not wise to paint over compression fitting nuts as it makes them hard to undo should it be necessary to remove the radiator.

Cove cornice

If you have put up new gypsum cove cornice as part of the redecorating, seal the surface with plaster primer prior to painting. The choice is yours as to whether the cove is painted to match the walls or the ceiling.

Gutters and pipes

Moving outside, the same basic principles apply as for interior painting, except that more care is needed to ensure that all surfaces exposed to the elements are well protected. One unfilled crack may be all that is needed for damp to get behind your defences and push protective coatings off from behind, so careful preparation is essential.

For exterior painting, start at gutter level, and work down. To reach this level you need a ladder which will take you three rungs above gutter level. This is so that there is always a hand-hold when working from the ladder. It is highly dangerous to adjust the ladder below the gutter then reach up, for the gutter should never be used as a support. This is particularly so with plastic guttering.

Make sure the ladder is standing on a secure base, and place a sandbag over the feet of the ladder to prevent slipping. Alternatively lash a rope around any nearby downpipe to the base of the ladder. To prevent sliding at the top, it is wise to anchor the top by means of a ring bolt in the fascia board through which nylon cord can be passed, then secured to the ladder. This is even more advisable with plastic guttering as its surface is very smooth. Do not worry about a ladder resting on plastic guttering, the plastic is quite able to take the strain.

The gutter brackets are normally screwed into a fascia board, and this needs to be painted. Ideally, remove the guttering so you can get at it. This is easy with plastic units, but with heavy cast iron sections, you will have to do the best you can. As with all timber, bare patches must be primed before undercoating and top coating. Two top coats are advisable. Try not to overload your brushes or you will get drips on to the brickwork.

Holding your paint at this height is always a problem, and a paint kettle will prove useful if used in conjunction with an S-hook looped over a suitable rung. Alternatively you can buy a simple ladder tray which, when hooked over the rungs of the ladder, forms a platform for paint and spare brushes. It is never advisable to hold a can of paint in your hand while painting with the other. Always keep one hand for the ladder!

With the gutter cleaned and repaired, make sure it is dry inside before painting. At this level you have the opportunity to

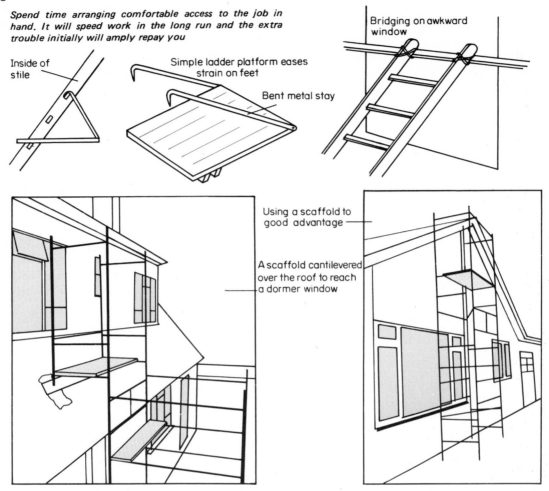

Spend time arranging comfortable access to the job in hand. It will speed work in the long run and the extra trouble initially will amply repay you

Inside of stile

Simple ladder platform eases strain on feet

Bent metal stay

Bridging on awkward window

Using a scaffold to good advantage

A scaffold cantilevered over the roof to reach a dormer window

use up any left-overs of good quality exterior gloss paint for the inside of the gutter. No one will see it up there—except the birds. If a heavy bituminous paint has been used previously, use the same again. Unfortunately bitumen will bleed through other paint coatings unless it is isolated by an aluminium sealer.

When changing colour, remember it is the undercoat which must hide the under-colour. Two or more coats if necessary. Finish with two coats of gloss.

Down-pipes get similar treatment. It is wise to hold a piece of card behind the pipe you are painting so you do not get paint on the brickwork.

Window frames

Next on the list are the upstairs windows. Here the problem is to use a ladder without resting it on the glass. It is often possible to lash a piece of wood across the top of the ladder so the wood rests either side of the frame, holding the ladder clear. Better still is to use two ladders with supports called 'cripples', on to which a stout scaffold board can be rested. This gives you a working platform along which you can move as necessary. If you are unused to working at heights, a scaffold pole fixed as a rail will discourage you from stepping back to admire your work!

An even better arrangement is a scaffold tower of the type developed for home use. This is easily erected from tubular sections, and it provides a safe working platform with safety rail all round. What you need is a hard, level area upon which to erect the scaffold; a wide path or patio would be suitable. If the tower can be moved along on wheels as supplied on some types so much the better.

Such a tower is fairly expensive, but often a group of neighbours will share the cost. If you prefer, you can hire one from a local hire shop. In this case plan your work so that you do not keep it longer than you need. Incidentally the tubular units can be utilised for interior work too, such as on stairs or to reach a high ceiling. You can make up a temporary bench, pasting table or trestle, while one outfit converts into a car port or garden shed by the addition of roof pieces and a stout plastic cover.

The actual painting of window frames is the same as for internal painting. If you wish to close your windows at the end of the day, start by painting those surfaces which have to meet when the windows are shut. If there is some doubt as to how dry the paint is, sandwich clean polythene between window and frame, and do not shut windows tight. Take your paint on to the putty of the window frames, extending it just fractionally on to the glass. This is to seal any fine gap between putty and glass where driving rain so often gets in. Paint the underside of the sills, and the ends. Ensure that there is a clear drip strip under the sill. This is usually a groove cut in the underside of the sill, and it is designed to force water to drip off rather than be carried over to the brickwork.

If the groove is clogged by too many old coats of paint, scrape it clean, prime and re-paint.

Never leave any bare wood or metal unprotected at the end of a day. At the very least put on a good priming coat to keep out damp. Do not be tempted to paint over damp wood; to seal the damp in will only encourage rot. If you must paint, a blowtorch will speed things up, but you must keep it on the move all the time to avoid scorching the wood.

Downstairs windows get the same basic treatment, except that a pair of well splayed steps will be far easier to work from than even a small section of ladder. Spend time establishing a firm, level base for the steps. Never take chances. If you are not happy even at these heights, it pays to invest in steps which have an extended hand rail so there is always something to grip. As with a ladder, never lean over to reach your work, always move the steps.

Door and door frames

Door frames are treated as for window frames. Treat the door as a separate unit, and paint it well. A suggested sequence for painting is shown in the illustration.

Timber garage doors can receive similar treatment, but metal doors are best painted with a polyurethane-based paint which is much tougher than normal paint. Because it dries hard, check the instructions on the can as to the time lapse between coats. If it is left too long to harden, subsequent coats will not bond to the undercoat.

Types of paint

One final word. At the time of writing, acrylic gloss has not been widely tried for exterior use, though at least one company markets it for this purpose. It has the advantage of quick drying; a real asset during winter months.

For full details of wall painting, including other types of paint suitable for exterior use, see Chapter 7.

Chapter 6
Interior walls

Careful preparation of the walls is necessary, as detailed in Chapter 4, before any form of new decoration is applied. It is assumed that any defects causing damp will have been dealt with. Painting of walls is described in detail in Chapter 5, so in this chapter we will deal principally with other forms of wall decoration.

Before the walls are tackled, all paintwork adjoining the walls—such as door frames, picture rails and skirting boards and window frames will have been done.

Insulation

The next consideration is whether a cold wall needs some insulation to reduce the risk of condensation. Only the external walls need be worried about, for internal partitions will not normally get very cold.

If you plan to treat a wall, measure up and buy sufficient expanded polystyrene wall veneer to cover it. At the same time, buy the special adhesive needed to fix it; preferably a rubberised or pva adhesive. You will see that the veneer is of different width to a standard roll of wallcovering so you will not get any matching of seams.

Apply adhesive to the wall surface, cut your veneer slightly oversize and press it on to the adhesive. A paint roller is a useful tool for pressing it in place. Note that if you apply too much hand pressure you will compress the veneer. Now paste the next wall area and apply a further length of

For smoothing textured papers

Paste

Size

Trough for pre-pasteds

Tools for papering

Tools you will need for papering. No paste, brush or pasting table needed with pre-pasted wall-coverings

veneer. If the edges of the wall veneer are true you can merely butt one piece of veneer to the next. If you encounter irregularities, it pays to overlap the second piece a fraction over the first, then cut through both with a sharp craft knife, using a straight-edge. Peel away the surplus pieces, and you will have a neat butt joint between both pieces.

Carry on until the whole wall has been covered, making sure all edges are well down. Trim off any surplus top and bottom, and the wall is ready for decorating. The remaining walls should be sized.

Wallpapering

Let us look at standard wallpapering first. For this you will need your pasting table and all the tools illustrated.

Assuming you choose a good medium weight paper, you need a paste with plenty of body and not too much water content. Bear in mind that you need to allow time for the paper to expand before you hang it. Once you become a little experienced at handling the paste brush, you will find you can paste one length of paper, fold it, put it aside and paste a further piece while the first is soaking. This way you will avoid bubbles.

Start work at a window wall, and measure the width of your paper is less about 12 mm (½ in) and make a mark on the wall. This will force 12 mm of paper around the corner, and the idea of this is to allow for any inaccuracy in the corner. Now hold your bob so that it hangs over the pencil mark you made on the wall, and make a further pencil mark. This ensures that you will be hanging the first piece to a true vertical. Never rely on the corner being true, for any error encountered here would by duplicated all along the run of the wall.

Now hold your paper to the wall and decide where you want the pattern to start. Make a fine mark and allow 40 mm (1¾ in) or so extra for trimming. Now measure your length and allow a further 40 mm at the base for trimming. Cut the length with scissors.

Lay the piece on the pasting table with the top to your right and pattern down. The top of the piece will at this point be on the floor. Apply paste, herringbone fashion, working from the centre out, making sure you cover every spot.

When all the paper on the table has been coated, pull the paper to the left and make a fold, pasted surface to pasted surface, then allow the fold to move to the left until all the unpasted paper is on the table. Finish pasting the length and allow it to soak. You can fold the top in at this stage and move the paper while you clean your table ready for the next piece. Never allow the paste to dry on the table.

Now move to the wall, release the top fold, and offer your right hand to the wall so that paper edge lines up with the pencil marks. Press the paper lightly to the wall with your right hand—still holding the left hand well away from the wall, then use your right hand to ensure the paper lines up with the pencil marks. Allow your left hand to take the rest of the paper to the wall, then use the smoothing brush down the centre of the paper to press the paper to the wall.

Work outwards from this point, then press the top against the picture rail and the bottom against the skirting board. Use your closed scissors to make the paper into the crease, pull the paper away and trim it top and bottom, allowing 3 mm (1/8 in) the crease so that paper just turns. This will hide any crack there may·be at rail or skirting level.

Push the paper back to the wall, and ease the surplus round to the adjoining wall. Press it into the corner with the brush.

The plumb bob and line ensures that the first piece on the wall is truly vertical

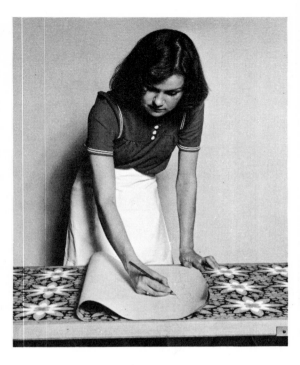

If it is not clear from the pattern, mark which is the top of the length

With one piece cut to length, match and cut two or three more lengths, again marking the tops

Paste from the centre out, herringbone fashion, making sure you do not miss any patches

Check to see the edges are down and that you have no bubbles, and that the first piece is in place.

Offer the roll to the first hung piece and note where the pattern match comes. If you are going to waste a fair piece of paper in matching, put that roll down and try some of the others. By using different rolls, it is often possible to cut waste quite dramatically which, in the long term, may save cutting into a new roll of paper. Hold your match in place, then mark top and bottom, with the spare 40 mm (1¾ in), top and bottom for trimming. Cut your length, paste, fold and allow to soak.

Obviously, if the pattern fits well into the room height, it may be possible to cut three or four pieces at a time. But if you have any problems with matching, it is still best to match one at a time, working from whichever rolls offer the best economy.

Carry your new piece to the wall, but

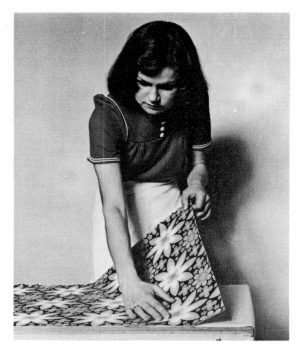

Fold the pasted area in, paste to paste, wipe the table and pull the remaining paper in place

Fold in again and leave the length to soak. When hanging, the smaller fold will be released

Position the paper and smooth out from the centre, just enough to hold the length in place. Release the lower fold

Use a brush to smooth the length in place, making sure no air is trapped underneath

Crease the paper into the skirting board and picture rail and trim off with scissors. Wipe off excess paste

this time it is the left hand which contacts the wall first, matching the pattern to the previous piece and easing the paper close to the first. With the paper in place, run the brush down the centre and out towards the far edge of the paper. Make sure that the seams match without pressing too tight, and if there are problems, pull the length away and try again. Do not try to force the paper into place, for at best you will stretch it and at worst tear it.

With the length in place, trim as before and wipe away any surplus paste. It is far harder to remove once it becomes dry.

Papering continues in this manner until some obstruction is encountered. If it is a further window, you need to do some careful measuring so that you can cut out any surplus piece, allowing at least 25 mm (1 in) over-size for trimming. Pasting will not be quite so easy as for a whole sheet, and you must be sure to wipe surplus

Slide the next piece in place so the pattern matches perfectly before pressing the paper down

A seam roller will ensure edges are pressed down. Don't press too hard on textured papers

Mark around obstructions with a light pencil mark. Don't press too hard

Cut out surplus allowing a few mm to turn on to the painted surface

paste from the table before pulling new paper into place.

When the piece is in place, press surplus paper into the edges of the frame as you did for the rail and skirting, and trim as before, allowing for a 3 mm (1/8) turn.

Light switches present another hazard which you will soon learn to deal with. Paste the paper as normal, hang it as for a flat wall, but do not press it tight down. Find the centre of the switch plate and, using your fine scissors, make a cut from the centre out. If the switch is a modern square one, cut towards each corner, but stop just short of the corner. If you encounter an older round switch plate, make star cuts all the way round as illustrated.

With a square plate, cut away surplus paper to within 6 mm (¼ in) of the edges of the plate, then loosen the holding screws enough to allow the surplus of

Wipe off surplus paste, then press the piece into place. Ensure no air is trapped

Finally smooth into place with the brush. Ensure all paste is removed from paintwork

paper to go behind the plate. Finish pressing down the paper, then use a lolly stick to ease the paper behind. A knife blade is unwise unless you have the power switched off!

With the round plate, you will have to press the edges of your star against the plate, make a crease, then trim off the surplus paper less a 3 mm (1/8 in) turn on to the plate. It sounds a complicated business, but once you have done one, it comes quite easily on any others you encounter.

Should you meet any bulges or other irregularities which prevent the paper laying properly, tear the paper over the difficult area, then press it back in place. This sounds drastic, but it gives a far more disguised repair than cutting with scissors. Never try to cut wet paper with a knife, however sharp; you will inevitably tear the paper.

On internal corners, it may be simplest to go right into the corner to cover the paper turn off the adjoining wall. The only exception is where the corner is really true and you can get a perfect match. Wherever you encounter external corners, it is wise to cut your paper width so that it turns about 25 mm (1 in) then join on the cut piece once you are round the corner. If angles are perfect, you may get a whole width to turn, but where there are inaccuracies in the plastering, you can end up with big problems where even tearing may not help much.

Ready-pasteds

One great advance in decorating in recent years has been the introduction of pre-pasted wallcoverings, where the adhesive comes as a dry layer on the back of the covering. With the rolls you get a special waxed trough, supplied as a flat sheet, but pre-creased so that it very easily converts into a strong water container.

The great advantage here, of course, is that no pasting table, bucket of paste or brush is required. The trough is filled about three-quarters full of cold water, then the wallcovering is cut as normal with spare at each end for final trimming. Roll the length loosely from the bottom with the pattern inwards. To activate the paste, press the loose-rolled length down into the water ensuring the back of the paper is completely wetted. Then slowly pull the length from the trough, allowing surplus water to drain back into the container. The trough should be positioned close to the wall, immediately below the area to be covered.

You may find a surplus of paste on the back of the piece, for the problem the manufacturers have is to supply sufficient paste for any situation. On a highly porous plaster you need far more paste than on a previously painted wall. The surplus is no real problem. Merely ease it out of the joints and wipe it clear with a sponge. The covering is positioned as for any other system, then smoothed down with a sponge.

The only trouble you may encounter is if you have to overlap a piece of vinyl wallcovering over another length. The paste supplied does not grip very well on vinyl and the surfaces may curl away from each other. In this case, let the vinyl dry, then put down the seams using a latex adhesive. This is clean to use, it will not stain, and any surplus can be rubbed off.

Specialist coverings

When buying special materials, like grass cloths, ask if there are any special points to watch. Are special adhesives required? Are the lengths and widths of rolls the same as for papers? Do pieces have to be trimmed? Will they match? A few tips are given below.

Flocks. These are now available in vinyl wallcoverings, and this makes them far easier to keep clean. Try to avoid getting paste on the flock pile, but if you do, wipe the flock clean with a damp sponge. Allow the paper to soak for about 15 minutes before hanging. Never press the paper down with your fingers when hanging, you may depress the flock pattern. Use the flat of your hand or a clean paint roller.

Cork decorated papers. It is best to line a wall which is to be covered with this material. Although hung in the same way as wallpaper, it does need trimming before hanging, using a long steel straight-edge and sharp trimming knife. Let the material become really supple before hanging, and keep paste off the cork face.

Grass cloths. Walls are best lined before a grass cloth is applied. Again the material needs trimming with a steel straight-edge and sharp knife. Use a prepared paste and allow the material to become supple before hanging. Do not turn the material at internal angles. Butt it into the corner. Turn about 50 mm (2 in) on external corners.

Hessian. Unless you have experience of this material, choose a hessian with a paper backing. This makes it much easier to handle. Backed types are pasted as for normal wallpaper, but if you choose an unbacked material, paste the wall then press the hessian on to the paste. Use a clean paint roller to press the material to the wall. Do not overlap the joints.

Silks. It is best to line walls first. Use a prepared paste and ensure that it does not get on the silk face. Fold the material only in pleats. Do not crease it or roll it or you will get marks you cannot lose, Keep your fingers off the delicate surface as much as possible, and do not overlap at the joints.

Murals. Special instructions are supplied with these. It is important to get the first piece truly vertical and to spend time getting a good join between sections. A prepared paste is usually advised, but

thinned down. It is important to work from the centre with a roller to ease out all air bubbles. Avoid folding or creasing the paper.

Wall tiling

The use of ceramic tiles increased tremendously with the introduction of the thin tile designed to be stuck in place with adhesive instead of the traditional bedding in cement mortar. The d-i-y tile was introduced in the size 5/32 in thick by 4¼ in square and at the time of writing it is still sold to these dimensions despite metrication.

As long as a surface is clean and dry, and is stable enough to support tiles, it may be covered. This includes old tiled surfaces where, perhaps, a rather ugly 6 in tile was used in the past. To remove these tiles is a terrible job, but tiling over is simple. The biggest problem is hiding a fair sized ledge formed where a wall was half-tiled, but this may be done with a hardwood edging strip, holding the top edge of both old and new tiling.

Tiles are available in plains and textures, and while plain tiles had a very good run there is an increasing interest in patterns and textures, despite the fact they cost more.

In some cases a combination of both may be the answer. An area of plain tiling relieved by the occasional patterned tile. Apart from simple patterns, picture tiles are available to enhance an area such as a splashback. Reproductions of vegetables, fish or plants. Then there are special tiles incorporating hooks, toilet roll holders and soap trays for use in the bathroom.

Leaflets are supplied with tiles explaining the method of applying, but here are the general rules.

Measure up one tile height from the floor or skirting board, and fix a straight-

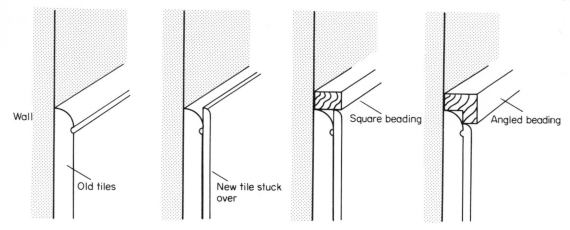

Wall

Old tiles

New tile stuck over

Square beading

Angled beading

You can tile over old tiles. Here is how to finish off at the top of a half-tiled area

Tips on wall tiling. The most vital point is to ensure that you start dead level. You cannot lose irregularities!

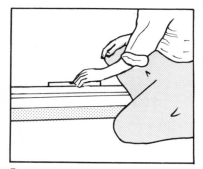

Fix a starting batten check with a level

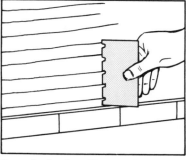

Spread adhesive with a special comb

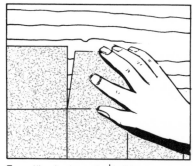

Ease tiles in place, don't slide

Apply grouting to gaps

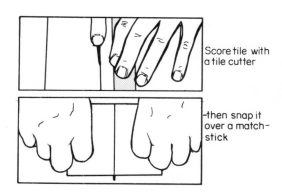

Score tile with a tile cutter

-then snap it over a match-stick

edge at this point with nails not driven right home. You will need a spirit level to get the board truly horizontal. If you find certain points are now wider than a tile width, due to floor irregularities, lower the batten a shade. It will be easier to nibble away a small portion from one or two tiles than cut slivers to insert into gaps.

Use the straight-edge as your base for the first row of tiles. Apply tile adhesive to the wall and spread it with the special serrated comb supplied. The comb ensures an even and not too liberal spread of adhesive. Press each tile into the adhesive, lowering it but not sliding it into place. If you slide the tile, you will force adhesive up between the joints. Wipe away any surplus adhesive before it sets.

Many tiles have built-in spacing nibs to ensure correct spacing between tiles, but if you encounter ones which have not, use thin strip of card as spacers, removing the strips once the tiles have set. Don't remove the batten too soon or the weight of the tiles may cause them to drop slightly.

Special tiles are available in certain ranges for finishing off edges. This must be borne in mind when ordering. These have one or two rounded edges without nibs.

Cutting tiles. This is quite simple, because only the top glaze is really hard. The 'biscuit' underneath snaps quite easily. Use a straight-edge and sharp tile cutter to score the tile on the glazed face, then lay the tile pattern up over a couple of matchsticks. Press either side of the line of cut, and the tile will break clean. Alternatively use a pliers-type cutter which has special jaws. If you grip the tile in the jaws in the correct manner and apply pressure, the tile will snap clean along the score mark.

For cutting shapes, such as where a pipe must pass through a hole cut in a tile, there is a special tile cutting blade which fits in a miniature hacksaw frame. It is also very useful for removing a very thin sliver from a tile where it would be hard to score and snap.

Grouting. Once tiling is complete, the gaps are filled with a special grouting powder mixed with water. It can be worked into the gaps with a small piece of sponge, then when dry, the surplus polished away

with a ball of newspaper. This is a very good tile cleaner; more effectice than a rag. The illustration shows how hardwood beading can be used to cover the edge of a half-tiled wall.

Plastic tiles

Apart from ceramic tiles, you can also get dense polystyrene wall tiles and decorative aluminium or stainless steel ones.

These are designed for fixing by adhesive, and they can look most attractive. They are much lighter than ceramic tiles, but it must also be said that they have not the tough surface of the ceramic tile. Plastic tiles can be scratched by abrasive cleaners, they are affected by heat such as from a cigarette, and certain cleaners, like brush cleaning cleaning liquids, can affect the surface.

Wall panelling

Here again, detailed instructions are supplied; the details vary according to type. The most common way of fixing wall panelling is to first batten the walls at regular intervals, as recommended by the supplier, then secure the panelling to the battens with panel pins. Fixing is usually through a section of a panel which is hidden when the adjoining panel is pushed into place.

One problem is that the battens add to the thickness of the wall so that the ledge at skirting board level disappears. There is also the problem of the depth of door frames, and repositioning light switches and wall lights. On the credit side this is the ideal time to plan extra wiring for items like wall lights as the new cable can be hidden behind the panelling without having to channel the walls.

An alternative to battening, which is becoming more popular as the price of timber has increased dramatically, is the use of a special panel adhesive so that wall panelling is stuck direct to the wall. Obviously, walls must be flat, clean and dry, but assuming this is the case, the total depth to worry about is now only the thickness of the actual panel material, which is considerably less than panel plus wall battens.

Apart from timber effects, panels imitating brick or stone are now popular for adding character to a wall area. Before buying, check how points like brick joints are dealt with on the panels. Do they actually interlock, or do they match in such a way as to appear to interlock? Very often an effect can be ruined by obvious joints between panels, which you would not get with the real thing.

Removing a picture rail

There may be occasions where a picture rail may get in the way of a new panel covering, or you may wish to take your decoration right up to the ceiling to increase the apparent height of the room. Removal of the rail is possible, but it does call for a little caution if you do not wish to make too much of a mess.

A picture rail is usually secured by means of cut nails, and these are often reluctant to leave the wall; they may have rusted in. Try to lever the rail away with a claw hammer resting on a thin block of wood. If the nails will not move, do not use force or you will pull away a large chunk of plaster. Locate the nail positions and use a

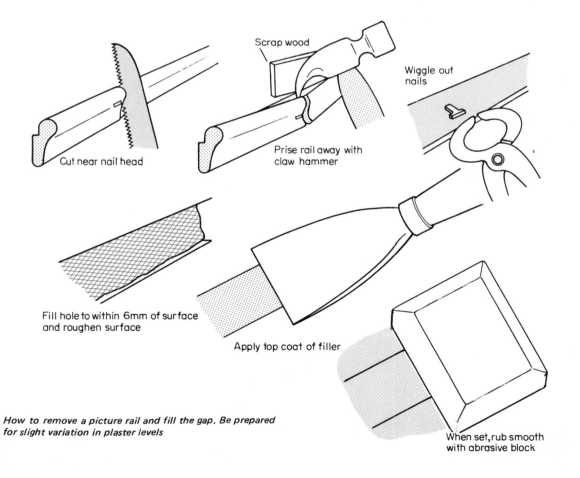

Scrap wood

Wiggle out nails

Cut near nail head

Prise rail away with claw hammer

Fill hole to within 6mm of surface and roughen surface

Apply top coat of filler

When set, rub smooth with abrasive block

How to remove a picture rail and fill the gap. Be prepared for slight variation in plaster levels

multi-purpose sheet saw to cut through the rail, as near the nail as possible, down to plaster level. Now use the claw hammer to rip the wood away from the nails.

With the wood out of the way, you can wiggle the nails out with pliers or a wrench. If you measure up, you may find you have problems with plaster levels, for the final coat may have been skimmed on after rail fixing. Clean out the gap, damp and fill with a compound such as Keene's cement, using two layers if the hole is deep.

Take the filler just above surface level, then use a permanent abrasive pad, which has particles of abrasive bonded into a metal sheet, to take down the plaster surface until it is level. If there is a difference in levels, you may have to compromise a little. Normally this does not show; the only exception being if that wall surface is lit by a wall light and the light source is close to the wall.

Applying a textured wall coating

This is really neither paint nor paper, for it is a way of using a thick compound to give a relief surface to a wall. It should be looked upon as a permanent finish which, once applied, cannot be papered in future.

Accepting this fact, the textured coating offers a very simple way of adding character to a plain wall, and of hiding the defects in a rather poor wall surface.

Further details of actually applying the finish are given in Chapter 8 dealing with ceilings.

Chapter 7 Exterior walls

Before any decisions are made as to how the external walls should be decorated, you should consider very carefully the reasons behind decorating the areas involved.

First, how will your ideas fit in with the surrounding area? Will what you plan to do enhance the road you live in, or will your place stand out like a sore thumb? Of course, we are all individualists at heart, but too much can be a bad thing. This is particularly true if you live in a semi-detached house. Does your neighbour plan to come into the scheme with you, or will his place look completely run down when your decorating is finished? Ideally, both should be treated together as if it were one detached house, but if this is not possible, some form of compromise is advisable.

How best should the walls be treated? The desire may be to hid the old red bricks, but a straight coat of paint on top of the bricks could make the place look cheap and nasty. It would be better to consider a coat of tyrolean finish (see later) over which you can paint, for in this way the wall has in fact been rendered before painting.

Never paint over a good facing brick to give the place a fresh look. As stated above, painted brickwork, in the main, looks cheap and nasty and once paint has been applied to the bricks, you will never be able to remove it.

Are the walls very cold? Perhaps you have solid walls which are therefore harder to insulate. Obviously, applying coats of paint may make the wall drier, but it will add

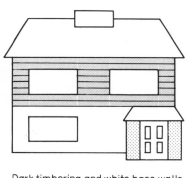

Dark timbering and white base walls

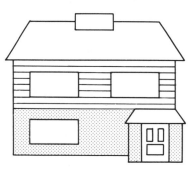

White plastic cladding and pastel lower walls

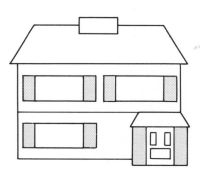

All white walls and contrasting timber shutters

Natural brick walls and contrasting shutters and window boxes

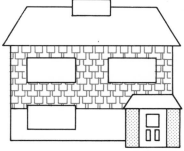

Cedar shingles and white lower walls

Variations on a theme. Choice of materials can transform the exterior of your home

little to the insulative effect. It may be worth considering at least part timber cladding, shingles, plastic weatherboard or perhaps vertical tiling which, if used correctly, and in conjunction with insulation materials, could vastly improve the insulation of the wall.

In view of the need for higher insulation standards, there are specialist companies who are considering ways of applying external insulation, then applying a coat of wall texture over the top. This is not a job for the handyman.

Where decorative brickwork is involved, if the walls are in any way porous, this will in itself lead to a colder house. In this case, the application of a clear silicone water repellent to the walls will help.

Ladders and scaffolds

When you have in mind just what needs doing, access to the job is the next important consideration. Working from an individual ladder can be very tiring, and because the ladder has to slope, different parts of the wall surface will be nearer or further from you. There is also the dangerous tendency to lean off the ladder to reach areas which would otherwise involve moving the ladder along. Far better make some form of safe working platform upon which you can stand.

A scaffold kit, supplied in knock-down form as a number of tubular sections, is ideal. It can be erected on any hard, flat surface, and it will provide a safe working platform at any height, with plenty of storage space for all the gear you need. It pays to add a safety rail to prevent your stepping off.

True, kits are expensive, but they can be hired for any given period and, if the work is planned correctly, hiring could prove well worthwhile. Wheels can be added to make the platform more mobile and sec-

tions of the kit can be used to form a workbench or a simple low platform for jobs nearer the ground. If this is not possible, you can use two ladders with items called builders' cripples to form a strong support for a stout scaffold board. Again this would be far more comfortable than standing on an individual ladder.

As mentioned earlier, never take chances with work above ground level. Safety must be the number one priority. Assuming you now have safe access, let us look at some of the surfaces we have to decorate.

Plain brick walls

As already mentioned, a thorough wash down with plain water and a scrubbing brush may be all that is needed.

Really grubby areas can be scrubbed with a piece of matching brick, or you may remove the grime with a wire brush, but remember to be sure to protect your eyes. Seal the surface with a silicone water repellent to keep out rain and also to discourage the settlement of dirt on the wall surface.

Renewing pointing

It often improves the appearance of the wall if the pointing looks attractive. Rake out the mortar with a tool made from a piece of steel sharpened to a point and bent to form a small rake. Go in at least 12 mm (½ in), brush out all loose material, then re-point using a mortar mix. This is available by the bag and all you need do is add water. Add a minimum amount so the mortar does not drip on to the brickwork. It should be dry enough to leave no marks. Shape the face of the mortar to match the surrounding brickwork.

For a hollow joint you will need a piece of mild steel rod bent to a curve. For a more traditional weathered joint, you can achieve this with a small pointing trowel.

Tyrolean finish

If yours is an older house with rather poor quality brick walls, it may pay to consider hiding the brick. A machine called a tyrolean projector can be hired from many hire shops, and this is designed to throw a wet mortar mix on to the wall to give a very attractive dash effect. This hides the brickword completely, including joints.

This system offers an excellent alternative to the more traditional spar dash or pebbledash finish which really calls for more expertise. It is quite a lengthy job and is really best left to a contractor who specialises in this kind of work. Once the tyrolean finish has set, it can be painted to suit.

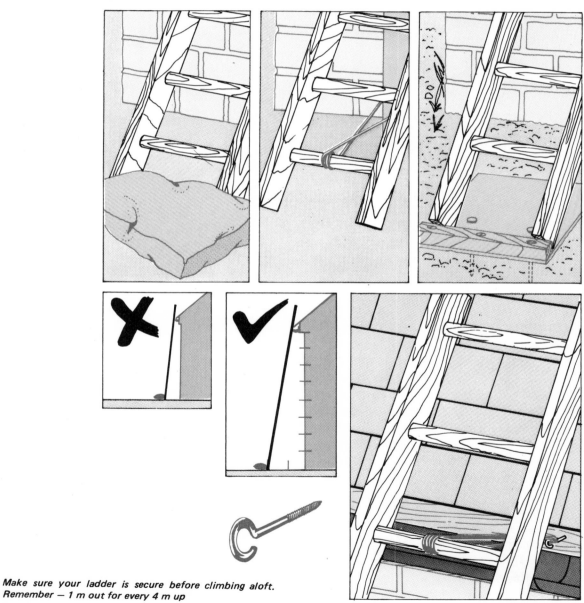

Make sure your ladder is secure before climbing aloft. Remember — 1 m out for every 4 m up

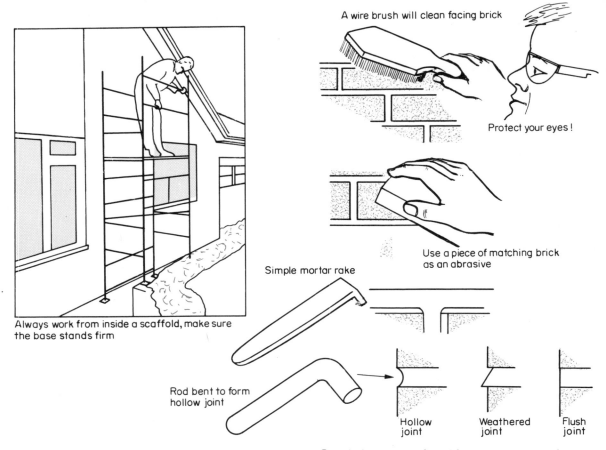

Always work from inside a scaffold, make sure the base stands firm

A wire brush will clean facing brick

Protect your eyes!

Use a piece of matching brick as an abrasive

Simple mortar rake

Rod bent to form hollow joint

Hollow joint

Weathered joint

Flush joint

Re-pointing an area of good facing brick can transform its appearance. Never add chemicals to any washing water

Rendered walls

Assuming the wall has been prepared as discussed in Chapter 4, a rendered wall can be painted with any one of a number of masonry paints. Exterior grade emulsion paint is fine as long as it does not have to fill hair-line cracks, for it has no bulking out like some of the paints. A coat thinned to 50% with water will do as a priming coat, then followed with two top coats. The emulsion can be applied by brush, at least 127 mm wide or, alternatively exterior grade paint roller.

The advantage of a good emulsion is that with age it 'chalks' on the surface, which means that just enough of the surface finish breaks down to bring off dirt and grime when it rains.

This makes it fairly self-cleaning, as important point in industrial areas.

Alternatively, you can use a cement-based paint, supplied as a powder and mixed with water as required. It can be applied by brush; a dustpan brush is very useful for any masonry paint. It is easy to hold and gives good coverage quickly.

A stone-based paint is more durable than a cement paint, and the next step up in durability and coverage is a masonry paint to which an additive such as mica or nylon fibre has been added. This combines decoration with extra strength, and the paint will hide minor blemishes and fill hairline cracks.

Be sure to wipe up any spills as you progress. All these rendering materials are far

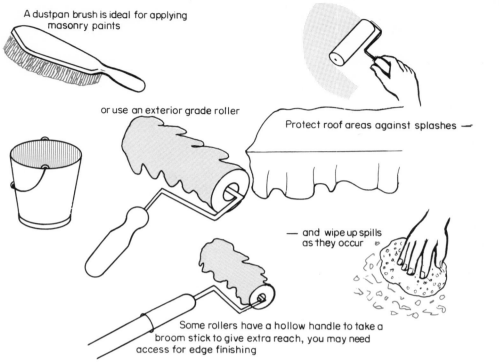

A dustpan brush is ideal for applying masonry paints

or use an exterior grade roller

Protect roof areas against splashes —

— and wipe up spills as they occur

Some rollers have a hollow handle to take a broom stick to give extra reach, you may need access for edge finishing

If you choose a roller for exterior work, be sure it is designed for the job. Foam and mohair are not suitable for this work

easier to remove when wet than when set hard. It also pays to protect surfaces like porch roofs, paths and flower beds, which are far easier to protect than to clean up afterwards.

Pebbledash

Pebbledash is always more difficult to decorate because of its deep textured surface. Assuming it is in good shape, a hose down with the jet on not too fierce a spray will remove loose dirt.

After drying, a masonry paint can be applied. Paint can be worked in by stippling with a well-loaded brush, or you can use a shaggy exterior grade paint roller. It is best to have a smaller brush handy for areas around windows and doors. As the

Work masonry paint into a surface and go gently so as not to damage dash surfaces

To apply masonry paint, stipple pebbledash with a paint brush

or use a shaggy pile roller

Scrub vertical tiling using clean water, detergent leave stains

brush will be contaminated with a certain amount of grit, it is wise to keep it for this kind of work and not transfer it to gloss work. The same basic treatment applies to a spar dash finish. Do not be too rough on older surfaces or you will dislodge stone chippings.

As soon as painting is finished, be sure to clean up all rollers and brushes used for masonry finishes. It is not wise to leave them soaking.

Tiles

Vertical tiling will usually respond to a scrub down with clean water. Do not be tempted to add detergents to the water as this often leaves whitish streaks which are impossible to remove when the tiles are dry.

If the tiles look very jaded, there are tile-coloured floor paints based upon rubber which will give a very good finish. The secret is to select one which really does not make the tiles look as if they have been painted. Keep the colour muted and preferably of the same colour as the tiles. Apply a thin coat well rubbed into the surface of the tiles so you get no brush marks.

Tile polish of the kind used for steps is an alternative, but it has not such a long life as a paint.

Shingles

Cedar shingles can look rather jaded on a house front once the warm colour of new cedar bleaches out and you are left with an uninteresting grey tone. The colour can be restored by using a preservative designed for red cedar which contains a stain. This is able to impart some of the warmth of the original wood while at the same time preserving it.

A coat of varnish over the timber will further preserve it against the weather, though you must bear in mind that the varnish would have to be removed should you wish to apply another coat of stain preservative. Obviously this is designed to soak into the wood, not sit on the surface.

Timber cladding also needs treatment, and this is mentioned in Chapter 10 'Wood-finishing'.

Plastic cladding

Plastic cladding is really designed to be self-cleaning as it has a smooth surface. To remove grime, all it should need is a wash with water containing a household detergent. It is not wise to use an abrasive material, as this will provide a rough surface to which dirt will adhere. It is far better to use something like a metal polish wadding to remove obstinate marks, as this will improve the gloss, not remove it.

Plastic cladding can be painted as long as it is clean and dry. Only a top coat is necessary unless you plan a change of colour. Be prepared to keep painting it in the future, as paint would not be easy to remove. Obviously a blowtorch is out of the question, and many chemical strippers will attack the surface of the plastic. In the main, it is best to leave it in its natural colour.

Stone facings

Natural stone facings are popular today, and these too need care when decorating. Again, only clean water should be used, in conjunction with a stiff scrubbing brush. If you need to rub the stone, find a piece of matching stone and use this as a pumice block, keeping it constantly wetted with water.

A stone facing may be painted, but again once done you will have to continue painting in the future. Probably the best finish is a stone-based masonry paint applied sparingly with a brush and worked well into the stone. But be warned, it can make your natural stone look like an artificial finish. Far better stick to the natural thing if at all possible.

Drives and paths

Although this is really another aspect of decorating, when thinking about exterior walls it is wise to consider paths and driveways.

These may not be decorated in the strict sense of the word, but you may consider coating paths with a cold macadam finish. This is available in black and a few warm colours, and it is supplied by the bag ready for spreading and rolling out. A special primer is supplied to bond the macadam to the path, and once it has started to harden, loose chippings of a contrasting colour are available to sprinkle on and relieve the solid colour a little.

Converting the paths from a normal concrete colour to perhaps black can contrast well with walls painted white.

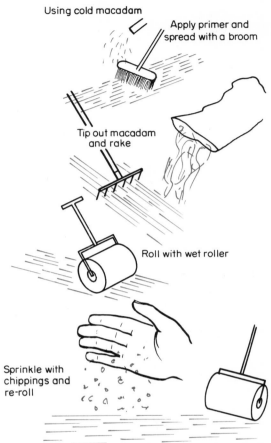

Using cold macadam

Apply primer and spread with a broom

Tip out macadam and rake

Roll with wet roller

Sprinkle with chippings and re-roll

Old paths and drives can be given a new look with cold macadam. Few tools are required

Chapter 8
Ceilings

As mentioned in an earlier chapter, the ceiling is best tackled before other decorating, and even before old wallpaper is stripped off the wall. In this way, any splashes will be removed with the old wall covering. It is at this stage you decide whether to add a cove cornice.

Fixing a cove cornice

The cove cornice bridges the gap between wall and ceiling, and adds a very neat finish to a room. This join between wall and ceiling is always a weak spot in house construction, and any slight movement in the fabric may appear as a crack which it is impossible to seal. As it cannot be sealed, the coving effectively hides it.

The simplest type of coving is made of expanded polystyrene lengths around 1 metre (or 1 yd) long, and apart from straight runs, internal and external corners are available. Fixing is very simple and is done by special adhesive. Do not be tempted to use any adhesive as some of the rubberised ones have solvents which dissolve expanded polystyrene. While very simple and light to handle, the main snag is that joints between pieces are very difficult, if not impossible, to hide because of the nature of the material. It is best just to accept the joints will be visible.

A better effect is gained by using a gypsum plaster coving covered in a stiffish paper. This is also available in short lengths, but joints can be hidden as long as the ceiling is not too irregular. If you can, it is better to get the longest lengths so that it is possible to do most room lengths or widths in one piece. Obviously this will look far neater than any other treatment.

The coving has to be stuck in place with a special adhesive and despite the considerable weight of a length of coving, the adhesive holds it firm without any other support. The adhesive must go on to bare wall and ceiling, so existing wallcoverings must be cut back to the recommended width, and the same on the ceiling.

The trickiest job is cutting mitres on the ends of the pieces, and while a templet is supplied, it pays to experiment on a spare piece of coving to ensure that you cut it correctly. Slight inaccuracies do not matter too much as the gap can be filled quite easily, but mis-use of the templet can result in a large oval hole!

Once in place, the coving is primed with a plaster primer, and is then ready for decorating along with the rest of the room. Coving offers a nice deep ledge up to which ceiling and wall coverings can come.

Painting the ceiling

Assuming that the ceiling has been cleaned and prepared, if the plaster is in really good shape, you can paint straight on to it, but any slight irregularities at joints may show up.

In the main, a ceiling always looks more attractive if it is first papered then painted; though of course there is nothing to stop you papering it to match the walls if you wish.

The paper may be smooth, rather like a good lining paper, or you can choose one of the Anaglypta range of textured finishes, offering anything from a simple pebbledash design through to some very pleasing plaster daub effects. These look even better when room lighting is near the ceiling, as the light picks up the texture.

Papering the ceiling

The operation for ceiling papering is similar to dealing with the walls, except that lengths involved are usually greater. So folding prior to papering has to be given more thought.

The first essential prior to papering is to arrange a working platform so your head is about 75 mm (3 in) from the ceiling. You can do this with a pair of steps and a suitable box, between which you support a scaffold board. Alternatively two pairs of steps will do. Do not try to work from one pair of steps; it just will not work!

Start papering at a window wall, parallel with the window and working away from it. The reason is that, should one piece overlap at some point, the overlap will be highlighted by light from the window. If you worked in the reverse direction, a similar overlap would appear as a dark shadow. Measure out from the window wall a subtract about 6 mm (¼ in) so that the paper will turn on to the wall by this amount. If you are working to a cove cornice, this turn need not be allowed for, as there will be no crack to hide between wall and ceiling.

How to fix a cove cornice. Experiment with scrap material first so you can make good internal and external joints

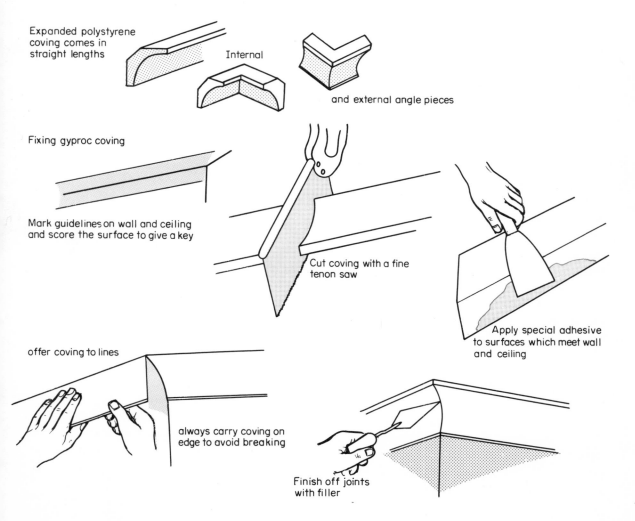

Expanded polystyrene coving comes in straight lengths

Internal

and external angle pieces

Fixing gyproc coving

Mark guidelines on wall and ceiling and score the surface to give a key

Cut coving with a fine tenon saw

Apply special adhesive to surfaces which meet wall and ceiling

offer coving to lines

always carry coving on edge to avoid breaking

Finish off joints with filler

Cut star shaped slits to fit around the ceiling rose, trim as for a wall switch

A broom will keep a heavy paper in place

Until you are experienced, get help with ceiling paper hanging — especially when dealing with heavy papers

Make two marks, then snap a chalk line right across the ceiling. This is the line to which the first piece of paper will be hung. You can buy quite elaborate chalk lines contained in a special case which holds the chalk, but for just occasional use it is sufficient to rub a length of coarse string with a coloured chalk. Secure one end of the string to a pin tapped into the ceiling. Hold the other end so the string is taut, then snap the string so that it leaves a mark.

Place the first cut piece of paper to the right of the pasting table with paper on the table ready to paste. Work from the centre out, herringbone fashion so you do not push paste under the length. As pasting is complete, fold the pasted part, concertina fashion, on to itself until the whole length is ready. If the paper is a fairly heavy one, allow it to soak before hanging.

Prior to papering, it is advisable to size the ceiling with a special glue size. This adds considerably to the adhesion of any paste used, and it also adds 'slip' to the paper, making it far easier to slide into place. This is important when you are working in a very awkward position with your hand above your head!

Now support the folded paper over a spare roll of paper as illustrated and use this as a carrier. Climb your scaffold, and offer the end to the ceiling, allowing the first fold to drop out. Position the paper to the line, ignoring the wall side at this stage, then slowly move along the scaffold board, letting out the folds. With a heavy paper it may help to have another pair of hands with a broom. They merely need to use the broom head to stop the hung piece pulling away from the ceiling, which it may try to do. You really appreciate the force of gravity when doing this job!

Once the length has been positioned along the line, use the smoothing brush to brush it down, making sure all wrinkles and any trapped air are eliminated. The ends are creased with scissors as with wallpaper, the paper pulled away and the surplus trimmed off. Allow a slight turn if the paper adjoins the wall. If a coving is involved, trim the paper accurately with no turn.

Now proceed with the next length, matching it to the edge of the previous length. You may well encounter an obstruction fairly soon in the form of a ceiling rose. If you do, it pays to do some accurate measuring and mark the position on the dry piece of paper. Make a number of star cuts in the paper, then paste the whole piece in the normal way.

When you get near the ceiling rose, merely feed the flex through the hole, and ease the paper around the rose. Press the cut pieces to the rose base, then trim off with small scissors. Again you can allow a slight turn on to the rose so no gap is visible. Be sure to wipe paste off the rose, before it hardens.

If you work with a textured Anaglypta, avoid the temptation to press the paper hard to the ceiling. This will flatten out the pattern to the extent that when you see the completed ceiling you will have tramlines of flattened pattern. Apply just enough pressure to make sure the paper is down. As with any heavy material, allow an Anaglypta plenty of time to soak before hanging. If it bubbles on the ceiling, allow more soaking time on subsequent pieces.

Fixing expanded polystyrene

An alternative to paper is sheet expanded polystyrene supplied by the roll. This is available in a number of patterns and the idea is that it is hung rather like ceiling paper, butting each piece to the next.

There is quite a difference in technique of hanging this. The adhesive is a special one which is applied to the ceiling and not the sheet. The polystyrene cannot be bent or folded, so it must be cut quite accurately to length. An obstruction, such as a ceiling rose, needs very careful marking out as it will have to fit exactly. It pays to cut the hole on the small size, then once the flex has been fed through and you have established the hole is in the right place, you can enlarge the hole with a craft knife.

Do not press hard on the sheet or you will indent it and it may not recover. Fill any slight gaps with a cellulose filler rubbed in with a rag. Gaps are easy to lose.

Once all these materials are in place the ceiling can be painted, using either brush, roller or pad brushes. It pays to apply at least two coats, one of which should be done in daylight so you can see if you have missed anything.

Ceiling tiles

Where a ceiling is sound, but looks pretty poor, ceiling tiles can transform it. There are a number of types of tiles, but the most used for d-i-y work are made of expanded polystyrene. They come in two main sizes, 300 mm² and 600 mm² approx. There are many patterns and textures available. For a large room, obviously the larger tiles are ideal as you need less, and each covers a larger area. They are not so convenient in a smaller room where cutting may be involved.

If you intend to paint your tiles, it pays to do so before putting them up. It is much easier, particularly as far as edges are concerned, and it is certainly less tiring on the arms.

Be sure to apply tile adhesive over the whole ceiling area and not by the old five blob method. A tile stuck overall is not a fire risk, even when not made of self-extinguishing grade expanded polystyrene. It is a fire risk if stuck by the blob method, as it has been shown that flaming pieces tend to drop away from the blobs of adhesive.

It is also essential that emulsion paint or a fire-retardant paint is used for decoration. Never use gloss paint as this has been shown to add considerably to the fire risk.

If you have to trim tiles, use a razor blade and straight-edge, or a very sharp knife. A blunt blade will rip at the plastic, causing it to crumble rather than cut.

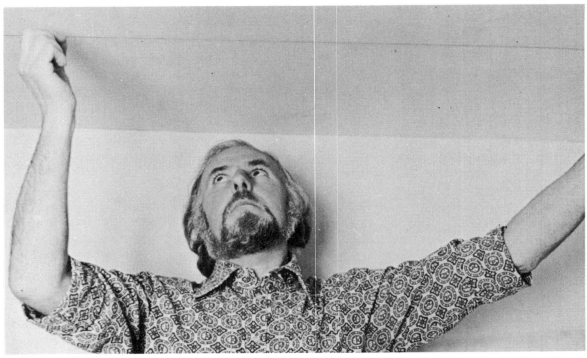

Snap a chalk line on the ceiling to give you a starting point

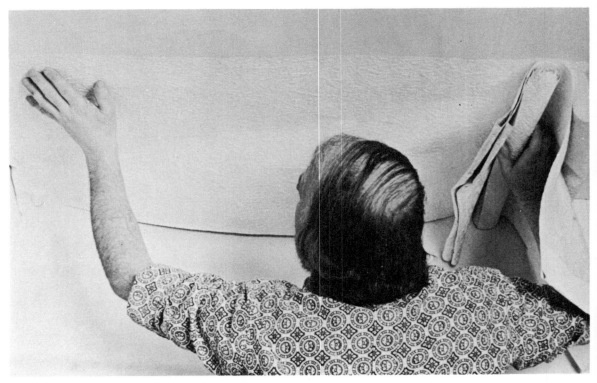

Align your first length with the chalk mark, sliding the paper to the line

Use a spare roll of paper to support the pasted paper, releasing the folds one by one

Mark the surplus paper with a fine pencil line. Don't press to hard

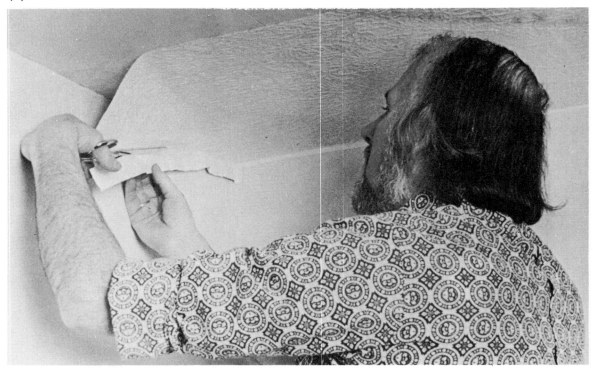

Trim surplus so you leave a few mm to turn on to the walls to hide cracks

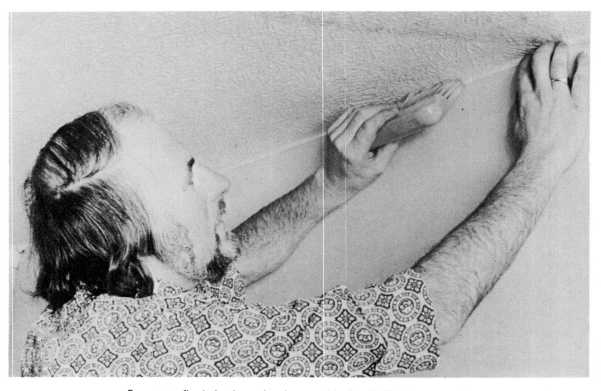

Press paper firmly in place using the smoothing brush. Check seams are down

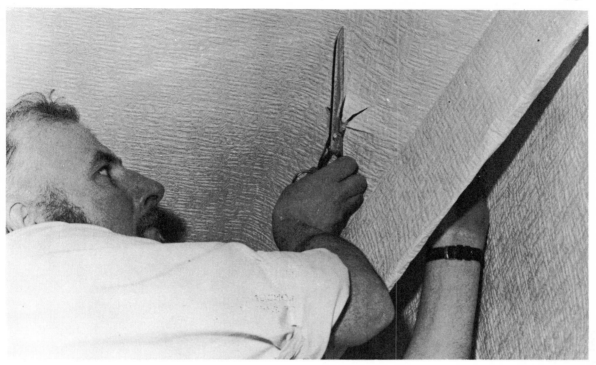

Make a star-shaped cut to pass light rose through

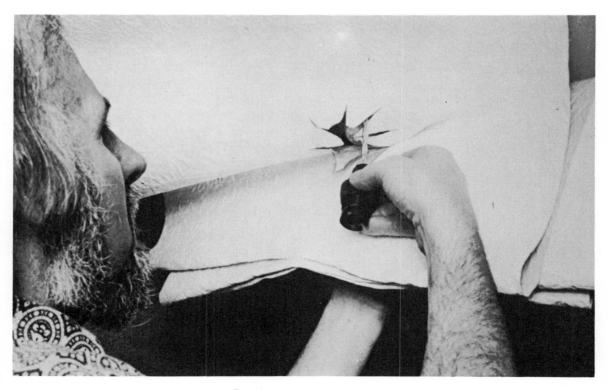

Ease the rose through the hole

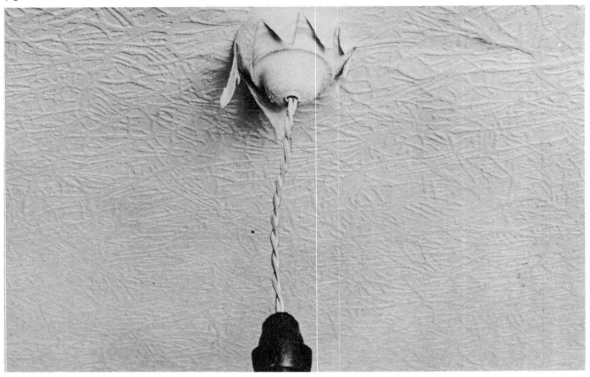

Press paper around the fitting and mark lightly with a pencil

Trim off surplus paper, press paper down and wipe paste from the fitting

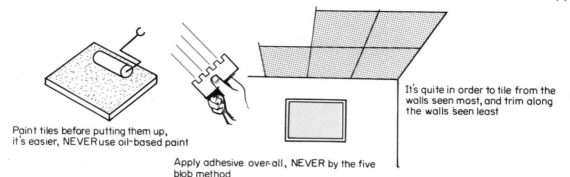

Paint tiles before putting them up, it's easier, NEVER use oil-based paint

Apply adhesive over-all, NEVER by the five blob method

It's quite in order to tile from the walls seen most, and trim along the walls seen least

Fixing ceiling tiles. As a fire precaution always apply tile adhesive over the whole ceiling. Tiles would melt but not drop away. The old method of applying a blob of adhesive to each corner of the tile should never be used

Opinions vary, but I do not consider it necessary to start in the centre of a ceiling and work out with tiles. Work from the two walls seen most as you enter the room, towards the walls noticed least—at these walls you can do your trimming. This method looks neater than perhaps having to trim all around the room.

Decorative finishes

Where a ceiling is not too well covered— perhaps with plasterboard where the joins are still visible—you can improve the appearance with a decorative compound. This comes in tubs, and you spread it thickly on the ceiling, using a wide brush.

Do not brush it out like ordinary paint. Cover an area no more than about ½ metre by 1½ metres (2-5ft approx), then start to texture the surface. A sponge inserted into a plastic bag, then pressed on the material and eased away produces a simple stipple. Twisting the sponge before pulling away produces a swirl. A plastic roller run lightly over the surface produces a bark effect and, of course, there are many variations on a theme. It pays to experiment on a piece of board before you start, so you know just what effect you want.

With one area done, continue, area by area, matching each into the pattern. The material sets in about 2 hours in a cool room. It pays not have the room too warm, or the material will dry out too fast.

Be sure to clean up as you go, as the material is not easy to remove once it has set. Do bear in mind that once you have a textured ceiling it is very hard to remove. You cannot paper over it.

Timbered ceilings

For something completely different, a timbered ceiling can look very attractive. Where old plaster is in a very bad state it may pay to pull the whole lot down so that the joists are exposed, but bear in mind that this is a very dusty, dirty operation.

If everything is holding up but just looks bad, it is better to leave the plaster in place, but probe the plaster with a fine drill or sharp awl and mark the exact position of the ceiling joists. Then, if you run your timber at right angles to the joints, you know exactly the location of your fixing points.

Tongued and grooved boarding as used for floors is quite adequate. Select it for grain pattern and firm knots. Fixing can be by fine panel pins angled through the tongue so that the next groove hides the

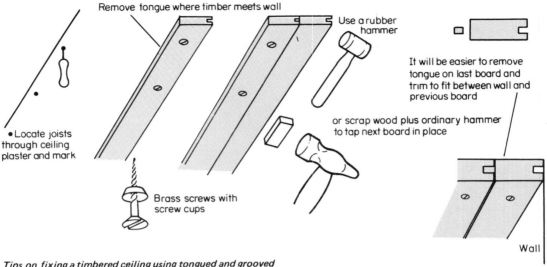

Tips on fixing a timbered ceiling using tongued and grooved boards. Quite a lot of weight is involved, so firm anchoring is essential

nails, or you could make a decorative feature of fixing and use brass screws. Countersink holes at set joist intervals in the boards, tap each in place with a rubber hammer, then drill a start hole and screw the board in place. Line up all the screw slots as you would with boat-building. It makes for a very neat finish. Brass screw cups may be used to further enhance the decorative effect. These go in place in the countersunk hole before the screw is put in.

A polyurethane seal can be used on the boards, or you could use one of the very attractive wood stains which gives a matt finish. As mentioned for ceiling tiles, the simplest way to finish the boards is before they are put up. It makes for much easier working.

False ceilings

Yet another approach to ceiling decoration where a high ceiling is involved is to lower the ceiling by making up a lightweight panel and suspending it from the main ceiling. The panel can be around 300 mm (12 in) smaller all round than the room size, then the space above used to house lighting. In this way the room can be lit indirectly, boosting the light with table lamps and standard lamp.

Alternatively, a package illuminated ceiling can be purchased which fits the whole room. Translucent panels fit in a special grid, and illumination is from above. Lighting can be plain, for areas such as a kitchen, or coloured to give mood lighting in a lounge.

Chapter 9 Floors

Floorcoverings have by far the heaviest wear of all the decorative surfaces in our homes. The first thing to remember is that the life you get from a floorcovering bears a direct relationship to the state of the floor upon which it is laid. To give a simple example, if you lay sheet vinyl on to a rough concrete floor, it will only be a matter of weeks before it shows signs of wear. If that same vinyl were bonded to a sheet of new chipboard, it would last for many years with no sign of wear at all.

So the first essential is to ensure that the floor, whether timber or solid, is in good condition. A very rough concrete floor may need a screed spread over it to provide a brand new surface. A badly worn timber floor may need resurfacing with a sanding machine, or perhaps have sheet hardboard laid over the whole lot to provide a new surface. All irregularities in the surface must be dealt with. Sharp nibs of concrete, or projecting nail heads. Anything which would damage the new floorcovering.

Faults like rot damage, structural weaknesses, damp and very badly worn areas are dealt with in another book in this series on 'Home Repair and Maintenance'. For the sake of decorating, we will assume the floors are in good shape.

The next important factor is what kind of floorcovering is to be laid. This may be a matter of preference or of pocket, but there are practical considerations too. We will now consider a few of these.

Choosing floorcovering

There are many grades of carpet very closely linked with the price you are asked to pay, and before you choose, ask at your local showroom for details of the gradings. These will range from the cheaper materials with very little body, where you can see the backing just by moving the tufts, through to a really expensive, dense pile. One may be adequate in the spare bedroom where there is little wear, but it would be hopeless on, say the main staircase. While the expensive one would be ideal for a well used lounge, it would be a waste of money in the spare bedroom.

Certain carpeting with artificial fibres is perfectly usable in the bathroom, if used in conjunction with a bath mat. It will make the room far more cosy, and the carpet will not be affected by damp conditions. On the other hand, the kitchen is not the ideal place for carpeting; with the likelihood of spills, it could soon look a mess. Cork or cushioned vinyl would be a better bet; this is easy to keep clean, yet warm to the feet. It is best to avoid a hard, smooth vinyl in the kitchen, for though it will wear well and be easy to clean, water spilled on it will make it extremely slippery.

If you are just starting a home and money is scarce, do not despise simple materials to start with. Oil-tempered hardboard can make a very attractive surround to a carpet Square. Treat it with a polyurethane seal and it will gleam—until such a time as you can afford a fitted carpet.

Think carefully before deciding whether to use tiles or sheet materials. The tile serves a very useful purpose in that it is very easy to lay, but you must accept pattern limitations. If you want the best of patterns, you will find these in the sheet materials. One problem we used to have with sheet vinyl was that, in most rooms, you needed two pieces to cover a floor; involving a seam.

However, with the introduction of much wider sheets, it is now possible to cover most rooms, such as kitchens and dining areas, in one piece. In addition, there is a far greater flexibility of material, so some cushioned vinyls can be folded like a carpet. This means that sheet materials are not so hard to lay as they used to be.

Above all, with carpeting, do not skimp on underlay. This too has a very real bearing on the feel and the wear of the carpet. Buy the very best you can afford.

Hardboard

This can be used to resurface a rather worn timber floor, but before putting it down, consider whether you need access at any point. It is made more difficult when the floor is covered by a sheet material. To prevent movement it can be spot bonded to the floor with a flooring adhesive. Tiles or sheet materials can then be laid over the top.

Sealing off a floor like this does not add to the risk of floor rot through damp. It is assumed the underfloor is well ventilated, and this is all that matters. The hardboard will eliminate draughts between boards, which is a good thing in these days of heat conservation.

Apart from using it as an underlay, hardboard can be laid as a decorative sheet material, as already suggested.

Before laying hardboard, sprinkle board backs with water

Stack back-to-back and leave for 24 hours in the room to condition This will avoid buckling

Hardboard can be used to completely cover a worn floor. Be sure to condition the hardboard before use, or it will buckle

Parquet

For a touch of elegance in hall, dining room or lounge, parquet is still a favourite, and this includes strip flooring.

To cater for the d-i-y market much thinner sections have been introduced which offer more than adequate wear for the average home and, of course, this brings the price down. There are two main systems offered; the first where thin sections are stuck down on to a hardboard base. The parquet is ready-prepared in squares and these are merely butted together to give the desired effect.

The second method involves prepared squares which have tongues and grooves built into the edges, and the floor is built up by tapping the squares together so the tongues and grooves mate. By this method, no adhesive is necessary, and it would be possible for the floor to be lifted; though it is not always easy to separate the units.

Strip flooring is also produced for the d.i.y market, and this also is available with interlocking edges, where the interlock is invisible when the units are pressed together. Full laying details of all these materials are supplied at the time of purchase.

Hard tiles

While the old quarry tile, so often seen in country homes, has lost favour, floor tiling has again become popular in recent years. This may well be influenced by holidays abroad in countries with hot summers, where the decorative floor tile is much in favour.

A very wide pattern and texture range is now available, and tiles can look very good in areas such as the bathroom, downstairs cloakroom and dining area. A few years back they would have been considered cold to the feet, but with full central heating, this argument no longer applies.

The tiles are, of course, far heavier than the ceramic tiles for walls, and they need more care in cutting. Special adhesives are also available and, for areas where damp may be encountered, waterproof grouting is available.

Sheet vinyl

As already suggested, vinyl floorcoverings have seen some dramatic changes in recent years. The main change has been the introduction of foamed backings, making the material far warmer to the touch, and enabling the manufacturers to build in texture to the pattern. This textured vinyl is the most popular today.

Also, there is less tendency for the sheet to shrink after laying, though this is a characteristic of vinyl which should be kept in mind. The old linoleums used to stretch as they bedded down; vinyl will try to shrink. So final cutting is best delayed until you are sure what is happening.

The latest vinyls are extremely pliable and it is possible to buy a floorcovering which is as supple as carpet, and can be folded and carried like a carpet. When spread out, all wrinkles will disappear. With the older vinyls, a crease could well remain and be impossible to lose. This new material is obviously easier to lay; particularly .in a small room, where the sheet will have to be folded while fitting.

Sheet vinyl can be loose laid and then merely held by an adhesive or a double sided carpet tape just around the edges.

For really hard wear, it can be stuck over-all but this obviously adds problems if you have to lift it. This is particularly the case with foamed backings, as the foam tends to tear away.

Try to avoid joins in foam-backed materials in traffic lanes. The join edges are more prominent because the foam backing flexes.

Carpet

This falls into three main categories for the handyman. The traditional Axminsters and Wiltons with their woven backings, used with a traditional jute or foam underlay. These are available as squares for loose laying, or off the roll for close-carpeting where the carpet must be pulled really tight if it is to look good and wear well.

There is a new family of carpets with a built-in foam underlay where the foam is bonded to the carpet. They offer a new approach to close carpeting as they do not need the same amount of tensioning as the traditional carpeting, and the quality range is greater. There are some very poor carpets produced with the minimum of tufts bonded into a poor backing and, in this field, it is a case of you get what you pay for.

Perhaps it should be added, that carpet laying is quite a skilled job, and if you are buying an expensive carpet where expert free fitting is offered as an incentive to buy, take advantage of the offer. The company will then be responsible for careful measuring and cutting.

Carpet tiles

Another interesting development has been the introducion of carpet tiles. These simplify laying and certainly make cutting and fitting that much easier. There is also the consideration that a room does not need to be completely cleared. Tiles can be laid in one half of the room; furniture moved over, then covering completed in the cleared area.

Obviously the pattern range must be limited, but patterns are available in carpet tiles. At the other end of the scale are the plain tiles with a definite direction of pile. By alternating the pile direction, an interesting squared pattern can be built up.

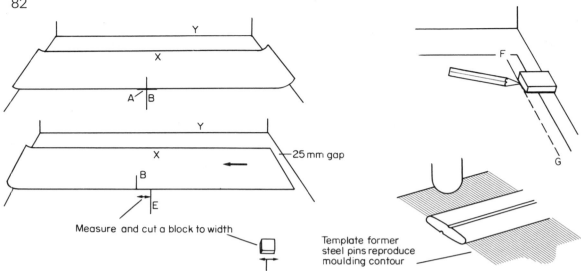

Measure and cut a block to width

How to cut sheet vinyl to fit your floor. The text describes the procedure which should be followed

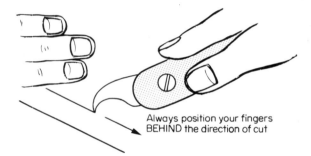

Template former
steel pins reproduce
moulding contour

Some tiles need to be fixed with tape, but others rely on the pressure of being pushed together to hold them in place, and, with the really shaggy piles, it is impossible to see that the floor consists of tiles. Another bonus of the tiled floor is that should one tile become worn or damaged, it can be lifted and replaced. The 'great problem inherent in the fitted carpet is that it cannot be moved when areas start to wear.

Always position your fingers
BEHIND the direction of cut

Take extreme care when cutting sheet floorcoverings

Laying sheet vinyl

If you can cover the whole floor with one piece of vinyl, do so, for it makes a much more attractive covering. If two pieces are needed, consider carefully where the join will be. If possible, keep the join out of the main traffic areas. Check also to see that the pattern matches correctly and how big the repeat is. Will the pattern still match if a small piece has to be run the other way to fill a space? All these points will influence how much floorcovering you buy.

It is always wise to get the vinyl really warm before starting work. It will be that much easier to handle. Should you encounter a stubborn fold, play the warmth of a hairdryer on the vinyl to further soften it. Do not let anyone walk over folded vinyl, or you may get creases and marks that you cannot do anything about. As mentioned earlier, this does not apply with the new flexible materials.

Fitting sheet material calls for care; particularly in measuring. Remember the old adage—measure twice, cut once. There is nothing more infuriating than cutting a sheet too small.

Use a sharp craft knife and steel straight-edge to cut the vinyl about 25 mm (1 in) longer at each end than the required length. This will allow for trimming. Take great care with the knife, always cutting with your hands behind the direction of cut. Never, never cut towards your fingers!

Lay the sheet in place with the extra 25 mm curling up each end wall, as in the illustration. Make sure the edge X is neatly in line with wall Y. Assuming you are working with more than one length, mark the edge of the sheet on the floor at A, then draw a line at right angles to the edge mark, as at B, marking both sheet and floor.

Pull the sheet away from the wall at C so the sheet clears the wall by 25 mm, making sure the sheet still lines up with line A. Now measure the distance between line B on the sheet and the bit of line it left behind at E. Cut a simple block of wood with its width equal to this distance, and use it as a guide to scribe a line FG along the edge of the floor covering. Keep the block in touch with the wall, and it will faithfully reproduce on the vinyl any slight irregularity in the wall. Trim your vinyl to this line, and you will see it now fits neatly to the wall at that end.

Now move to the other end and repeat the process, and the sheet will fit perfectly. Use the same technique for further pieces.

If you are working with a whole sheet, covering the whole floor, you will have to modify the system by marking line B on the far wall instead of on the floor, and it will be harder to ensure you pull the floor-covering back by 25 mm. Be sure to keep edge X against wall Y. Once you have fitted the sheet in one direction, the trimming in the other direction will be easier.

Of course, there will be odd shapes to cut—perhaps around door mouldings or a projecting cupboard. To ensure an accurate fit, make a simple cardboard templet which fits exactly, then transfer this to the vinyl.

For intricate mouldings, there is a useful little tool called a template former. This is a frame, housing dozens of steel pins free to move within the frame. By pressing the pins on to a moulding, it will faithfully reproduce the shape, which can then be drawn on to the floorcovering. When cutting to awkward shapes, always err on the safe side and take off a little less than may be necessary. It is easy to trim a little more off—but impossible to stick a bit back on!

With the covering fitted, secure joints with double-sided carpet tape, or use a latex adhesive.

Laying carpet

Obviously, laying carpet squares is not a problem, but securing a fitted carpet calls for some expertise. The simplest way of fixing is to use special carpet fixing battens which incorporate a series of spikes upon which the carpet can be held. The length of spike varies according to the type of carpet you have to fix, so this is a point to check when buying. The battens will come with instructions as to how far from the wall the batten must be fixed, and how much surplus carpet can be tucked down behind the batten.

The battens are nailed, screwed or glued to the floor according to type, with the teeth projecting towards the wall. Then the underlay is fitted up to, but not over, the battens. It is wise to stretch and anchor the underlay to the floor so it cannot wrinkle. On timber floors, simply pull the underlay taut and tack it down, keeping the tacks about 100 mm (4 in) away from the battens. On concrete floors, use a latex adhesive to hold the underlay in place. Trim any surplus underlay away from the battens so nothing sticks up.

There is a definite technique in hooking carpet on to the pins, and this will be

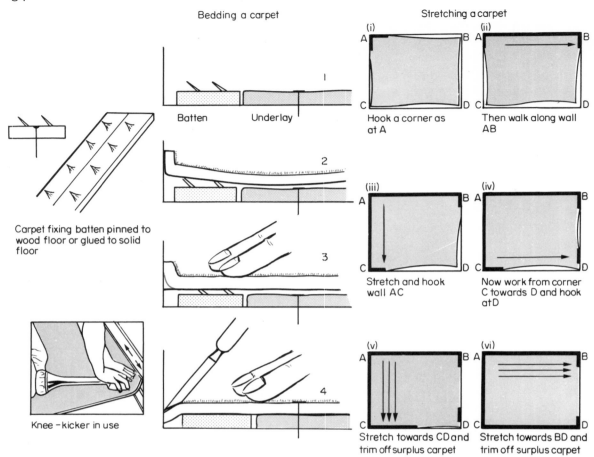

Bedding a carpet

Batten   Underlay

Carpet fixing batten pinned to wood floor or glued to solid floor

Knee – kicker in use

Stretching a carpet

(i) Hook a corner as at A

(ii) Then walk along wall AB

(iii) Stretch and hook wall AC

(iv) Now work from corner C towards D and hook at D

(v) Stretch towards CD and trim off surplus carpet

(vi) Stretch towards BD and trim off surplus carpet

Tips on fitting carpet. However inconvenient, it is wise to lift fitted carpets before decorating. This can be done very easily if the batten method of fitting the carpet has been used

explained in the instructions with the battens, but in the main, the carpet must be eased up the wall about 9 mm (3/8 in), then use your fingers to press the carpet on to the batten. As the spikes start to grip, press the carpet down with an old blunt chisel blade, easing the surplus carpet down behind the batten, but not pressing it right down, or you will find this releases the carpet from the pins at this stage.

Use the same technique to hold the carpet, as illustrated, first at one corner, then along one wall. From this point on, you need the help of a special tool called a knee kicker. This has a spiked pad which grips the carpet, and a padded end which you can push with your knee to apply pressure while leaving both hands free to manipulate the carpet.

This tool applies the necessary pressure to stretch the carpet while you ease the edge over the pins as before—except that this time you will have the natural stretch of the carpet helping you get the carpet on to the pins.

As work progresses, a surplus of carpet will be forced up at least two walls, and once the carpet is correctly stretched, the surplus can be trimmed with a sharp knife, and the remaining edges eased down behind the battens to give a very neat finish.

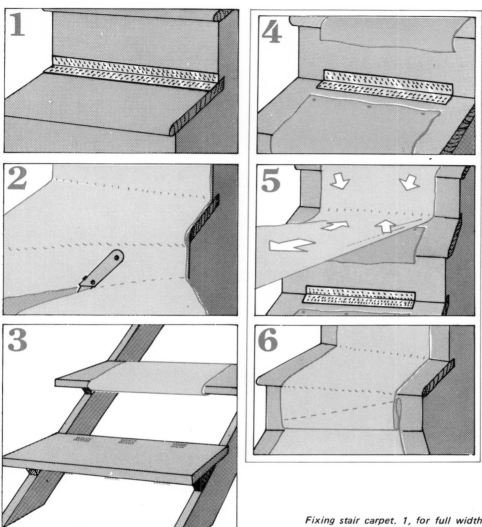

Fixing stair carpet. 1, for full width fitting, carpet grip goes full width. 2, carpet will have to be tailored on turns. 3, on open treads, Velcro tape can be used.to hold carpet pads in place. 4, on narrower carpet make sure that the grip strips and underfelt will not show. 5, this is how to press the carpet on to the grip teeth. 6, on turns, carpet can be folded as shown and tucked under at the riser

To make a neat finish at doorways, special edging bars are available. These can be single bars for just hiding the carpet edge, or they may be in the form of a double bar to match up with an adjoining carpet. There are also edging bars which will combine carpet and vinyl floorcovering.

Laying staircarpets

The same kind of spiked grip offers an ideal way of holding stair carpet, though for stairs the grip has a different shape. It incorporates an angled bar with teeth facing into the angle. The bars are screwed in place in the angle of each tread, each being just a fraction short of the carpet

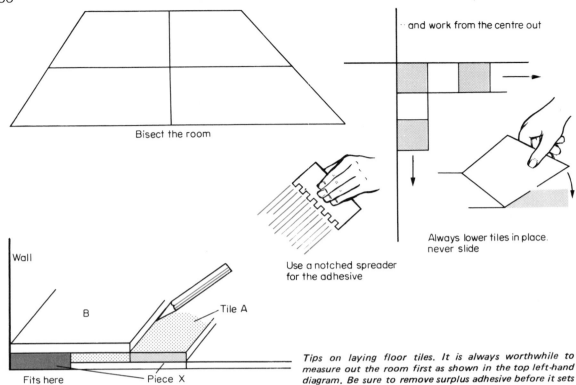

Bisect the room

and work from the centre out

Use a notched spreader
for the adhesive

Always lower tiles in place.
never slide

Wall

B

Tile A

Fits here

Piece X

Tips on laying floor tiles. It is always worthwhile to
measure out the room first as shown in the top left-hand
diagram. Be sure to remove surplus adhesive before it sets

width. Then the stair treads should be pinned in place using carpet tacks. You need only tack at the edge nearest the grip. Allow the other edge to lay free over the stair nosing.

Now lay the carpet down the stairs with the correct amount left at the top, then ease the carpet into the first grip. Keep the carpet taut and ease it into the next grip—and so on down the stairs. At the turn, the carpet can be folded and tacked as shown to lose the surplus. This assumes that one day you will want to lift the carpet and re-position it to spread the wear. Similarly, any surplus at the bottom can be folded and pinned to the last stair riser.

With the tendency for full width fitted carpet on stairs, it is common practice to cut the carpet and tailor each piece to fit. This certainly gives a very neat result, but

it does mean that carpet cannot be re-positioned as it starts to wear.

The open tread staircase presents yet another problem—that of holding a pad neatly, yet firmly in place. There are two main methods you can use. First, special carpet press studs which are designed to screw into the treads for one half, while the other half is sewn to the underside of the carpet. The second method makes use of a special tape called Velcro. This consists of two tapes, one of which is covered with thousands of tiny hooks, while the other has thousands of loops. When pressed together the hooks engage the loops, and the two tapes will not part unless ripped apart.

One half of the tape is glued to the stair tread, while its mating tape is stuck to the underside of the carpet. This results in a very neat job which does not involve drilling into the treads.

Floor tiles

As has already been suggested, laying tiles does not present so many hazards as laying sheet materials. The first job is to find the centre of the room by measuring then using the chalk line to snap marks on the floor. You can then work from the intersection of the lines outwards.

Most tile companies supply a useful squared paper on which you can mark the size of your room, and the proposed pattern. From this you can calculate just how many tiles of each design you need. It will also act as a guide when you lay the tiles. Many plain tiles have a grain pattern added, and it is best to run the grain of each tile at right angles to its neighbours.

Apply adhesive to a small area of floor and press the tiles on to the adhesive. Do not slide them in place or you will force adhesive up between the tiles. If any comes on to the surface of the tiles, wipe it off while wet. Laying is simple until you reach the borders of the room, when it will be necessary to trim tiles to fit. The diagram on page 86 shows an accurate way of doing this.

To cut a perfect fit, lay tile A on top of one of the last full row of tiles. Then slide B over A until it comes into contact with the wall. Now mark the edge of tile B on tile A. Cut tile A, and you will find piece X fits the gap perfectly. Continue cutting until the border is complete.

Most floor tiling can be done in this way, but there is an exception with loose laid floor tiles. These are laid from a wall surface out so that tiles can be placed under pressure. This will be explained on the pack, and it applies in the main to certain types of carpet tile, particularly in the upper price bracket.

When cutting tiles to fit around mouldings or other projections, the same technique is used as for sheet materials, and again the tool mentioned earlier, called a template former, is useful.

Chapter 10 Wood-finishing

We have talked a great deal about decorative finishes which involve a covering-up process, but there are cases where the natural beauty of an item, such as a timber door, needs to be seen and not hidden. This involves different decorating techniques.

These techniques are gaining more popularity as it is realised that natural finishing joinery calls for less work initially and far less maintenance in the future. What is needed, however, is good quality work in the first place, for poor joints and bad cracks cannot be hidden beneath a dense coat of paint. They will be on show for all to see.

Preparing the timber

Before any timber surface can be finished, it must be stripped back to bare wood, removing all old primer and surface filler. If the wood is discoloured, it may be possible to start again by using a wood bleach. These are still available from companies which specialise in woodfinishing products. Then, when clean, the timber should be rubbed smooth with a fine glasspaper, working with the wood grain to prevent surface scratches.

Any holes and gaps are filled with a wood stopping of similar colour. If the wood is to be stained, it is essential that the filler you use will in fact take the stain too. For example, filling a crack in whitewood with putty would give a well hidden repair until a dark stain were applied. Then, the stain would soak in the timber but be rejected by the oily putty, leaving a whitish mark.

Creosote and other stains

For external use, there is a wide range of stains, most of which are incorporated in preservatives. Creosote is probably the best known one, and this is still widely used for fencing of all kinds, and for sheds and other timber buildings. Its only disadvantages are that during its drying it can stain clothing, and it can burn plants with which it may come into contact.

Also, there is little colour variety, whereas in other proprietary ranges a colour card can be offered, giving good imitations of a whole range of wood colours from pine to mahogany.

Other stains offer a pigmented range which have yet to really catch on in this country. Yellows, and oranges through to black can be offered, all of which colour and preserve at the same time.

For staining joinery there are three main types available. Water-based, methylated-spirit-based and oil-based. The water and spirit stains are usually sold as crystals, and they have the disadvantage that they cause the grain of the wood to swell. This means more rubbing down after the stain is dry. The water-based stain is popular with beginners because if too dark a colour is used, it can be lightened by rubbing with a damp rag. The most popular types of stain are the oil-based ones. They have good penetration, are quick drying and do not raise the wood grain.

Apart from normal stains, a whole range of polyurethane finishes incorporating stains is available. These colour and decorate in one process, and they have become very popular in recent years for whitewood furniture. These finishes are also available in large aerosol cans.

For Western red cedar, there are special stain preservatives which restore something of the natural colour of the wood. The warm glow of new cedar can soon be changed to grey with weathering.

Wood finishes

Now a brief word on finishes available.

French polish is still available in simplified form for amateur use, but it is seldom used by furniture manufacturers. It has the advantage that drying time is quick but you do need a fair bit of practice to produce a good finish. It is also easily marked by heat, solvents and abrasion, and it does not like damp. It is better to use one of the products mentioned below.

Polyurethanes

These come in three main types; two-pack, moisture cured and air drying. The first is not widely used by amateurs, but is quite widely used in the furniture trade because of its durability. The moisture-cured types give a good durable surface, but drying time can vary considerably, as this depends on the moisture content of the air.

The most popular is the air-drying type, available as a high gloss, satin or matt finish. This gives a hard finish with good resistance to water, solvents and abrasion, but does not produce a mirror-like gloss expected by the professional furniture maker.

Two-part cold cure lacquers

This is a resin-based material to which a hardener is added as the material is required. It produces a very hard non-yellowing finish which is ideal for surfaces like table tops, which must be able to withstand hard wear.

Linseed oil

This material, like distemper, is best omitted from the range you plan to use —even though it has always been looked upon as a traditional finish for items like natural timber doors. Raw linseed oil takes days to dry, gathering dust in the process, and boiled linseed oil, while drying faster, goes gummy and dark with age.

It is far better to use one of the proprietary teak oils as these are reinforced with resins and other oils to give a more effective and durable finish to timber. If you encounter a nice door coated linseed oil, strip it back to bare wood before redecorating.

Waxes

With the wide range of materials available today, it is best not to use wax as a decorative finish. Once applied to bare wood, few materials will take over the top. Also, as the film is soft, it tends to pick up dust and dirt. Its best use is as a final polish over a surface decorated with a polyurethane seal.

Choice of finish

Many of the products referred to above may have interior and exterior grades available. So if you have a particular job in mind, check to see whether your choice is suitable. For example, weatherboarding would need a really good exterior grade polyurethane— or perhaps better still a good oil varnish. Yacht varnish still needs a lot of beating when it comes to durability.

With all exterior work, it is vital to see that all surfaces of the timber are protected with finish—and particularly the end grain. If water can find a way behind your protective coating, it will often push the new finish off. Damp wood expands, and the expansion alone can break down the toughest of finishes.

Chapter 11
Wrinkles and tips

These are the ideas which may be picked up through experience—either your own or those you come into contact with. Add your own to the list! Some of these tips have been mentioned previously but have been brought together here for convenience.

If paint has to be stored, cut a circle of foil and float it on the surface of the paint before closing the tin. This will keep the air away from the paint.

With small quantities of paint left in large tins, transfer the paint to a screw top jar which it fills, and mark the jar. Never, never turn a tin upside down. You merely end up with a skin on the bottom instead of the top.

To strain paint, use clean nylon stocking (or tights). Fix a piece around the can lid and push the stocking into the paint. You can then pick up strained paint from inside the stocking.

For applying very messy adhesives to small areas, make up a simple brush from coarse string pushed through a short piece of copper piping. The frayed string acts as bristles which can be cut off as they are spoiled.

If you use a paintbrush for dusting off, be sure to mark it for that purpose. Do not use it to paint.

Before you start papering, write on the wall the number of rolls you had to use and how much of other materials the room used. (you can adjust your figures before the last piece goes up if necessary) This will be useful when next the room is decorated.

If you have to patch wallpaper, always tear the patch—do not cut it out with scissors as this produces a hard edge. Learn to tear so you get a feathered edge under the pattern of the paper.

Wherever paper creases through a fault in the wall surface, tear the paper—do not cut it. This way you can disguise the remedy.

Always wipe wet paste from rails and skirtings as you work. It saves time spent afterwards trying to soften dry paste.

Store brushes overnight in cooking foil. Load the brush with paint then wrap it up tightly. It will be ready for use next day. While storing in water does omit air, it can cause swelling of the brush and rusting of the ferrule.

After using brush cleaner, let the sediment settle then drain off the remaining cleaner. This can be used again.

Soften old brushes by suspending them in paint stripper. You may need to work the brush a number of times to allow the stripper to get right into the bristles.

In order to economise on brush cleaner, pour a little in a sound plastic bag. Insert the brush head, secure the mouth of the bag with an elastic band, then work the bristles through the bag.

When suspending a brush in cleaner, drill a hole through the handle and push a piece of wire through. Rest the wire on the jar. Never rest the bristles on the base of the jar. It deforms them.

When painting inside a pipe (not often necessary) wrap a heavy stone in old towelling, tie it to a length of string, and mould the towel to the internal diameter of the pipe. Pour some paint on the towelling and work it up and down in the pipe.

Do not seal the joins between lengths of down-pipe. These joints act as tell-tales if the pipe gets blocked. You can tell at which point the blockage has occurred. If you block them there is no way of telling.

Always secure a ladder base so that it cannot slip when you climb up. If possible anchor it at the top. Never lean off a ladder, and beware of plastic guttering. It is strong enough to take a ladder but is far more slippery than cast iron.

When moving cast iron guttering, get help. Rope the guttering so it can be lowered easily. The weight can very easily throw you off balance.

Never stand a ladder on soft soil. Stand it on a board, and weight the ladder so it can't move off the board.

Clean up paint splashes on tiles and paths as you go. It comes off so much easier than dry paint. Protect border plants and flowers from splashes—especially from masonry paints.

Take care with blowtorches—especially out of doors. The flame can be invisible in bright sunlight. Keep it out of eaves where there may be nests. Avoid open windows, and always take down curtains.

Protect your eyes when working with wire brushes, grinding wheels or chemicals such as paint stripper. Also, when cutting or dressing stone.

Always have adequate ventilation when using materials such as flooring adhesives which produce fumes. Ventilate all clothing used, and avoid naked lights and pilot lights.

Do not have paper on the floor when using a blowtorch for paint stripping. Have a bucket handy in which you can drop burning paint.

Be sure to shake aerosols well before use to mix in any sediment which could clog the valve. Always up-end the can after use and press until only solvent appears. This cleans the jet. Never puncture old aerosols, and do not throw them on a bonfire.

Never use sheet or tile vinyls straight in from the cold. Let them warm up and become pliable. They will be so much easier to handle.

Never have rooms over-warm when decorating. It can speed up drying times of adhesives and paints to the point where you get problems.

When drilling holes in tiles, use your slowest drill speed. A piece of adhesive tape stuck on the tile will help the drill tip make a start without wandering.

Do not try to chip concrete from surfaces like brick or tile. You will probably damage them. Get the solution that builders use for dissolving concrete on tools. It will remove the concrete without affecting the under-surface.

To lift old vinyl tiles, lay a piece of cooking foil over the tile and apply a hot iron. The heat with soften the vinyl and probably the adhesive below, allowing you to pull the tile away. Use a hot scraper to remove any residue of adhesive from the floor.

Remove scuff marks from vinyl floor-coverings and parquet with a very fine wire wool dipped in turps substitute. Rub lightly until the marks disappear. On parquet, only work with the wood grain to avoid scratches.

CHART FOR ESTIMATING WALLCOVERING

Measurement round walls, including doors and windows. The figures in the columns below give the number of rolls required

(ft)	28	32	36	40	44	48	52	56	60	64	68	72	76	80	84	88	92	96	100
Ceiling height (m)	8·53	9·75	10·97	12·19	13·41	14·63	15·85	17·07	18·29	19·51	20·73	21·95	23·16	24·28	25·60	26·82	18·04	29·26	30·48
2·13–2·29 m	4	4	5	5	6	6	7	7	8	8	9	9	9	10	10	10	11	12	12
2·30–2·44	4	4	5	5	6	6	7	8	8	9	9	10	10	11	11	12	12	13	13
2·45–2·59	4	5	5	6	6	7	7	8	8	9	9	10	10	11	12	13	13	13	14
2·60–2·74	4	5	5	6	6	7	7	8	9	9	10	11	11	12	12	13	13	14	14
2·75–2·90	4	5	6	6	7	8	8	9	9	10	10	11	12	12	13	13	14	15	15
2·91–3·05	5	5	6	7	7	8	9	9	10	10	11	12	12	13	14	14	15	15	16
3·06–3·20	5	5	6	7	8	8	9	10	10	11	12	12	13	14	14	18	16	16	17
3·21–3·35	5	6	7	7	8	9	9	10	11	11	12	13	13	14	15	16	16	17	18
3·36–3·50	5	6	7	8	8	9	10	10	11	12	13	13	14	15	16	16	17	18	18

CHART FOR ESTIMATING ROLLS REQUIRED FOR CEILINGS

Ceilings Measurement in metres round room	Number of rolls	Measurement in metres round room	Number of rolls	Measurement in metres round room	Number of rolls	Measurement in metres round room	Number of rolls
11.0	2	16.0	4	21.0	6	26.0	9
12.0	2	17.0	4	22.0	7	27.0	10
13.0	3	18.0	5	23.0	7	28.0	10
14.0	3	19.0	5	24.0	8	29.0	11
15.0	4	20.0	5	25.0	8	30.0	11

Index

95

(*The photographs used in this book are by courtesy of Crown Decorative Products*)

FOR YOUR REFERENCE

A great deal of decorating time can be saved if you have at your fingertips information concerning the quantities of materials you will need. It will also ensure that you order just what you require—not too much or too little.

Use the following pages to keep an accurate account of the materials used in various locations, and details of room, window and door sizes.

Apart from the obvious details required, space has been left for any particular points you may wish to record: cables buried in walls for wall lights, boards which lift to reveal cable runs or gas points, location of stop taps, drain cocks, junction boxes, fuse boxes. In fact any reference which may be needed at some future date.

Do not be bound by the headings given; add your own extra ones as needed—and use the squared paper to mark out areas, choosing a scale to suit your rooms. For most rooms, one square can represent 1 ft or 30 cm.

If you require space for additional information use the abbreviated check list on the back cover.

HOUSE EXTERIOR

Gutter lengths:			amount of paint:		
Downpipe lengths:			amount of paint:		
Window sizes: types (metal/wood/casement/sash)					
Door sizes: Patio door size: Wall areas for each wall face (N.S.E.W) amount of paint required per coat					

Garage size:
   window sizes:
   door sizes and type (make)					

Details of fuse boxes in garage
   fuse ratings:
   consumer unit fuse ratings:
 	
Number of socket outlets:					

LOUNGE AND DINING ROOM

Floor area: floorcovering type:			amount needed:		

Wall area (total)
   wallcovering type:
   amount of wall paint:
			no. of rolls:
			(bear in mind pattern repeat
			and pattern size)		

Ceiling area:
   amount of paint:
   number of ceiling tiles:
   amount of ceiling paper used:
	size:				

Radiator types: Socket outlets: (single):	number: (double):		sizes:		

Window sizes:
   curtain track lengths:
   amount of curtain material:
   no. of curtains made:
   net curtain sizes:
			type of track:		

Lighting: wattage of lamps required: Problem areas, special points to note:					

KITCHEN

Floor area: floorcovering type:			amount needed:		

Wall area (total)
   wallcovering type:
   amount of wall paint:
			no. of rolls:
			(bear in mind pattern repeat
			and pattern size)		

Ceiling area:
   amount of paint:
   number of ceiling tiles: sizes:
   amount of ceiling paper used:					

Radiator types: number: sizes: Socket outlets: (single): (double): Window sizes: curtain track lengths: type of track:					
amount of curtain material: no. of curtains made: net curtain sizes: Lighting: wattage of lamps required:					
Appliances: ref. number: guarantee number (a) (b) (c) (d)					
(e) Boiler type: service period: Problem areas, special points to note:					

BATHROOM, CLOAKROOM

Floor area: floorcovering type:			amount needed:		

Wall area (total)
  wallcovering type:
  amount of wall paint:
			no. of rolls:
			(bear in mind pattern repeat
			and pattern size)		

Ceiling area:
  amount of paint:
  number of ceiling tiles:
  amount of ceiling paper used:
		sizes:			

Radiator types: Socket outlets:		number: (single):	sizes: (double):		

Window sizes:
  curtain track lengths:
  amount of curtain material:
  no. of curtains made:
  net curtain sizes:
			type of track:		

Lighting: wattage of lamps required: Problem areas, special points to note:					

HALL AND STAIRWAY

Floor area: floorcovering type:			amount needed:		
Wall area (total) wallcovering type: amount of wall paint:			no. of rolls: (bear in mind pattern repeat and pattern size)		
Ceiling area: amount of paint: number of ceiling tiles: amount of ceiling paper used:		sizes:			
Radiator types:		number:	sizes:		
Socket outlets:		(single):	(double):		
Window sizes: curtain track lengths: amount of curtain material: no. of curtains made:			type of track:		
net curtain sizes:					
Lighting: wattage of lamps required:					
Number of stairs: Hall carpet size: Landing carpet size: Thermostat setting: Problem areas, special points to note:			length of stair carpet:		

BEDROOMS

Main bedroom: Floor area: floorcovering type:			amount needed:		

Wall area (total)
    wallcovering type:
    amount of wall paint:
			no. of rolls:
			(bear in mind pattern repeat
			and pattern size)		

Ceiling area:
    amount of paint:
    number of ceiling tiles:
    amount of ceiling paper used:
 	
Radiator types:
	sizes:
	
	number:
		sizes:			

Socket outlets:
 	
Window sizes:
    curtain track lengths:
    amount of curtain material:
    no. of curtains made:
    net curtain sizes:
 	
Lighting:
    wattage of lamps required:
	(single):	(double):
		
		type of track:			

Problem areas, special points to note: Use of following squared page(s) to provide similar details for other bedrooms, extensions or loft rooms.					

OTHER BEDROOMS